# Expert SQL Server Transactions and Locking

## Concurrency Internals for SQL Server Practitioners

Dmitri Korotkevitch

APRESS®

***Expert SQL Server Transactions and Locking***

Dmitri Korotkevitch
Land O Lakes, Florida, USA

ISBN-13 (pbk): 978-1-4842-3956-8
https://doi.org/10.1007/978-1-4842-3957-5

ISBN-13 (electronic): 978-1-4842-3957-5

Library of Congress Control Number: 2018958877

Managing Director, Apress Media LLC: Welmoed Spahr
Acquisitions Editor: Jonathan Gennick
Development Editor: Laura Berendson
Coordinating Editor: Jill Balzano

Cover image designed by Freepik (www.freepik.com)

Distributed to the book trade worldwide by Springer Science+Business Media New York, 233 Spring Street, 6th Floor, New York, NY 10013. Phone 1-800-SPRINGER, fax (201) 348-4505, email orders-ny@springer-sbm.com, or visit www.springeronline.com. Apress Media, LLC is a California LLC and the sole member (owner) is Springer Science + Business Media Finance Inc (SSBM Finance Inc). SSBM Finance Inc is a **Delaware** corporation.

For information on translations, please email rights@apress.com, or visit http://www.apress.com/rights-permissions.

Apress titles may be purchased in bulk for academic, corporate, or promotional use. eBook versions and licenses are also available for most titles. For more information, reference our Print and eBook Bulk Sales web page at http://www.apress.com/bulk-sales.

Any source code or other supplementary material referenced by the author in this book is available to readers on GitHub via the book's product page, located at www.apress.com/9781484239568. For more detailed information, please visit http://www.apress.com/source-code.

Printed on acid-free paper

*To my friends from Chewy.com: Thanks for all the excitement you bring to my life nowadays!*

# Table of Contents

# About the Author

**Dmitri Korotkevitch** is a Microsoft Data Platform MVP and Microsoft Certified Master (SQL Server 2008) with many years of IT experience, including years of working with Microsoft SQL Server as an application and database developer, database administrator, and database architect. He specializes in the design, development, and performance-tuning of complex OLTP systems that handle thousands of transactions per second around the clock providing SQL Server consulting services and training to clients around the world.

Dmitri regularly speaks at various Microsoft and SQL PASS events. He blogs at http://aboutsqlserver.com, rarely tweets as @aboutsqlserver, and can be reached at dk@aboutsqlserver.com.

# About the Technical Reviewer

 **Mark Broadbent** is a Microsoft Data Platform MVP and Microsoft Certified Master in SQL Server with more than 30 years of IT experience and more than 20 years' experience working with SQL Server. He is an expert in concurrency control, migration, and HADR, and a lover of Linux, Golang, Serverless, and Docker. In between herding cats and dogs and being beaten at video games by his children, he can be found blogging at `https://tenbulls.co.uk` and lurking on Twitter as `@retracement`.

# Acknowledgments

Writing is an extremely time-consuming process, and it would be impossible for me to write this book without the patience, understanding, and continuous support of my family. Thank you very much for everything!

I am enormously grateful to Mark Broadbent, who helped with the technical review of this book. His advice and persistence dramatically improved the quality of my work. It's been a pleasure to work together, Mark!

On the same note, I would like to thank Victor Isakov, who helped with the technical review of my other books. Even though Victor did not participate in this project, you can see his influence all over the place.

I would like to thank Nazanin Mashayekh, who read the manuscript and provided many great pieces of advice and suggestions. Nazanin lives in Tehran, and she has years of experience working with SQL Server in various roles.

And, of course, I need to thank the entire Apress team, especially Jill Balzano, April Rondeau, and Jonathan Gennick. Thank you for all your help and effort to keep us organized!

Obviously, neither of my books would exist without the great product we have. Thank you, Microsoft engineering team, for all your hard work and effort! I would also like to thank Kalen Delaney for her *SQL Server Internals* books, which helped me and many others to master SQL Server skills.

Finally, I would like to thank all my friends from the SQL Server community for their support and encouragement. I am not sure if I would have had the motivation to write without all of you!

Thank you, all!

# Introduction

Some time ago, one of my colleagues asked me, "What do you like about SQL Server the most?" I had heard this question many times before, and so I provided my usual answer: "SQL Server Internals. I like to understand how the product works and solve complex problems with this knowledge."

His next question was not so simple though: "How did you fall in love with SQL Server Internals?" After some time thinking, I answered, "Well, I guess it started when I had to work on the locking issues. I had to learn SQL Server Internals to troubleshoot complex deadlocks and blocking conditions. And I enjoyed the sense of satisfaction those challenges gave me."

This is, in fact, the truth. The Concurrency Model has always been an essential part of my SQL Server journey, and I have always been fascinated by it. Concurrency is, perhaps, one of the most confusing and least understood parts of SQL Server, but, at the same time, it is also quite logical. The internal implementation is vaguely documented; however, as soon as you grasp the core concepts, everything starts to fit together nicely.

It is also fair to say that concurrency topics have always been my favorites. My first few SQL Saturday presentations and first few blog posts were about locking and blocking. I even started to write my first book, the first edition of *Pro SQL Server Internals*, from Chapter 17—the first chapter in the "Locking, Blocking, and Concurrency" part—before going back to write the beginning.

Those few chapters, by the way, were the first and worst chapters I have ever written. I am very glad that I had an opportunity to revisit them in the second edition of *Internals* book. Nevertheless, I was unable to cover the subject as deeply as I wanted to due to deadlines and space constraints (I am sure that Apress regularly ran out of paper printing the 900-page manuscript in its current form). Thus, I am very glad that I can present you with a separate book on SQL Server locking, blocking, and concurrency now.

If you have read *Pro SQL Server Internals* before, you will notice some familiar content. Nevertheless, I did my best to expand the coverage of the old topics and added quite a few new ones. I also made many changes in the demo scripts and added the new Blocking Monitoring Framework code, which dramatically simplifies troubleshooting concurrency issues in the system.

This book covers all modern versions of SQL Server, starting with SQL Server 2005, along with Microsoft Azure SQL Databases. There may be a few very minor version-specific differences; however, conceptually the SQL Server Concurrency Model has not changed much over the years.

Nor do I expect it to dramatically change in the near future, so this book should be applicable to at least several future versions of SQL Server.

Finally, I would like to thank you again for choosing this book and for your trust in me. I hope that you will enjoy reading it as much as I enjoyed writing it!

# How This Book Is Structured

This book consists of 14 chapters and is structured in the following way:

- Chapter 1, "Data Storage and Access Methods," describes how SQL Server stores and works with the data in disk-based tables. This knowledge is the essential cornerstone to understanding the SQL Server Concurrency Model.

- Chapter 2, "Transaction Management and Concurrency Models," provides an overview of optimistic and pessimistic concurrency and focuses on transaction management and error handling in the system.

- Chapter 3, "Lock Types," explains the key elements of SQL Server concurrency, such as lock types.

- Chapter 4, "Blocking in the System," discusses why blocking occurs in the system and shows how to troubleshoot it.

- Chapter 5, "Deadlocks," demonstrates the common causes of deadlocks and outlines how to address them.

- Chapter 6, "Optimistic Isolation Levels," covers optimistic concurrency in SQL Server.

- Chapter 7, "Lock Escalations," talks about lock escalation techniques that SQL Server uses to reduce locking overhead in the system.

- Chapter 8, "Schema and Low-Priority Locks," covers the schema locks that occur during schema modifications in the database. It also explains low-priority locks that may help to reduce blocking during index and partition management in recent versions of SQL Server.

- Chapter 9, "Lock Partitioning," discusses lock partitioning, which SQL Server uses in systems that have 16 or more logical CPUs.

- Chapter 10, "Application Locks," focuses on application locks that can be created in the code programmatically.

- Chapter 11, "Designing a Transaction Strategy," provides guidelines on how to design transaction strategies in the system.

- Chapter 12, "Troubleshooting Concurrency Issues," discusses the holistic system troubleshooting process and demonstrates how to detect and address concurrency issues in the system.

- Chapter 13, "In-Memory OLTP Concurrency Model," provides an overview of how concurrency works in In-Memory OLTP environments.

- Chapter 14, "Locking and Columnstore Indexes," explains the locking that occurs with updateable columnstore indexes.

# Downloading the Code

You can download the code used in this book from the "Source Code" section of the Apress website (`www.apress.com`) or from the "Publications" section of my blog (`http://aboutsqlserver.com`). The source code consists of the SQL Server Management Studio solution, which includes a set of projects (one per chapter).
There is also a separate solution with the Blocking Monitoring Framework code.

I am planning to update and enhance the Blocking Monitoring Framework on a regular basis in the future. You can always download the latest version from `http://aboutsqlserver.com/bmframework`.

# CHAPTER 1

# Data Storage and Access Methods

It is impossible to grasp the SQL Server concurrency model without understanding how SQL Server stores and accesses the data. This knowledge helps you to comprehend various aspects of locking behavior in the system, and it is also essential when troubleshooting concurrency issues.

Nowadays, SQL Server and Microsoft Azure SQL Databases support three different technologies that dictate how data is stored and manipulated in the system. The classic Storage Engine implements row-based storage. This technology persists the data in disk-based tables, combining all columns from a table together into data rows. The data rows, in turn, reside on 8 KB data pages, each of which may have one or multiple rows.

Starting with SQL Server 2012, you can store data in a columnar format using columnstore indexes. SQL Server splits the data into *row groups* of up to 1,048,576 rows each. The data in the row group is combined and stored on a per-column rather than a per-row basis. This format is optimized for reporting and analytics queries.

Finally, the In-Memory OLTP Engine, introduced in SQL Server 2014, allows you to define memory-optimized tables, which keep all data entirely in memory. The data rows in memory are linked to the data row chains through the memory pointers. This technology is optimized for heavy OLTP workload.

We will discuss locking behavior in In-Memory OLTP and columnstore indexes later in the book, after we cover the concurrency model of the classic Storage Engine. This knowledge is a cornerstone of understanding how SQL Server behaves in a multi-user environment.

The goal of this chapter is to give a high-level overview of row-based storage in SQL Server. It will explain how SQL Server stores the data in disk-based tables, illustrate the structure of B-Tree indexes, and demonstrate how SQL Server accesses data from them.

1

© Dmitri Korotkevitch 2018

D. Korotkevitch, *Expert SQL Server Transactions and Locking*, https://doi.org/10.1007/978-1-4842-3957-5_1

You should not consider this chapter as a deep dive into the SQL Server Storage Engine. It should provide, however, enough information to discuss the concurrency model in SQL Server.

# Anatomy of a Table

The internal structure of a disk-based table is rather complex and consists of multiple elements and internal objects, as shown in Figure 1-1.

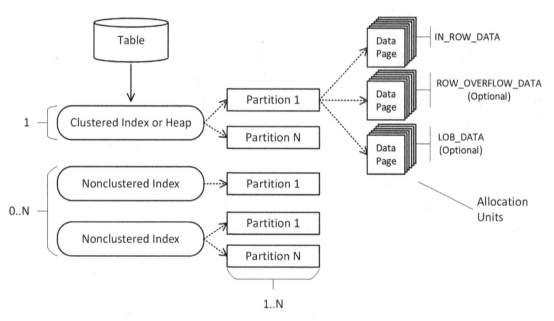

***Figure 1-1.*** *Internal structure of a table*

The data in the tables is stored either completely unsorted (those tables are called *heap tables* or *heaps*) or sorted according to the value of a clustered index key when a table has such an index defined.

In addition to a single clustered index, every table may have a set of nonclustered indexes. These indexes are separate data structures that store a copy of the data from a table sorted according to index key column(s). For example, if a column was included in three nonclustered indexes, SQL Server would store that data four times—once in a clustered index or heap and in each of the three nonclustered indexes.

You can create either 250 or 999 nonclustered indexes per table, depending on SQL Server version. However, it is clearly not a good idea to create a lot of them due to the overhead they introduce. In addition to storage overhead, SQL Server needs to insert or delete data from each nonclustered index during data modifications. Moreover, the update operation requires SQL Server to modify data in every index in which updated columns were present.

Internally, each index (and heap) consists of one or multiple *partitions*. Every partition, in a nutshell, is an internal data structure (index or heap) independent from other partitions in the object. SQL Server allows the use of a different partition strategy for every index in the table; however, in most cases, all indexes are partitioned in the same way and aligned with each other.

---

**Note**   Every table/index in SQL Server is partitioned. Non-partitioned tables are treated as single-partition tables/indexes internally.

---

As I already mentioned, the actual data is stored in *data rows* on 8 KB *data pages* with 8,060 bytes available to users. The pages that store users' data may belong to three different categories called *allocation units* based on the type of data they store.

IN_ROW_DATA allocation unit pages store the *main* data row objects, which consist of internal attributes and the data from fixed-length columns, such as int, datetime, float, and others. The in-row part of a data row must fit on a single data page and, therefore, cannot exceed 8,060 bytes. The data from variable-length columns, such as (n)varchar(max), (n)varbinary(max), xml, and others, may also be stored in-row in the main row object when it fits into this limit.

In cases when variable-length data does not fit in-row, SQL Server stores it off-row on different data pages, referencing them through in-row pointers. Variable-length data that exceeds 8,000 bytes is stored on LOB_DATA allocation unit data pages (LOB stands for *large objects*). Otherwise, the data is stored in ROW_OVERFLOW_DATA allocation unit pages.

Let's look at an example and create a table that contains several fixed- and variable-length columns and insert one row there, as shown in Listing 1-1.

***Listing 1-1.***  Data row storage: Creating the test table

```
create table dbo.DataRows
(
    ID int not null,
    ADate datetime not null,
    VarCol1 varchar(max),
    VarCol2 varchar(5000),
    VarCol3 varchar(5000)
);

insert into dbo.DataRows(ID, ADate, VarCol1, VarCol2, VarCol3)
values
(
    1
    ,'1974-08-22'
    ,replicate(convert(varchar(max),'A'),32000)
    ,replicate(convert(varchar(max),'B'),5000)
    ,replicate(convert(varchar(max),'C'),5000)
);
```

The data from fixed-length columns (ID, ADate) will be stored in-row on an IN_ROW_
DATA allocation unit page. The data from VarCol1 column is 32,000 bytes and will be
stored on LOB_DATA data pages.

The VarCol2 and VarCol3 columns have 5,000 bytes of data each. SQL Server would
keep one of them in-row (it would fit into the 8,060-byte limit) and place the other one
on the single ROW_OVERFLOW_DATA page.

---

**Note**    Off-row column pointers use 16 or 24 bytes in-row, which counts toward
the 8,060 maximum row size. In practice, this may limit the number of columns
you can have in a table.

---

Figure 1-2 illustrates this state.

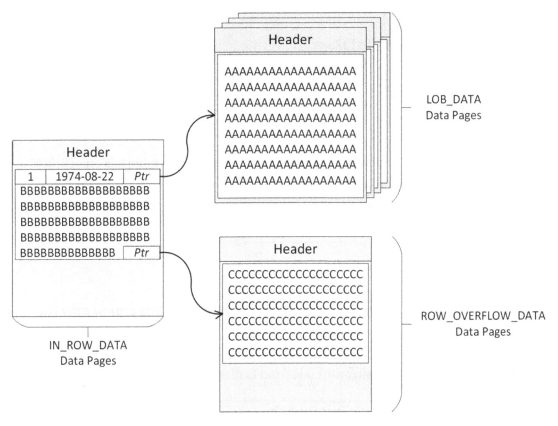

***Figure 1-2.*** *Data row storage: Data pages after the first INSERT*

The sys.dm_db_index_physical_stats data management function is usually used to analyze index fragmentation. It also displays the information about data pages on a per–allocation unit basis.

Listing 1-2 shows the query that returns the information about the dbo.DataRows table.

***Listing 1-2.*** Data row storage: Analyzing the table using sys.dm_db_index_physical_stats DMO

```
select
    index_id, partition_number, alloc_unit_type_desc
    ,page_count, record_count, min_record_size_in_bytes
    ,max_record_size_in_bytes, avg_record_size_in_bytes
from
```

```
sys.dm_db_index_physical_stats
(
    db_id()
    ,object_id(N'dbo.DataRows')
    ,0  /* IndexId = 0 -> Table Heap */
    ,NULL /* All Partitions */
    ,'DETAILED'
);
```

Figure 1-3 illustrates the output of the code. As expected, the table has one IN_ROW_ DATA, one ROW_OVERFLOW_DATA, and four LOB_DATA pages. The IN_ROW data page has about 2,900 free bytes available.

| | index_id | partition_number | alloc_unit_type_desc | page_count | record_count | min_record_size_in_bytes | max_record_size_in_bytes | avg_record_size_in_bytes |
|---|---|---|---|---|---|---|---|---|
| 1 | 0 | 1 | IN_ROW_DATA | 1 | 1 | 5111 | 5111 | 5111 |
| 2 | 0 | 1 | ROW_OVERFLOW_DATA | 1 | 1 | 5014 | 5014 | 5014 |
| 3 | 0 | 1 | LOB_DATA | 4 | 4 | 7894 | 8054 | 8014 |

*Figure 1-3.* *Data row storage: sys.dm_db_index_physical_stats output after the first INSERT*

Let's insert another row using the code from Listing 1-3.

*Listing 1-3.* Data row storage: Inserting the second row

```
insert into dbo.DataRows(ID, ADate, VarCol1, VarCol2, VarCol3)
values(2,'2006-09-29','DDDDD','EEEEE','FFFFF');
```

All three variable-length columns store five-character strings, and, therefore, the row would fit on the already-allocated IN_ROW_DATA page. Figure 1-4 illustrates data pages at this phase.

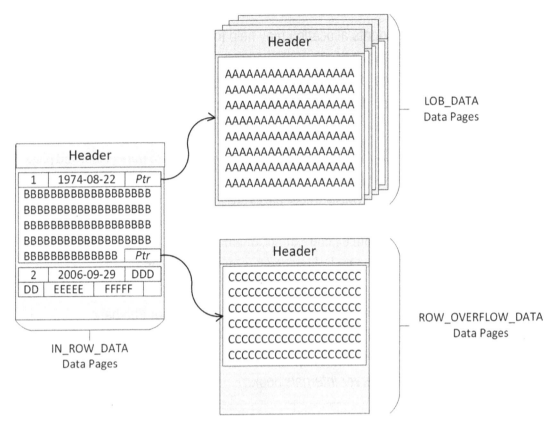

**Figure 1-4.** *Data row storage: Data pages after the second INSERT*

You can confirm it by running the code from Listing 1-2 again. Figure 1-5 illustrates the output from the view.

| | index_id | partition_number | alloc_unit_type_desc | page_count | record_count | min_record_size_in_bytes | max_record_size_in_bytes | avg_record_size_in_bytes |
|---|---|---|---|---|---|---|---|---|
| 1 | 0 | 1 | IN_ROW_DATA | 1 | 2 | 42 | 5111 | 2576.5 |
| 2 | 0 | 1 | ROW_OVERFLOW_DATA | 1 | 1 | 5014 | 5014 | 5014 |
| 3 | 0 | 1 | LOB_DATA | 4 | 4 | 7894 | 8054 | 8014 |

**Figure 1-5.** *Data row storage: sys.dm_db_index_physical_stats output after the second INSERT*

SQL Server logically groups eight pages into 64KB units called *extents*. There are two types of extents available: *mixed extents* store data that belongs to different objects, while *uniform extents* store the data for the same object.

By default, when a new object is created, SQL Server stores the first eight object pages in mixed extents. After that, all subsequent space allocation for that object is done with uniform extents.

> **Tip**   Disabling mixed extents allocation may help to improve `tempdb` throughput in the system. In SQL Server prior to 2016, you can achieve that by enabling server-level trace flag T1118. This trace flag is not required in SQL Server 2016 and above, where `tempdb` does not use mixed extents anymore.

SQL Server uses a special kind of pages, called *allocation maps,* to track extent and page usage in database files. *Index Allocation Maps (IAM)* pages track extents that belong to an allocation unit on a per-partition basis. Those pages are, in a nutshell, bitmaps, where each bit indicates if the extent belongs to a specific allocation unit from the object partition.

Each IAM page covers about 64,000 extents, or almost 4 GB of data in a data file. For larger files, multiple IAM pages are linked together into *IAM chains.*

> **Note**   There are many other types of allocation maps used for database management. You can read about them at `https://docs.microsoft.com/en-us/sql/relational-databases/pages-and-extents-architecture-guide` or in my *Pro SQL Server Internals* book.

# Heap Tables

Heap tables are tables without a clustered index. The data in heap tables is unsorted. SQL Server does not guarantee, nor does it maintain, a sorting order of the data in heap tables.

When you insert data into heap tables, SQL Server tries to fill pages as much as possible, although it does not analyze the actual free space available on a page. It uses another type of allocation map page called *Page Free Space (PFS)*, which tracks the amount of free space available on the page. This tracking is imprecise, however. SQL Server uses three bits, which indicate if the page is empty, or if it is 1 to 50, 51 to 80, 81 to 95 or above 95 percent full. It is entirely possible that SQL Server would not store a new row on the page even when it has available space.

When you select data from the heap table, SQL Server uses IAM pages to find the pages and extents that belong to the table, processing them based on their order on the IAM pages rather than on the order in which the data was inserted. Figure 1-6 illustrates this point. This operation is shown as *Table Scan* in the execution plan.

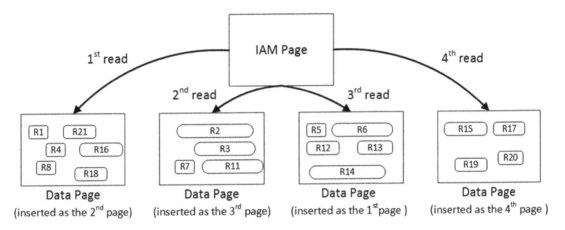

***Figure 1-6.*** *Selecting data from the heap table*

When you update the row in the heap table, SQL Server tries to accommodate it on the same page. If there is no free space available, SQL Server moves the new version of the row to another page and replaces the old row with a special 16-byte row called a *forwarding pointer*. The new version of the row is called a *forwarded row*. Figure 1-7 illustrates this point.

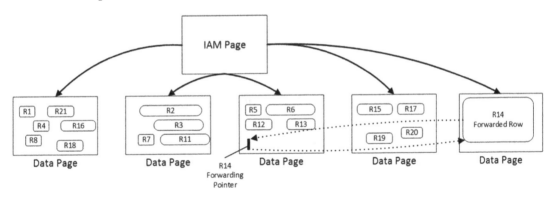

***Figure 1-7.*** *Forwarding pointers*

There are two main reasons why forwarding pointers are used. First, they prevent updates of nonclustered index keys, which reference the row. We will talk about nonclustered indexes in more detail later in this chapter.

In addition, forwarding pointers help minimize the number of duplicated reads; that is, the situation when a single row is read multiple times during the table scan. Let's look at Figure 1-7 as an example and assume that SQL Server scans the pages in left-to-right order. Let's further assume that the row in page 3 was modified at the time when SQL

Server reads page 4 (after page 3 has already been read). The new version of the row would be moved to page 5, which has yet to be processed. Without forwarding pointers, SQL Server would not know that the old version of the row had already been read, and it would read it again during the page 5 scan. With forwarding pointers, SQL Server skips the forwarded rows—they have a flag in their internal attributes indicating that condition.

Although forwarding pointers help minimize duplicated reads, they introduce additional read operations at the same time. SQL Server follows the forwarding pointers and reads the new versions of the rows at the time it encounters them. That behavior can introduce an excessive number of I/O operations when heap tables are frequently updated and have a large number of forwarded rows.

---

**Note**   You can analyze the number of forwarded rows in the table by checking the `forwarded_record_count` column in the `sys.dm_db_index_physical_stats` view.

---

When the size of the forwarded row is reduced by another update, and the data page with the forwarding pointer has enough space to accommodate the updated version of the row, SQL Server may move it back to its original data page and remove the forwarding pointer row. Nevertheless, the only reliable way to get rid of all forwarding pointers is by rebuilding the heap table. You can do that by using an `ALTER TABLE REBUILD` statement.

Heap tables can be useful in staging environments where you want to import a large amount of data into the system as quickly as possible. Inserting data into heap tables can often be faster than inserting it into tables with clustered indexes. Nevertheless, during a regular workload, tables with clustered indexes usually outperform heap tables as a result of heap tables' suboptimal space control and extra I/O operations introduced by forwarding pointers.

---

**Note**   You can find the scripts that demonstrate forwarding pointers' overhead and suboptimal space control in heap tables in this book's companion materials.

---

# Clustered Indexes and B-Trees

A clustered index dictates the physical order of the data in a table, which is sorted according to the clustered index key. The table can have only one clustered index defined.

Let's assume that you want to create a clustered index on the heap table with the data. As a first step, which is shown in Figure 1-8, SQL Server creates another copy of the data and sorts it based on the value of the clustered key. The data pages are linked in a double-linked list, where every page contains pointers to the next and previous pages in the chain. This list is called the *leaf level* of the index, and it contains the actual table data.

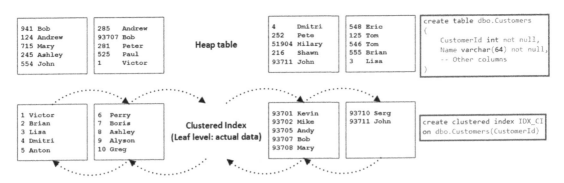

*Figure 1-8.* *Clustered index structure: Leaf level*

---

**Note**    The pages reference each other through page addresses, which consist of two values: `file_id` in the database and sequential number of the page in the file.

---

When the leaf level consists of multiple pages, SQL Server starts to build an *intermediate level* of the index, as shown in Figure 1-9.

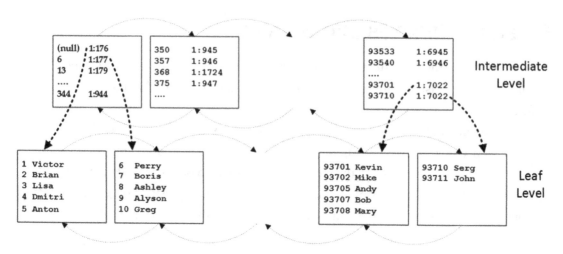

***Figure 1-9.*** *Clustered index structure: Intermediate levels*

The intermediate level stores one row per each leaf-level page. It stores two pieces of information: the physical address and the minimum value of the index key from the page it references. The only exception is the very first row on the first page, where SQL Server stores NULL rather than the minimum index key value. With such optimization, SQL Server does not need to update non-leaf level rows when you insert the row with the lowest key value in the table.

The pages on the intermediate level are also linked in a double-linked list. SQL Server adds more and more intermediate levels until there is a level that includes just a single page. This level is called the *root level*, and it becomes the entry point to the index, as shown in Figure 1-10.

---

**Note**   This index structure is called a *B-Tree Index*, which stands for *Balanced Tree*.

---

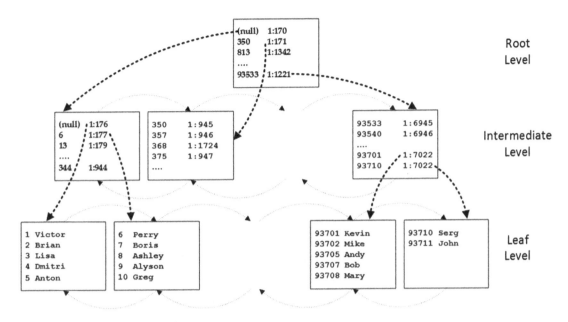

***Figure 1-10.*** *Clustered index structure: Root level*

As you can see, the index always has one leaf level, one root level, and zero or more intermediate levels. The only exception is when the index data fits into a single page. In that case, SQL Server does not create the separate root-level page, and the index consists of just the single leaf-level page.

SQL Server always maintains the order of the data in the index, inserting new rows on the data pages to which they belong. In cases when a data page does not have enough free space, SQL Server allocates a new page and places the row there, adjusting pointers in the double-linked page list to maintain a logical sorting order in the index. This operation is called *page split* and leads to index fragmentation.

Figure 1-11 illustrates this condition. When *Original Page* does not have enough space to accommodate the new row, SQL Server performs a page split, moving about half of the data from *Original Page* to *New Page*, adjusting page pointers afterward.

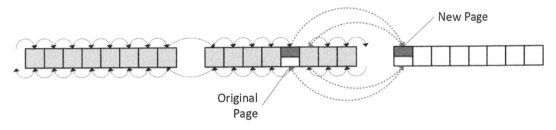

***Figure 1-11.*** *Leaf-level data pages after page split*

A page split may also occur during data modifications. SQL Server does not use forwarding pointers with B-Tree indexes. Instead, when an update cannot be done in-place—for example, during data row increase—SQL Server performs a page split and moves updated and subsequent rows from the page to another page. Nevertheless, the index sorting order is maintained through the page pointers.

SQL Server may read the data from the index in three different ways. The first is an *allocation order scan*. SQL Server accesses the table data through IAM pages similar to how it does this with heap tables. This method, however, could introduce data consistency phenomena—with page splits, rows may be skipped or read more than once—and, therefore, allocation order scan is rarely used. We will discuss conditions that may lead to allocation order scans later in the book.

The second method is called an *ordered scan*. Let's assume that we want to run the SELECT Name FROM dbo.Customers query. All data rows reside on the leaf level of the index, and SQL Server can scan it and return the rows to the client.

SQL Server starts with the root page of the index and reads the first row from there. That row references the intermediate page with the minimum key value from the table. SQL Server reads that page and repeats the process until it finds the first page on the leaf level. Then, SQL Server starts to read rows one by one, moving through the linked list of the pages until all rows have been read. Figure 1-12 illustrates this process.

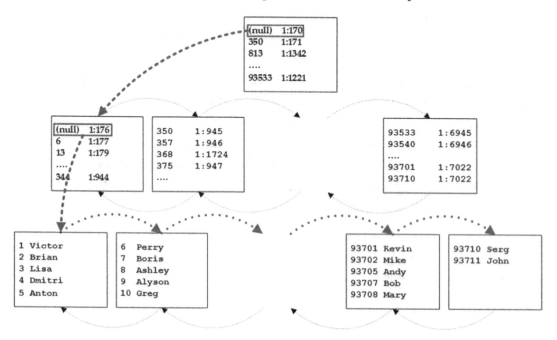

***Figure 1-12.*** *Ordered index scan*

Both allocation order scan and ordered scan are represented as *Index Scan* operators in the execution plans.

---

**Note**   The server can navigate through indexes in both directions, forward and backward. However, SQL Server does not use parallelism during backward index scans.

---

The last index access method is called *index seek*. Let's assume we want to run the following query: SELECT Name FROM dbo.Customers WHERE CustomerId BETWEEN 4 AND 7. Figure 1-13 illustrates how SQL Server may process it.

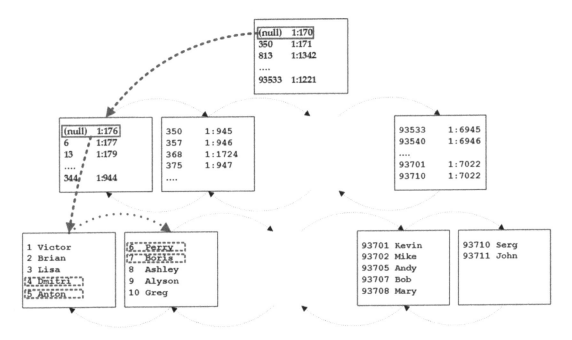

***Figure 1-13.*** *Index seek*

In order to read the range of rows from the table, SQL Server needs to find the row with the minimum value of the key from the range, which is 4. SQL Server starts with the root page, where the second row references the page with the minimum key value of 350. It is greater than the key value that we are looking for, and SQL Server reads the intermediate-level data page (1:170) referenced by the first row on the root page.

Similarly, the intermediate page leads SQL Server to the first leaf-level page (1:176). SQL Server reads that page, then it reads the rows with CustomerId equal to 4 and 5, and, finally, it reads the two remaining rows from the second page.

Technically speaking, there are two kinds of index seek operations. The first is called a *point-lookup* (or, sometimes, *singleton lookup*), where SQL Server seeks and returns a single row. You can think about the WHERE CustomerId = 2 predicate as an example.

The other type is called a *range scan*, and it requires SQL Server to find the lowest or highest value of the key and scan (either forward or backward) the set of rows until it reaches the end of scan range. The predicate WHERE CustomerId BETWEEN 4 AND 7 leads to the range scan. Both cases are shown as *Index Seek* operators in the execution plans.

As you can guess, index seek is more efficient than index scan because SQL Server processes just the subset of rows and data pages rather than scanning the entire index. However, an *Index Seek* operator in the execution plan may be misleading and represent a range scan that scans a large number of rows or even an entire index. For example, in our table, the WHERE CustomerId > 0 predicate requires SQL Server to scan the entire index; however, it would be represented as an *Index Seek* operator in the plan.

There is a concept in relational databases called *SARGable predicates*, which stands for *Search Argument-able*. The predicate is SARGable if SQL Server can utilize an index seek operation if the index exists. In a nutshell, predicates are SARGable when SQL Server can determine the single or range of index key values to process during predicate evaluation. Obviously, it is beneficial to write queries using SARGable predicates and utilize index seek whenever possible.

SARGable predicates include the following operators: =, >, >=, <, <=, IN, BETWEEN, and LIKE (in case of prefix matching). Non-SARGable operators include NOT, <>, LIKE (in case of non-prefix matching), and NOT IN.

Another circumstance for making predicates non-SARGable is using functions (standard or user-defined) against the table columns. SQL Server must call the function for every row it processes, which prevents an index seek from being used.

The same applies to data-type conversions where SQL Server uses the CONVERT_ IMPLICIT internal function. One common example of when it may happen is using the unicode nvarchar parameter in the predicate with a varchar column. Another case is having different data types for the columns that participate in a join predicate. Both of those cases could lead to the index scan even when the predicate operator appears to be SARGable.

# Composite Indexes

Indexes with multiple key columns are called *composite (or compound) indexes*. The data in the composite indexes is sorted on a per-column basis from leftmost to rightmost columns. Figure 1-14 shows the structure of a composite index defined on LastName and FirstName columns in the table. The data is sorted based on LastName (left-most column) first and then on FirstName within each LastName value.

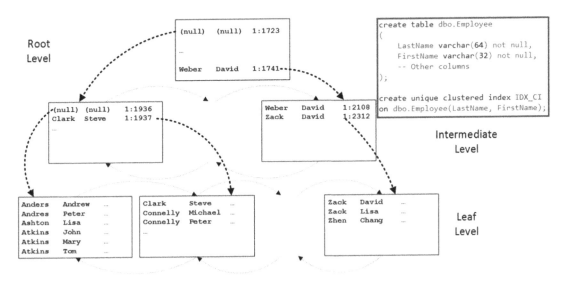

*Figure 1-14.* *Composite index structure*

The SARGability of a composite index depends on the SARGability of the predicates on the leftmost index columns, which allow SQL Server to determine the range of the index keys to process.

Table 1-1 shows examples of SARGable and non-SARGable predicates, using the index from Figure 1-14 as the example.

***Table 1-1.*** *SARGable and non-SARGable Predicates on a Composite Index*

| SARGable Predicates | Non-SARGable Predicates |
| --- | --- |
| LastName = 'Clark' and<br>FirstName = 'Steve' | LastName <> 'Clark' and<br>FirstName = 'Steve' |
| LastName = 'Clark' and<br>FirstName <> 'Steve' | LastName LIKE '%ar%' and<br>FirstName = 'Steve' |
| LastName = 'Clark' | FirstName = 'Steve' |
| LastName LIKE 'Cl%' | |

# Nonclustered Indexes

While a clustered index specifies how data rows are sorted in a table, nonclustered indexes define a separate sorting order for a column or set of columns and persist them as separate data structures.

You can think about a book as an example. Page numbers would represent the book's *clustered index*. The index at the end of the book shows the list of terms from the book in alphabetical order. Each term references the page numbers where the term is mentioned. That represents the *nonclustered index* of the terms.

When you need to find a term in the book, you can look it up in the term index. It is a fast and efficient operation because terms are sorted in alphabetical order. Next, you can quickly find the pages on which the terms are mentioned by using the page numbers specified there. Without the term index, the only choice would be to read all of the pages in the book one by one until all references to the term are found.

The nonclustered index structure is very similar to the clustered index structure. Let's create a nonclustered index on the Name column from the dbo.Customers table with CREATE NONCLUSTERED INDEX IDX_NCI ON dbo.Customers(Name) statement. Figure 1-15 shows the structure of both indexes.

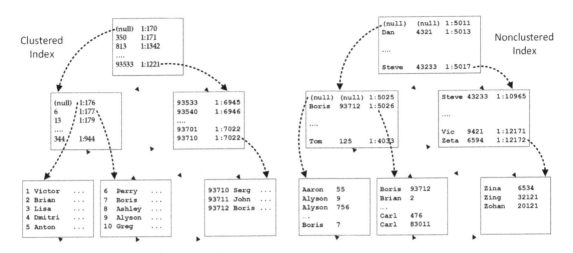

***Figure 1-15.*** *Clustered and nonclustered index structures*

The leaf level of the nonclustered index is sorted based on the value of the index key—Name in our case. Every row on the leaf level includes the key value and row-id value. For heap tables, row-id is the physical location of the row defined as the file:page:slot address, where slot identifies location of the row on the data page.

For tables with a clustered index, row-id represents the value of the clustered index key of the row. This is a very important point to remember. *Nonclustered indexes do not store information about physical row location when a table has a clustered index defined. They store the value of the clustered index key instead.*

Like clustered indexes, the intermediate and root levels of nonclustered indexes store one row per page from the level they reference. That row consists of the physical address and the minimum value of the key from the page. In addition, for non-unique indexes, it also stores the row-id of such a row.

Let's look at how SQL Server uses nonclustered indexes, assuming that you run the following query: SELECT * FROM dbo.Customers WHERE Name = 'Boris'.

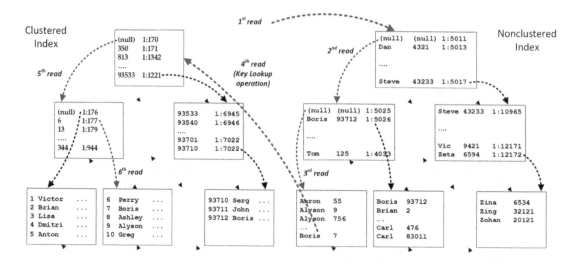

***Figure 1-16.*** *Nonclustered index usage: Step 1*

As shown in the first step in Figure 1-16, SQL Server starts with the root page of the nonclustered index. The key value *Boris* is less than *Dan,* and SQL Server goes to the intermediate page referenced from the first row in the root-level page.

The second row of the intermediate page indicates that the minimum key value on the page is *Boris*, although the index had not been defined as unique and SQL Server does not know if there are other *Boris* rows stored on the first page. As a result, it goes to the first leaf page of the index and finds the row with the key value *Boris* and `row-id` equal to 7 there.

In our case, the nonclustered index does not store any data besides `CustomerId` and `Name,` and SQL Server needs to traverse the clustered index tree and obtain the data from other columns from a table, returning them to the client. This operation is called *Key Lookup*. In heap tables, where clustered indexes do not exist, SQL Server accesses data rows using `row-id`, which stores a physical location of the row in the database. This operation is called *RID Lookup*.

In the next step shown in Figure 1-17, SQL Server comes back to the nonclustered index and reads the second page from the leaf level. It finds another row with the key value *Boris* and `row-id` of 93712, and it performs a key lookup again.

20

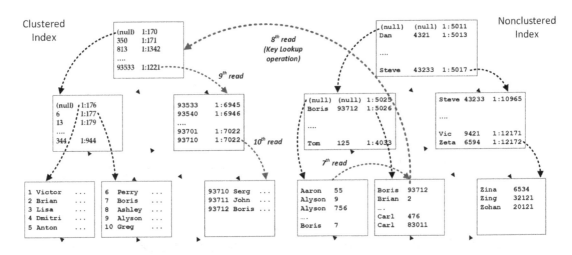

**Figure 1-17.** *Nonclustered index usage: Step 2*

As you can see, SQL Server had to read the data pages 10 times even though the query returned just two rows. The number of I/O operations can be calculated based on the following formula: (# of levels in nonclustered index) + (number of pages read from the leaf level of nonclustered index) + (number of rows found) * (# of levels in clustered index). As you can guess, a large number of rows found (key lookup operations) leads to a large number of I/O operations, which makes nonclustered index usage inefficient.

The same applies to heap tables. Reading the main data row from a heap (RID lookup operation) does not require SQL Server to traverse root and intermediate levels of clustered index B-Tree. Nevertheless, it is an expensive operation, especially with forwarding pointers. SQL Server does not update row-id in nonclustered indexes when a heap table row is moved to another page and forwarding pointer is created. Nonclustered indexes still reference the old row location, which may lead to additional I/O operation when SQL Server reads the forwarded row.

As a result, SQL Server is very conservative in choosing nonclustered indexes when it expects that a large number of key or RID lookup operations will be required. The threshold when SQL Server chooses to scan another index or table over performing key lookups varies; however, it is very low.

Finally, it is worth repeating that nonclustered indexes store a copy of the data from the index columns, which introduces update overhead. When columns are updated, SQL Server needs to update them in every index in which they are present. Similarly, every insert or delete operation requires SQL Server to perform it on each nonclustered index B-Tree.

Remember this overhead and avoid creating unnecessary nonclustered indexes in the system.

# Indexes with Included Columns

As we just discussed, SQL Server rarely uses nonclustered indexes when it expects that a large number of key or RID lookups is required. Those operations usually lead to a large number of reads, both logical and physical.

With key lookup operations, SQL Server accesses multiple data pages from a clustered index every time it needs to obtain a single row. Even though root and intermediate index levels are usually cached in the buffer pool, access to leaf-level pages produces random, and often physical, I/O reads, which are slow, especially in the case of magnetic disk drives.

This is also true for heap tables. Even though the `row-id` in a nonclustered index stores the physical location of the row in a table, and RID lookup operations do not need to traverse the clustered index tree, they still introduce random I/O. Moreover, forwarding pointers can lead to extra reads if a row has been updated and moved to another page.

The existence of key or RID lookups is the crucial factor here. Rows in a nonclustered index are smaller than those in a clustered index. Nonclustered indexes use fewer data pages and, therefore, are more efficient. SQL Server uses nonclustered indexes even when it expects that a large number of rows need to be selected, as long as key or RID lookups are not required.

As you will recall, nonclustered indexes store data from the index key columns and `row-id`. For tables with clustered indexes, the `row-id` is the clustered key value of the index row. The values in all indexes are the same: when you update the row, SQL Server synchronously updates all indexes.

SQL Server does not need to perform key or RID lookups when all of the data a query needs exists in a nonclustered index. Those indexes are called *covering indexes* because they provide all of the information that a query needs, and they are essentially *covering* the query.

Making nonclustered indexes *covering* is one of the most commonly used query-optimization techniques, which improves index efficiency and allows you to eliminate expensive key or RID lookups from execution plans. You can achieve it by including required columns in the index using the INCLUDE clause of the CREATE INDEX statement. The data from these columns are stored on the leaf level only, without being added to the index key and without affecting the sorting order of the index rows.

Figure 1-18 illustrates the structure of an index with included columns, defined as `CREATE INDEX IDX_Customers_Name ON dbo.Customers(Name)` `INCLUDE(DateOfBirth)`, on the table we defined earlier, which has `CustomerId` as the clustered index column.

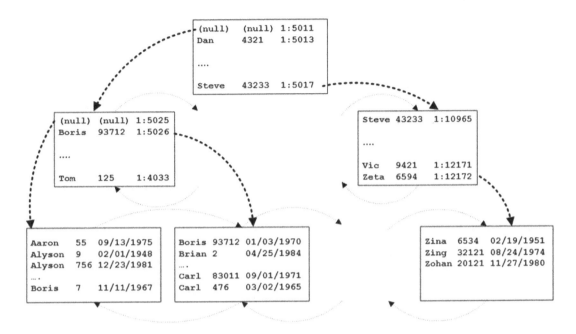

***Figure 1-18.*** *Structure of an index with included column*

Now, if all columns, which query references are present in the index, SQL Server may obtain all data from the leaf level of the nonclustered index B-Tree without performing key or RID lookups. It could use the index regardless of how many rows would be selected from there.

Although covering indexes are a great tool that can help optimize queries, they come at a cost. Every column in the index increases its row size and the number of data pages it uses on disk and in memory. That introduces additional overhead during index maintenance and increases the database size. Moreover, queries need to read more pages when scanning all or part of the index. It does not necessarily introduce a noticeable performance impact during small range scans when reading a few extra pages is far more efficient as compared to key lookups. However, it could negatively affect the performance of queries that scan a large number of data pages or the entire index.

Obviously, they also add update overhead. By adding a column to nonclustered indexes, you store the data in multiple places. This improves the performance of queries that select the data. However, during updates, SQL Server needs to change the rows in every index where updated columns are present. Remember this and be careful with including frequently modified columns to the indexes.

# Summary

The classic SQL Server Storage Engine stores data in disk-based tables using row-based storage. All columns from the table are stored together in the data rows, which reside on 8 KB data pages.

The data in the tables may be stored in two different ways—either completely unsorted in heap tables or sorted according to a clustered index key when such an index is defined. The tables with clustered indexes usually outperform heap tables during normal workload.

Every table may have a set of nonclustered indexes defined. Each nonclustered index is a separate data structure, which stores a copy of the data from a table sorted according to index key columns. Nonclustered indexes may improve performance of the queries at the cost of the update overhead they introduce.

SQL Server uses key lookup and RID lookup operations to obtain data from columns that are not present in nonclustered indexes. These operations are expensive, and SQL Server does not use nonclustered indexes if it expects that a large number of such operations is required. You can include additional columns in the indexes, making them covering and eliminating key and RID lookups from execution plans.

There are two main data access patterns SQL Server uses when working with indexes. Index scans read the entire index by scanning all pages from there. Alternatively, index seek processes read just a subset of the index rows and pages. Index seek is more efficient than index scan, and it is beneficial to use SARGable predicates that may utilize index seek when an index exists.

# CHAPTER 2

# Transaction Management and Concurrency Models

Transactions are the key concept in data management systems; they guarantee the consistency and durability of the data in the database. It is impossible to implement a database system without proper transaction management in place.

This chapter will explain the importance of transactions, provide an overview of both pessimistic and optimistic concurrency models, and outline transaction isolation levels and the possible data consistency phenomena they may introduce. Finally, the chapter will discuss several questions related to transaction management and error handling in SQL Server.

## Transactions

Microsoft SQL Server has been designed to work in multi-user environments, just like any other general-purpose database server. The Database Engine should handle simultaneous workloads from multiple users and provide the required level of data consistency when users query and modify the same data.

There is a key concept in database and data management systems called *transactions*. Transactions are the single unit of work that reads and modifies data in a database and helps to enforce the consistency and durability of the data there. Every transaction in a properly implemented transaction management system has four different characteristics: *atomicity, consistency, isolation,* and *durability*, often referenced as *ACID*.

- *Atomicity* guarantees that each transaction executes as a single unit of work using an "all or nothing" approach. All changes done within a transaction are either committed or rolled back in full. Consider the classic example of transferring money between checking and savings

25

© Dmitri Korotkevitch 2018
D. Korotkevitch, *Expert SQL Server Transactions and Locking*, https://doi.org/10.1007/978-1-4842-3957-5_2

bank accounts. That action consists of two separate operations: decreasing the balance of the checking account and increasing the balance of the savings account. Transaction atomicity guarantees that both operations either succeed or fail together, and a system will never be in an inconsistent state where money was deducted from the checking account but never added to the savings account.

- *Consistency* ensures that any database transaction brings the database from one consistent state to another and that none of the defined database rules and constraints were violated.

- *Isolation* ensures that the changes made in the transaction are isolated and invisible to other transactions until the transaction is committed. By the book, transaction isolation should guarantee that the concurrent execution of multiple transactions brings the system to the same state as if those transactions were executed serially. However, in most database systems, such a requirement is often relaxed and controlled by *transaction isolation levels*, which we will discuss later in the chapter.

- *Durability* guarantees that after a transaction is committed, all changes done by the transaction stay permanent and will survive a system crash. SQL Server achieves durability by using *write-ahead logging* to harden log records in the transaction log. A transaction is not considered to be committed until all log records generated by the transaction are hardened in the log file.

The isolation requirements are the most complex to implement in multi-user environments. Even though it is possible to completely isolate different transactions from each other, this could lead to a high level of blocking and other concurrency issues in systems with volatile data. SQL Server addresses this situation by introducing several transaction isolation levels that relax isolation requirements at the cost of possible concurrency phenomena related to read data consistency:

- **Dirty Reads:** A transaction reads uncommitted (dirty) data from other uncommitted transactions.

- **Non-Repeatable Reads:** Subsequent attempts to read the same data from within the same transaction return different results. This data inconsistency issue arises when the other transactions modified, or even deleted, data between the reads done by the affected transaction.

- **Phantom Reads:** This phenomenon occurs when subsequent reads within the same transaction return new rows (the ones that the transaction did not read before). This happens when another transaction inserted new data in between the reads done by the affected transaction.

# Pessimistic and Optimistic Concurrency

Transaction isolation levels control another aspect of SQL Server behavior that dictates *concurrency models* for the transactions. Conceptually, there are two concurrency models used in database systems:

- *Pessimistic concurrency* works under the assumption that multiple users who access the same data would all eventually like to modify the data and override each other's changes. The Database Engine prevents this from happening by locking the data for the duration of the transaction as soon as the first session accesses and/or modifies it.

- *Optimistic concurrency*, on the other hand, assumes that, while multiple users may access the same data, the chance of simultaneous updates is low. The data would not be locked; however, multiple updates would trigger write–write conflicts and roll back affected transactions.

Let's illustrate the difference between those models with an example. Consider, again, that we have a transaction that wants to transfer money between checking and savings accounts. As you remember, this would lead to two update operations—decreasing the balance of checking and increasing the balance of savings. Let's also assume that you have another session that wants to perform a withdrawal from the checking account in parallel with the transfer. This operation would decrease the balance of the checking account (updating the same row) along with other actions.

With pessimistic concurrency, the first session that updates (and in some cases even reads) the checking account balance would lock this row, preventing other sessions from accessing or updating it. The second session would be blocked until the first session completed the transaction, and it would read the new checking account balance afterward.

With optimistic concurrency, neither of the sessions would be blocked. However, one of the sessions would not be able to commit and would fail with a *write–write conflict* error.

Both concurrency models have benefits and downsides. Pessimistic concurrency may introduce blocking in the system. Optimistic concurrency, on the other hand, requires proper write-write conflict handling, and it often introduces additional overhead during data modifications.

SQL Server supports both pessimistic and optimistic concurrency models, controlling them by transaction isolation levels.

# Transaction Isolation Levels

With disk-based tables, SQL Server supports six different transaction isolation levels, as shown in Table 2-1. The table also demonstrates possible concurrency phenomena for each of the transaction isolation levels.

*Table 2-1.* *Transaction Isolation Levels and Concurrency Phenomena*

| Isolation Level | Type | Dirty Reads | Non-Repeatable Reads | Phantom Reads | Write–Write Conflict |
|---|---|---|---|---|---|
| READ UNCOMMITTED | Pessimistic | YES | YES | YES | NO |
| READ COMMITTED | Pessimistic | NO | YES | YES | NO |
| REPEATABLE READ | Pessimistic | NO | NO | YES | NO |
| SERIALIZABLE | Pessimistic | NO | NO | NO | NO |
| READ COMMITTED SNAPSHOT | Optimistic for readers. Pessimistic for writers. | NO | YES | YES | NO |
| SNAPSHOT | Optimistic | NO | NO | NO | YES |

With pessimistic isolation levels, SQL Server relies strictly on locking to prevent access to the rows that were modified or sometimes even read by other sessions. With optimistic isolation levels, SQL Server uses *row versioning* and copies old versions of modified rows to a special area in `tempdb` called the *version store*. The other sessions would read old (already committed) versions of the rows from there rather than being blocked.

28

It is important to note that SQL Server still acquires locks on updated rows in optimistic isolation levels, preventing other sessions from updating the same rows simultaneously. We will talk about it in more detail in Chapter 6.

The READ COMMITTED SNAPSHOT isolation level combines both optimistic and pessimistic concurrency models. *Readers* (SELECT queries) use row versioning, while *writers* (INSERT, UPDATE, and DELETE queries) rely on locking.

Strictly speaking, READ COMMITTED SNAPSHOT is not a *true* isolation level but rather the database option (READ_COMMITTED_SNAPSHOT) that changes the default behavior of the readers (SELECT queries) in the READ COMMITTED isolation level. In this book, however, I will treat this option as a separate transaction isolation level.

---

**Note**   The READ_COMMITTED_SNAPSHOT database option is enabled by default in Microsoft Azure SQL Databases and disabled by default in regular versions of SQL Server.

---

You can set the transaction level on the session level using a SET TRANSACTION ISOLATION LEVEL statement. Most client libraries use READ COMMITTED (or READ COMMITTED SNAPSHOT when READ_COMMITTED_SNAPSHOT database option is enabled) as the default isolation level. You can also control isolation level on a per-table basis using a locking hint, which we will discuss in the next chapter.

# Working with Transactions

Let's look at several aspects of transaction management in the system, starting with transaction types.

## Transaction Types

There are three types of transactions in SQL Server—explicit, autocommitted, and implicit.

*Explicit transactions* are *explicitly* controlled by the code. You can start them by using the BEGIN TRAN statement. They will remain active until you *explicitly* call COMMIT or ROLLBACK in the code.

In the event there are no active transactions present, SQL Server would use *autocommitted transactions*—starting transactions and committing them for each statement it executes. It is very important to remember that autocommitted transactions work on a per-statement rather than per-module level. For example, when a stored procedure consists of five statements, SQL Server would have five autocommitted transactions executed. Moreover, if this procedure failed in the middle of execution, SQL Server would not roll back its previously committed autocommitted transactions. This behavior may lead to logical data inconsistencies in the system.

For logic that includes multiple data modification statements, autocommitted transactions are less efficient than explicit transactions due to the logging overhead they introduce. In this mode, every statement would generate transaction log records for implicit BEGIN TRAN and COMMIT operations, which would lead to a large amount of transaction log activity and degrade the performance of the system.

There is another potential performance hit caused by having an excessive number of autocommitted transactions. As I already mentioned, SQL Server implements write-ahead logging to support the transaction durability's hardening the log records on disk synchronously with data modifications. Internally, however, SQL Server batches log write operations and caches log records in memory in small 60 KB structures called *log buffers*. Committing a log record forces SQL Server to flush log buffers to disk, thus introducing a synchronous I/O operation.

Figure 2-1 illustrates this condition. INSERT_1, UPDATE_1, and DELETE_1 operations run in autocommitted transactions, generating additional log records and forcing the log buffer to flush on each COMMIT. Alternatively, INSERT_2, UPDATE_2, and DELETE_2 operations run in an explicit transaction, which leads to more efficient logging.

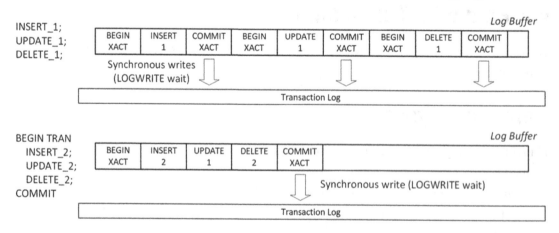

***Figure 2-1.*** *Transaction logging with autocommitted and explicit transactions*

The code in Listing 2-1 demonstrates this overhead in action. It performs the INSERT/UPDATE/DELETE sequence 10,000 times in a loop in autocommitted and explicit transactions, measuring execution time and transaction log throughput with the sys.dm_io_virtual_file_stats view.

***Listing 2-1.*** Autocommitted and explicit transactions

```
create table dbo.TranOverhead
(
    Id int not null,
    Col char(50) null,
    constraint PK_TranOverhead
    primary key clustered(Id)
);

-- Autocommitted transactions
declare
    @Id int = 1,
    @StartTime datetime = getDate(),
    @num_of_writes bigint,
    @num_of_bytes_written bigint

select
    @num_of_writes = num_of_writes
    ,@num_of_bytes_written = num_of_bytes_written
from
    sys.dm_io_virtual_file_stats(db_id(),2);

while @Id < 10000
begin
    insert into dbo.TranOverhead(Id, Col) values(@Id, 'A');

    update dbo.TranOverhead set Col = 'B' where Id = @Id;

    delete from dbo.TranOverhead where Id = @Id;

    set @Id += 1;
end;
```

```
select
    datediff(millisecond, @StartTime, getDate())
            as [Exec Time ms: Autocommitted Tran]
    ,s.num_of_writes - @num_of_writes as [Number of writes]
    ,(s.num_of_bytes_written - @num_of_bytes_written) / 1024
            as [Bytes written (KB)]
from
    sys.dm_io_virtual_file_stats(db_id(),2) s;
go

-- Explicit Tran
declare
    @Id int = 1,
    @StartTime datetime = getDate(),
    @num_of_writes bigint,
    @num_of_bytes_written bigint

select
    @num_of_writes = num_of_writes
    ,@num_of_bytes_written = num_of_bytes_written
from
    sys.dm_io_virtual_file_stats(db_id(),2);

while @Id < 10000
begin
    begin tran
        insert into dbo.TranOverhead(Id, Col) values(@Id, 'A');

        update dbo.TranOverhead set Col = 'B' where Id = @Id;

        delete from dbo.TranOverhead where Id = @Id;
    commit
    set @Id += 1;
end;
```

```
select
    datediff(millisecond, @StartTime, getDate())
          as [Exec Time ms: Explicit Tran]
    ,s.num_of_writes - @num_of_writes as [Number of writes]
    ,(s.num_of_bytes_written - @num_of_bytes_written) / 1024
          as [Bytes written (KB)]
```

Figure 2-2 illustrates the output of the code in my environment. As you can see, explicit transactions are about two times faster and generated three times less log activity than autocommitted ones.

| | Exec Time ms: Autocommitted Tran | Number of writes | Bytes written (KB) |
| --- | --- | --- | --- |
| 1 | 5470 | 30001 | 120624 |

| | Exec Time ms: Explicit Tran | Number of writes | Bytes written (KB) |
| --- | --- | --- | --- |
| 1 | 2040 | 10000 | 40624 |

***Figure 2-2.*** *Explicit and autocommitted transaction performance*

SQL Server 2014 and above allows you to improve transaction log throughput by using *delayed durability*. In this mode, SQL Server does not flush log buffers when COMMIT log records are generated. This reduces the number of disk writes at the cost of potential small data losses in case of disaster.

---

**Note**   You can read more about delayed durability at https://docs.microsoft.com/en-us/sql/relational-databases/logs/control-transaction-durability or in my *Pro SQL Server Internals* book.

---

SQL Server also supports *implicit transactions*, which you can enable with the SET IMPLICIT_TRANSACTION ON statement. When this option is enabled, SQL Server starts the new transaction when there are no active explicit transactions present. This transaction stays active until you explicitly issue a COMMIT or ROLLBACK statement.

From a performance and transaction log throughput standpoint, implicit transactions are similar to explicit ones. However, they make transaction management more complicated and are rarely used in production. However, there is a caveat—the SET ANSI_DEFAULT ON option also automatically enables implicit transactions. This behavior may lead to unexpected concurrency issues in the system.

# Error Handling

Error handling in SQL Server is a tricky subject, especially with transactions involved. SQL Server handles exceptions differently depending on error severity, active transaction context, and several other factors.

Let's look at how exceptions affect control flow during execution. Listing 2-2 creates two tables—dbo.Customers and dbo.Orders—and populates them with data. Note the existence of a foreign key constraint defined in the dbo.Orders table.

***Listing 2-2.*** Error handling: Tables creation

```
create table dbo.Customers
(
    CustomerId int not null,
    constraint PK_Customers
    primary key(CustomerId)
);

create table dbo.Orders
(
    OrderId int not null,
    CustomerId int not null,

    constraint FK_Orders_Customerss
    foreign key(CustomerId)
    references dbo.Customers(CustomerId)
);
go

create proc dbo.ResetData
as
begin
    begin tran
        delete from dbo.Orders;
        delete from dbo.Customers;
        insert into dbo.Customers(CustomerId) values(1),(2),(3);
        insert into dbo.Orders(OrderId, CustomerId) values(2,2);
    commit
```

```
end;
go
```

```
exec dbo.ResetData;
```

Let's run three DELETE statements in one batch, as shown in Listing 2-3. The second statement will trigger a *foreign key violation* error. The @@ERROR system variable provides the error number for the last T-SQL statement executed (0 means no errors).

***Listing 2-3.*** Error handling: Deleting customers

```
delete from  dbo.Customers where CustomerId = 1; -- Success
select @@ERROR as [@@ERROR: CustomerId = 1];
delete from  dbo.Customers where CustomerId = 2; -- FK Violation
select @@ERROR as [@@ERROR: CustomerId = 2];
delete from  dbo.Customers where CustomerId = 3; -- Success
select @@ERROR as [@@ERROR: CustomerId = 3];
go

select * from dbo.Customers;
```

Figure 2-3 illustrates the output of the code. As you can see, SQL Server continues execution after the non-critical *foreign key violation* error, deleting the row with CustomerId=3 afterward.

```
@@ERROR: CustomerId = 1
-----------------------
0
```

```
Msg 547, Level 16, State 0, Line 66
The DELETE statement conflicted with the REFERENCE constraint "FK_Orders_Customerss".
The conflict occurred in database "SQLServerInternals", table "dbo.Orders", column 'CustomerId'.
The statement has been terminated.

@@ERROR: CustomerId = 2
-----------------------
547
```

```
@@ERROR: CustomerId = 3
-----------------------
0
```

```
CustomerId
-----------
2
```

***Figure 2-3.*** *Deleting three customers in the batch*

The situation would change if you use a TRY..CATCH block, as shown in Listing 2-4.

***Listing 2-4.*** Error handling: Deleting customers in TRY..CATCH block

```
exec dbo.ResetData;
go

begin try
    delete from  dbo.Customers where CustomerId = 1; -- Success
    delete from  dbo.Customers where CustomerId = 2; -- FK Violation
    delete from  dbo.Customers where CustomerId = 3; -- Not executed
end try
begin catch
    select
        ERROR_NUMBER() as [Error Number]
        ,ERROR_LINE() as [Error Line]
        ,ERROR_MESSAGE() as [Error Message];
end catch
go

select * from dbo.Customers;
```

As you can see in Figure 2-4, the error was caught in the CATCH block, and the third deletion statement has not been executed.

| | Error Number | Error Line | Error Message |
|---|---|---|---|
| 1 | 547 | 4 | The DELETE statement conflicted with the REFERENCE constr... |

| | CustomerId |
|---|---|
| 1 | 2 |
| 2 | 3 |

***Figure 2-4.*** *Deleting three customers in TRY..CATCH block*

There are several functions that you can use in the CATCH block:

> ERROR_NUMBER() returns the number of the error that caused the CATCH block to run.

> ERROR_MESSAGE() provides an error message.

ERROR_SEVERITY() and ERROR_STATE() indicate the severity and state number of the error, respectively.

ERROR_PROCEDURE() returns the name of the stored procedure or trigger in which the error occurred. This can be useful if the code has nested stored procedure calls with TRY..CATCH in the outer module.

ERROR_LINE() provides the line number at which the error occurred.

Finally, the THROW operator allows you to re-throw an error from the CATCH block.

---

**Important**    Non-critical exceptions do not automatically roll back explicit or implicit transactions, regardless of whether a TRY..CATCH block is present. You still need to commit or roll back the transactions after the error.

---

Depending on the severity of the error, a transaction in which an error occurred may be committable or may become uncommittable and doomed. SQL Server would not allow you to commit uncommittable transactions, and you must roll it back to complete it.

The XACT_STATE() function allows you to analyze the state of a transaction; it returns one of three values:

0 indicates that there are no active transactions present.

1 indicates that there is an active *committable* transaction present. You can perform any actions and data modifications, committing the transactions afterward.

-1 indicates that there is an active *uncommittable* transaction present. You cannot commit such a transaction.

There is a very important SET option, XACT_ABORT, that allows you to control error-handling behavior in the code. When this option is set to ON, SQL Server treats every run-time error as severe, making transactions uncommittable. This prevents you from accidentally committing transactions when some data modifications failed with non-critical errors. Again, remember the example with the money transfer between checking and savings accounts. This transaction should not be committed if one of the UPDATE statements triggered an error, regardless of its severity.                                        37

When XACT_ABORT is enabled, any error would terminate the batch when a
TRY..CATCH block is not present. For example, if you run the code from Listing 2-3 again
using SET XACT_ABORT ON, the third DELETE statement would not be executed, and only
the row with CustomerId=1 will be deleted. Moreover, SQL Server would automatically
roll back doomed uncommitted transactions after the batch completed.

Listing 2-5 illustrates this behavior. The stored procedure dbo.GenerateError sets
XACT_ABORT to ON and generates an error within the active transaction. The @@TRANCOUNT
variable returns the nested level of the transaction (more on this later), and non-zero
values indicate that the transaction is active.

***Listing 2-5.*** SET XACT_ABORT behavior

```
create proc dbo.GenerateError
as
begin
    set xact_abort on
    begin tran
        delete from dbo.Customers where CustomerId = 2; -- Error
        select 'This statement will never be executed';
end
go

exec dbo.GenerateError;
select 'This statement will never be executed';
go

-- Another batch
select XACT_STATE() as [XACT_STATE()], @@TRANCOUNT as [@@TRANCOUNT];
go
```

Figure 2-5 illustrates the output of the code. As you can see, batch execution has
been terminated, and the transaction has been automatically rolled back at the end of
the batch.

```
Msg 547, Level 16, State 0, Procedure GenerateError, Line 7 [Batch Start Line 30]
The DELETE statement conflicted with the REFERENCE constraint "FK_Orders_Customerss".
The conflict occurred in database "SQLServerInternals", table "dbo.Orders", column 'CustomerId'.

XACT_STATE() @@TRANCOUNT
------------ -----------
0            0
```

**Figure 2-5.** *XACT_ABORT behavior*

A TRY..CATCH block, however, will allow you to capture the error even with XACT_ABORT set to ON. Listing 2-6 illustrates such a situation.

**Listing 2-6.** SET XACT_ABORT behavior with TRY..CATCH block

```
begin try
    exec dbo.GenerateError;
    select 'This statement will never be executed';
end try
begin catch
    select
        ERROR_NUMBER() as [Error Number]
        ,ERROR_PROCEDURE() as [Procedure]
        ,ERROR_LINE() as [Error Line]
        ,ERROR_MESSAGE() as [Error Message];

    select
        XACT_STATE() as [XACT_STATE()]
        ,@@TRANCOUNT as [@@TRANCOUNT];

    if @@TRANCOUNT > 0
        rollback;
end catch
```

As you can see in Figure 2-6, the exception has been trapped in the CATCH block, with the transaction still remaining active there.

| | Error Number | Procedure | Error Line | Error Message |
|---|---|---|---|---|
| 1 | 547 | GenerateError | 7 | The DELETE statement conflicted with the REFEREN... |

| | XACT_STATE() | @@TRANCOUNT |
|---|---|---|
| 1 | -1 | 1 |

***Figure 2-6.*** *XACT_ABORT behavior with TRY..CATCH block*

Consistent error handling and transaction management strategies are extremely important and allow you to avoid data consistency errors and improve data quality in the system. I would recommend the following approach as the best practice:

- Always use explicit transactions in the code during data modifications. This would guarantee data consistency in transactions that consist of multiple operations. It is also more efficient than individual autocommitted transactions.

- Set XACT_ABORT to ON before transaction is started. This would guarantee the "all-or-nothing" behavior of the transaction, preventing SQL Server from ignoring non-severe errors or committing partially completed transactions.

- Use proper error handling with TRY..CATCH blocks and explicitly roll back transactions in case of exceptions. This helps to avoid unforeseen side effects in case of errors.

It is impossible to perform the operations that generate transaction log records after a transaction becomes uncommittable. In practice, it means that you could not perform any data modifications—for example, log errors in the database in the CATCH block—until you roll back an uncommittable transaction. You can persist the data in table variables if needed.

---

**Tip**   As the opposite of temporary tables, table variables are not transaction-aware. The data in table variables would not be affected by a transaction rollback.

---

The choice between client-side and server-side transaction management depends on the application architecture. Client-side management is required when data modifications are done in the application code; for example, changes are generated by ORM frameworks. On the other hand, stored procedure-based data access tiers may benefit from server-side transaction management.

Listing 2-7 provides an example of a stored procedure that implements server-side transaction management.

***Listing 2-7.*** Server-side transaction management

```
create proc dbo.PerformDataModifications
as
begin
    set xact_abort on
    begin try
        begin tran
            /* Perform required data modifications */
        commit
    end try
    begin catch
        if @@TRANCOUNT > 0 -- Transaction is active
            rollback;
        /* Addional error-handling code */
        throw;  -- Re-throw error. Alternatively, SP may return the error
        code
    end catch;
end;
```

# Nested Transactions and Savepoints

SQL Server *technically* supports nested transactions; however, they are primarily intended to simplify transaction management during nested stored procedure calls. In practice, it means that the code needs to explicitly commit all nested transactions, and the number of COMMIT calls should match the number of BEGIN TRAN calls. The ROLLBACK statement, however, rolls back the entire transaction regardless of the current nested level.

The code in Listing 2-8 demonstrates this behavior. As I already mentioned, system variable @@TRANCOUNT returns the nested level of the transaction.

***Listing 2-8.*** Nested transactions

```
select @@TRANCOUNT as [Original @@TRANCOUNT];
begin tran
    select @@TRANCOUNT as [@@TRANCOUNT after the first BEGIN TRAN];
    begin tran
        select @@TRANCOUNT as [@@TRANCOUNT after the second BEGIN TRAN];
    commit
    select @@TRANCOUNT as [@@TRANCOUNT after nested COMMIT];
    begin tran
        select @@TRANCOUNT as [@@TRANCOUNT after the third BEGIN TRAN];
    rollback
select @@TRANCOUNT as [@@TRANCOUNT after ROLLBACK];
rollback; -- This ROLLBACK generates the error
```

You can see the output of the code in Figure 2-7.

```
Original @@TRANCOUNT
-------------------
0
@@TRANCOUNT after the first BEGIN TRAN
--------------------------------------
1
@@TRANCOUNT after the second BEGIN TRAN
---------------------------------------
2
@@TRANCOUNT after nested COMMIT
-------------------------------
1
@@TRANCOUNT after the third BEGIN TRAN
--------------------------------------
2
@@TRANCOUNT after ROLLBACK
--------------------------
0

Msg 3903, Level 16, State 1, Line 27
The ROLLBACK TRANSACTION request has no corresponding BEGIN TRANSACTION.
```

***Figure 2-7.*** *Nested transactions*

You can save the state of the transaction and create a *savepoint* by using a SAVE TRANSACTION statement. This will allow you to partially roll back a transaction, returning to the most recent savepoint. The transaction will remain active and will need to be completed with an explicit COMMIT or ROLLBACK statement later.

---

**Note**   Uncommittable transactions with XACT_STATE() = -1 cannot be rolled back to a savepoint. In practice, it means that you cannot roll back to a savepoint after an error if XACT_ABORT is set to ON.

---

The code in Listing 2-9 illustrates this behavior. The stored procedure creates the savepoint when it runs an active transaction and rolls back to this savepoint in case of a committable error.

*Listing 2-9.* Savepoints

```
create proc dbo.TryDeleteCustomer
(
    @CustomerId int
)
as
begin
    -- Setting XACT_ABORT to OFF for rollback to savepoint to work
    set xact_abort off

    declare
        @ActiveTran bit

    -- Check if SP is calling in context of active transaction
    set @ActiveTran = IIF(@@TranCount > 0, 1, 0);

    if @ActiveTran = 0
        begin tran;
    else
        save transaction TryDeleteCustomer;

    begin try
        delete dbo.Customers where CustomerId = @CustomerId;
```

43

```
        if @ActiveTran = 0
            commit;
        return 0;
    end try
    begin catch
        if @ActiveTran = 0 or XACT_STATE() = -1
        begin
            -- Roll back entire transaction
            rollback tran;
            return -1;
        end
        else begin
                -- Roll back to savepoint
            rollback tran TryDeleteCustomer;
            return 1;
        end
    end catch;
end;
```

The code in Listing 2-10 triggers a foreign key violation during the second
dbo.TryDeleteCustomer call. This is a non-critical error, and therefore the code is able to
commit after it.

***Listing 2-10.*** dbo.TryDeleteCustomer in action

```
declare
    @ReturnCode int

exec dbo.ResetData;

begin tran
    exec @ReturnCode = TryDeleteCustomer @CustomerId = 1;
    select
        1 as [CustomerId]
        ,@ReturnCode as [@ReturnCode]
        ,XACT_STATE() as [XACT_STATE()];
```

```
    if @ReturnCode >= 0
    begin
        exec @ReturnCode = TryDeleteCustomer @CustomerId = 2;
        select
            2 as [CustomerId]
            ,@ReturnCode as [@ReturnCode]
            ,XACT_STATE() as [XACT_STATE()];
    end
if @ReturnCode >= 0
    commit;
else
    if @@TRANCOUNT > 0
        rollback;
go

select * from dbo.Customers;
```

Figure 2-8 shows the output of the code. As you can see, SQL Server has been able to successfully delete the row with CustomerId=1 and commit the transaction at this state.

| | CustomerId | @ReturnCode | XACT_STATE() |
|---|---|---|---|
| 1 | 1 | 0 | 1 |

| | CustomerId | @ReturnCode | XACT_STATE() |
|---|---|---|---|
| 1 | 2 | 1 | 1 |

| | CustomerId |
|---|---|
| 1 | 2 |
| 2 | 3 |

*Figure 2-8.* *Output of Listing 2-10*

It is worth noting that this example is shown for demonstration purposes only. From an efficiency standpoint, it would be better to validate the referential integrity and existence of the orders before deletion occurred rather than catching an exception and rolling back to a savepoint in case of an error.

# Summary

Transactions are a key concept in data management systems and support atomicity, consistency, isolation, and durability requirements for data modifications in the system.

There are two concurrency models used in database systems. Pessimistic concurrency expects that users may want to update the same data, and it blocks access to uncommitted changes from other sessions. Optimistic concurrency assumes that the chance of simultaneous data updates is low. There is no blocking under this model; however, simultaneous updates will lead to write–write conflicts.

SQL Server supports four pessimistic (READ UNCOMMITTED, READ COMMITTED, REPEATABLE READ, and SERIALIZABLE) and one optimistic (SNAPSHOT) isolation levels. It also supports the READ COMMITTED SNAPSHOT isolation level, which implements optimistic concurrency for readers and pessimistic concurrency for data modification queries.

There are three types of transactions in SQL Server—explicit, autocommitted, and implicit. Autocommitted transactions are less efficient as a result of the transaction logging overhead they introduce.

Depending on the severity of the errors and a few other factors, transactions may be committable or may become uncommittable and doomed. You can treat all errors as uncommittable by setting XACT_ABORT option to ON. This approach simplifies error handling and reduces the chance of data inconsistency in the system.

SQL Server supports nested transactions. The number of COMMIT calls should match the BEGIN TRAN calls for the transaction to be committed. A ROLLBACK statement, on the other hand, rolls back the entire transaction regardless of the nested level.

# CHAPTER 3

# Lock Types

This chapter will discuss the key concept in SQL Server concurrency—*locks*. It will provide an overview of the major lock types in SQL Server, explain their compatibility, and, finally, demonstrate how different transaction isolation levels affect the lifetime of the locks in the system.

## Major Lock Types

SQL Server uses locking to support the isolation requirements of the transaction. Every lock, in a nutshell, is an in-memory structure managed by a SQL Server component called the *lock manager*. Each lock structure uses 64 bytes of memory on the 32-bit and 128 bytes on the 64-bit edition of SQL Server.

Locks are acquired and held on *resources*, such as data rows, pages, partitions, tables (objects), databases, and several others. By default, SQL Server uses row-level locking to acquire locks on the data rows, which minimizes possible concurrency issues in the system. You should remember, however, that the only guarantee SQL Server provides is enforcing data isolation and consistency based on transaction isolation levels. The locking behavior is not documented, and in some cases SQL Server can choose to lock at the page or table level rather than at the row level. Nevertheless, lock compatibility rules are always enforced, and understanding the locking model is enough to troubleshoot and address the majority of the concurrency issues in the system.

The key attribute in the lock structure is the *lock type*. Internally, SQL Server uses more than 20 different lock types. They can be grouped into several major categories based on their type and usage.

© Dmitri Korotkevitch 2018
D. Korotkevitch, *Expert SQL Server Transactions and Locking*, https://doi.org/10.1007/978-1-4842-3957-5_3

## CODE SAMPLES

The code examples in this and subsequent chapters will rely on the `Delivery.Orders` table defined here. This table has a clustered primary key on the `OrderId` column with no nonclustered indexes defined.

You can find the script that creates the table and populates it with the data in the companion materials of the book.

```
create schema Delivery;

create table Delivery.Orders
(
    OrderId int not null identity(1,1),
    OrderDate smalldatetime not null,
    OrderNum varchar(20) not null,
    Reference varchar(64) null,
    CustomerId int not null,
    PickupAddressId int not null,
    DeliveryAddressId int not null,
    ServiceId int not null,
    RatePlanId int not null,
    OrderStatusId int not null,
    DriverId int null,
    Pieces smallint not null,
    Amount smallmoney not null,
    ModTime datetime not null
        constraint DEF_Orders_ModTime
        default getDate(),
    PlaceHolder char(100) not null
        constraint DEF_Orders_Placeholder
        default 'Placeholder',

    constraint PK_Orders
    primary key clustered(OrderId)
)
go
```

```
declare
    @MaxOrderId int = 65536
    ,@MaxCustomers int = 1000
    ,@MaxAddresses int = 20
    ,@MaxDrivers int = 125

;with N1(C) as (select 0 union all select 0) -- 2 rows
,N2(C) as (select 0 from N1 as T1 cross join N1 as T2) -- 4 rows
,N3(C) as (select 0 from N2 as T1 cross join N2 as T2) -- 16 rows
,N4(C) as (select 0 from N3 as T1 cross join N3 as T2) -- 256 rows
,N5(C) as (select 0 from N4 as T1 cross join N4 as T2) -- 65,536 rows
,IDs(ID) as (select row_number() over (order by (select null)) from N5)
,Info(OrderId, CustomerId, OrderDateOffset, RatePlanId, ServiceId, Pieces)
as
(
    select
        ID, ID % @MaxCustomers + 1, ID % (365*24*60)
        ,ID % 2 + 1, ID % 3 + 1, ID % 5 + 1
    from IDs
    where ID <= @MaxOrderId
)
,Info2(OrderId, OrderDate, OrderNum, CustomerId, RatePlanId ,ServiceId
    ,Pieces ,PickupAddressId, OrderStatusId, Rate)
as
(
    select
        OrderId
        ,dateadd(minute, -OrderDateOffset, getdate())
        ,convert(varchar(10),OrderId), CustomerId
        ,RatePlanId
        ,ServiceId
        ,Pieces
        ,(CustomerId - 1) * @MaxAddresses + OrderId % 20
        ,case
            when OrderDateOffset > 5 * 24 * 60
            then 4
            else OrderId % 4 + 1
        end
```

```
        ,(OrderId % 5 + 1) * 10.
    from Info
)
insert into Delivery.Orders(OrderDate, OrderNum, CustomerId,
    PickupAddressId, DeliveryAddressId, ServiceId, RatePlanId,
    OrderStatusId, DriverId, Pieces, Amount)
select
    o.OrderDate
    ,o.OrderNum
    ,o.CustomerId
    ,o.PickupAddressId
    ,case
        when o.PickupAddressId % @MaxAddresses = 0
        then o.PickupAddressId + 1
        else o.PickupAddressId - 1
    end
    ,o.ServiceId
    ,o.RatePlanId
    ,o.OrderStatusId
    ,case
        when o.OrderStatusId in (1,4)
        then NULL
        else OrderId % @MaxDrivers + 1
    end
    ,o.Pieces
    ,o.Rate
from Info2 o;
```

# Exclusive (X) Locks

Exclusive (X) locks are acquired by *writers*—INSERT, UPDATE, DELETE, and MERGE
statements that modify data. Those queries acquire exclusive (X) locks on the affected
rows and hold them until the end of the transaction.

As you can guess by the name—*exclusive* means *exclusive*—only one session can
hold an exclusive (X) lock on the resource at any given point in time. This behavior
enforces the most important concurrency rule in the system—multiple sessions cannot
modify the same data simultaneously. That's it; other sessions are unable to acquire

exclusive (X) locks on the row until the first transaction is completed and the exclusive (X) lock on the modified row is released.

Transaction isolation levels do not affect exclusive (X) lock behavior. Exclusive (X) locks are acquired and held until the end of the transaction, even in READ UNCOMMITTED mode. The longer the transaction you have, the longer the exclusive (X) locks would be held, which would increase the chance that blocking would occur.

# Intent (I*) Locks

Even though row-level locking reduces blocking in the system, keeping locks only on the row level would be bad from a performance standpoint. Consider a situation where a session needs to have exclusive access to a table; for example, during the table alteration. In this case, if only row-level locking existed, the session would have to scan the entire table, checking if any row-level locks were held there. As you can imagine, this would be an extremely inefficient process, especially on large tables.

SQL Server addresses this situation by introducing the concept of intent (I*) locks. Intent locks are held on the data-page and table levels and indicate the existence of locks on the child objects.

Let's run the code from Listing 3-1 and check what locks are held after we update one row in the table. The code uses the sys.dm_tran_locks dynamic management view, which returns information about current lock requests in the system.

It is worth noting that I am using the READ UNCOMMITTED isolation level to demonstrate that exclusive (X) locks are acquired in any transaction isolation level.

*Listing 3-1.* Updating a row and checking the locks held

```
set transaction isolation level read uncommitted
begin tran
    update Delivery.Orders
    set Reference = 'New Reference'
    where OrderId = 100;

    select
        l.resource_type
        ,case
            when l.resource_type = 'OBJECT'
            then
```

```
                object_name
                (
                    l.resource_associated_entity_id
                     ,l.resource_database_id
                )
            else ''
        end as [table]
        ,l.resource_description
        ,l.request_type
        ,l.request_mode
        ,l.request_status
    from
        sys.dm_tran_locks l
    where
        l.request_session_id = @@spid;
commit
```

Figure 3-1 illustrates the output from the SELECT statement. As you can see, SQL Server held an exclusive (X) lock on the row (key) and intent exclusive (IX) locks on both the page and the object (table). *Those intent exclusive (IX) locks indicate the existence of the exclusive (X) row-level lock held.* Finally, there was also a shared (S) lock on the database, which indicates that the session was accessing it. We will cover shared (S) locks later in this chapter.

| | resource_type | table | resource_description | request_type | request_mode | request_status |
|---|---|---|---|---|---|---|
| 1 | DATABASE | | | LOCK | S | GRANT |
| 2 | PAGE | | 3:11 | LOCK | IX | GRANT |
| 3 | KEY | | (931e04457546) | LOCK | X | GRANT |
| 4 | OBJECT | Orders | | LOCK | IX | GRANT |

*Figure 3-1.* *Locks held after UPDATE statement*

The `resource_description` column indicates the resources on which those locks were acquired. For the page, it indicates its physical location (page 944 in the database file 1), and for the row (key) it indicates the hash value of the index key. For object locks, you can obtain the `object_id` from the `resource_associated_entry_id` column in the view.

When the session needs to obtain object- or page-level locks, it could check lock compatibility with the other locks (intent or full) held on the table or page rather than scanning the table/page and checking row-level locks there.

Finally, it is worth noting that in some cases SQL Server may acquire intent locks on other intermediate objects, such as table partitions or row groups in columnstore indexes.

# Update (U) locks

SQL Server uses another lock type, update (U) locks, during data modifications, acquiring them while searching for the rows that need to be updated. After an update (U) lock is acquired, SQL Server reads the row and *evaluates* if the row needs to be updated by checking the row data against query predicates. If this is the case, SQL Server converts the update (U) lock to an exclusive (X) lock and performs the data modification. Otherwise, the update (U) lock is released.

Let's look at an example and run the code from Listing 3-2.

***Listing 3-2.*** Updating multiple rows using clustered index key as the predicate

```
begin tran
    update Delivery.Orders
    set Reference = 'New Reference'
    where OrderId in (1000, 5000);
commit
```

Figure 3-2 provides the output from the Extended Events session that captures `lock_acquired` and `lock_released` events. SQL Server acquired aintent update (IU) locks on the pages and update (U) locks on the rows converting them to intent exclusive (IX) and exclusive (X) locks afterwards. The locks were held until the end of the transactions and were released at the time of COMMIT.

| name | mode | resource_descri... | resource_type |
|------|------|--------------------|---------------|
| lock_acquired | IX | | OBJECT |
| lock_acquired | IU | 1:4581 | PAGE |
| lock_acquired | U | (1f00de11a529) | KEY |
| lock_acquired | IX | 1:4581 | PAGE |
| lock_acquired | X | (1f00de11a529) | KEY |
| lock_acquired | IU | 1:4665 | PAGE |
| lock_acquired | U | (086dba16bcf4) | KEY |
| lock_acquired | IX | 1:4665 | PAGE |
| lock_acquired | X | (086dba16bcf4) | KEY |
| lock_released | X | (086dba16bcf4) | KEY |
| lock_released | IX | 1:4665 | PAGE |
| lock_released | X | (1f00de11a529) | KEY |
| lock_released | IX | 1:4581 | PAGE |
| lock_released | IX | | OBJECT |

**Figure 3-2.**  *Update (U) and exclusive (X) locks*

Update (U) locks' behavior depends on the execution plan. In some cases, SQL Server acquires update (U) locks on all rows first, converting them to exclusive (X) locks afterward. In other cases—when, for example, you update only one row based on the clustered index key value—SQL Server can acquire an exclusive (X) lock without using an update (U) lock at all.

The number of locks to acquire also greatly depends on the execution plan. Let's run the UPDATE Delivery.Orders SET Reference = 'Ref' WHERE OrderNum='1000' statement, filtering data based on the OrderNum column. Figure 3-3 illustrates the locks that were acquired and released along with the total number of locks processed.

| name | mode | resource_descri... | resource_type |
|---|---|---|---|
| lock_acquired | IU | 1:4746 | PAGE |
| lock_acquired | U | (c03154f3046a) | KEY |
| lock_released | U | (c03154f3046a) | KEY |
| lock_acquired | U | (20057a7cc0d6) | KEY |
| lock_released | U | (20057a7cc0d6) | KEY |
| lock_acquired | U | (d94911eb25da) | KEY |
| lock_released | U | (d94911eb25da) | KEY |
| lock_acquired | U | (e16c266249af) | KEY |
| lock_released | U | (e16c266249af) | KEY |

| package_name | event_name | count |
|---|---|---|
| sqlserver | lock_acquired | 1070885 |
| sqlserver | lock_released | 1070885 |

*Figure 3-3. Locks during query execution*

There are no indexes on the OrderNum column, so SQL Server needs to perform a *clustered index scan*, acquiring an update (U) lock on every row in the table. More than one million locks have been acquired even though the statement updated just a single row.

That behavior illustrates one of the typical blocking scenarios. Consider a situation where one of the sessions holds an exclusive (X) lock on a single row. If another session were to update a different row by running a non-optimized UPDATE statement, SQL Server would acquire an update (U) lock on every row it was scanning, and eventually it would be blocked trying to read the row with the exclusive (X) lock held on it. It does not matter that the second session does not need to update that row after all—SQL Server still needs to acquire an update (U) lock to evaluate if that row needs to be updated.

# Shared (S) locks

Shared (S) locks are acquired by the readers—SELECT queries—in the system. As you can guess by the name, shared (S) locks are compatible with each other, and multiple sessions can hold shared (S) locks on the same resource.

Let's run the code from Table 3-1 to illustrate that.

**Table 3-1.**  *Shared (S) Locks*

| Session 1 (SPID=53) | Session 2 (SPID=55) |
|---|---|
| set transaction isolation level<br>repeatable read | set transaction isolation level<br>repeatable read |
| begin tran<br>    select OrderNum<br>    from Delivery.Orders<br>    where OrderId = 500; | begin tran<br>    select OrderNum<br>    from Delivery.Orders<br>    where OrderId = 500; |
| select<br>    request_session_id<br>    ,resource_type<br>    ,resource_description<br>    ,request_type<br>    ,request_mode<br>    ,request_status<br>from sys.dm_tran_locks; | |
| commit; | commit |

Figure 3-4 illustrates the output from the sys.dm_tran_locks view. As you can see, both sessions acquired shared (S) locks on the database, intent shared (IS) locks on the table and page (1:955), and shared (S) locks on the row, all without blocking each other.

| | request_session_id | resource_type | resource_description | request_type | request_mode | request_status |
|---|---|---|---|---|---|---|
| 1 | 53 | DATABASE | | LOCK | S | GRANT |
| 2 | 55 | DATABASE | | LOCK | S | GRANT |
| 3 | 53 | PAGE | 1:955 | LOCK | IS | GRANT |
| 4 | 55 | PAGE | 1:955 | LOCK | IS | GRANT |
| 5 | 53 | KEY | (c07b8c04b989) | LOCK | S | GRANT |
| 6 | 55 | KEY | (c07b8c04b989) | LOCK | S | GRANT |
| 7 | 53 | OBJECT | | LOCK | IS | GRANT |
| 8 | 55 | OBJECT | | LOCK | IS | GRANT |

**Figure 3-4.**  *Locks acquired by the sessions*

# Lock Compatibility, Behavior, and Lifetime

Table 3-2 shows the lock compatibility matrix that shows compatibility between lock types.

***Table 3-2.*** *Lock Compatibility Matrix (I\*, S, U, X Locks)*

|      | (IS) | (S)  | (IU) | (U)  | (IX) | (X)  |
|------|------|------|------|------|------|------|
| (IS) | Yes  | Yes  | Yes  | Yes  | Yes  | No   |
| (S)  | Yes  | **Yes** | Yes  | **Yes** | No   | **No** |
| (IU) | Yes  | Yes  | Yes  | No   | Yes  | No   |
| (U)  | Yes  | **Yes** | No   | **No** | No   | **No** |
| (IX) | Yes  | No   | Yes  | No   | Yes  | No   |
| (X)  | No   | **No** | No   | **No** | No   | **No** |

The most important lock compatibility rules are:

1.  Intent (IS/IU/IX) locks are compatible with each other. Intent locks indicate the existence of locks on the child objects, and multiple sessions can hold intent locks on the object and page levels simultaneously.

2.  Exclusive (X) locks are incompatible with each other and any other lock types. Multiple sessions cannot update the same row simultaneously. Moreover, readers that acquire shared (S) locks cannot read uncommitted rows with exclusive (X) locks held.

3.  Update (U) locks are incompatible with each other as well as with exclusive (X) locks. Writers cannot evaluate if the row needs to be updated simultaneously nor access a row that has an exclusive (X) lock held.

4.  Update (U) locks are compatible with shared (S) locks. Writers can evaluate if the row needs to be updated without blocking or being blocked by the readers. It is worth noting that (S)/(U) lock compatibility is the main reason why SQL Server uses update (U) locks internally. They reduce the blocking between readers and writers.

57

As you already know, exclusive (X) lock behavior does not depend on transaction isolation level. Writers always acquire exclusive (X) locks and hold them until the end of the transaction. With the exception of the SNAPSHOT isolation level, the same is true for update (U) locks—writers acquire them on every row they scan while evaluating if the rows need to be updated.

The shared (S) locks' behavior, on the other hand, depends on transaction isolation level.

---

**Note**    SQL Server always works with data in the transaction context. In this case, when applications do not start explicit transactions with BEGIN TRAN / COMMIT statements, SQL Server uses autocommitted transactions for the duration of the statements. Even SELECT statements run within their own lightweight transactions. SQL Server does not write them to the transaction log, although all locking and concurrency rules still apply.

---

With the READ UNCOMMITTED isolation level, shared (S) locks are not acquired. Therefore, readers can read the rows that have been modified by other sessions and have exclusive (X) locks held. This isolation level reduces blocking in the system by eliminating conflicts between readers and writers at the cost of data consistency. Readers would read the current (modified) version of the row regardless of what happens next, such as if changes were rolled back or if a row were modified multiple times. This explains why this isolation level is often called a *dirty read*.

The code in Table 3-3 illustrates that. The first session runs a DELETE statement, acquiring an exclusive (X) lock on the row. The second session runs a SELECT statement in READ UNCOMMITTED mode.

***Table 3-3.*** *READ UNCOMMITTED Isolation Level Consistency*

| Session 1 | Session 2 |
|---|---|
| begin tran<br>   delete from Delivery.Orders<br>   where OrderId = 95; | |
| | -- Success / No Blocking<br>set transaction isolation level read<br>uncommitted;<br>select OrderId, Amount<br>from Delivery.Orders<br>where OrderId between 94 and 96; |
| rollback; | |

In the READ UNCOMMITTED isolation level, readers do not acquire shared (S) locks. Session 2 would not be blocked and would return the result set shown in Figure 3-5. It does not include the row with OrderId=95, which has been deleted in the uncommitted transaction in the first session even though the transaction is rolled back afterward.

| | OrderId | Amount |
|---|---|---|
| 1 | 94 | 30.00 |
| 2 | 96 | 10.00 |

***Figure 3-5.*** *READ UNCOMMITTED and shared (S) lock behavior*

It is worth noting again that exclusive (X) and update (U) locks' behavior is not affected by transaction isolation level. You will have writers/writers blocking even in READ UNCOMMITTED mode.

In the READ COMMITTED isolation level, SQL Server acquires and releases shared (S) locks immediately after the row has been read. This guarantees that transactions cannot read uncommitted data from other sessions. Let's run the code from Listing 3-3.

***Listing 3-3.*** Reading data in READ COMMITTED isolation level

```
set transaction isolation level read committed;
select OrderId, Amount
from Delivery.Orders
where OrderId in (90,91);
```

Figure 3-6 illustrates how SQL Server acquires and releases the locks. As you can see, row-level locks are acquired and released immediately.

| name | mode | resource_descri... | resource_type |
|---|---|---|---|
| lock_acquired | IS | | OBJECT |
| lock_acquired | IS | 1:386 | PAGE |
| lock_acquired | S | (bbd62f3afb44) | KEY |
| lock_released | S | (bbd62f3afb44) | KEY |
| lock_acquired | S | (a2ae6a22daf4) | KEY |
| lock_released | S | (a2ae6a22daf4) | KEY |
| lock_released | IS | 1:386 | PAGE |
| lock_released | IS | | OBJECT |

***Figure 3-6.*** *Shared (S) locks' behavior in READ COMMITTED mode*

It is worth noting that in some cases, in READ COMMITTED mode, SQL Server can hold shared (S) locks for the duration of the SELECT statement, releasing the locks only after it is completed. One such example is a query that reads the data from LOB columns from the table.

---

**Tip**    Do not select unnecessary columns or use the SELECT * pattern in the code. This may introduce performance overhead and increase locking in the system.

---

In the REPEATABLE READ isolation level, SQL Server acquires shared (S) locks and holds them until the end of the transaction. This guarantees that other sessions cannot modify the data after it is read. You can see this behavior if you run the code from Listing 3-3, changing the isolation level to REPEATABLE READ.

Figure 3-7 illustrates how SQL Server acquires and releases the locks. As you can see, SQL Server acquires both shared (S) locks first, releasing them at the end of the transaction.

| name | mode | resource_descri... | resource_type |
|------|------|--------------------|---------------|
| lock_acquired | IS | | OBJECT |
| lock_acquired | IS | 1:386 | PAGE |
| lock_acquired | S | (bbd62f3afb44) | KEY |
| lock_acquired | S | (a2ae6a22daf4) | KEY |
| lock_released | S | (a2ae6a22daf4) | KEY |
| lock_released | S | (bbd62f3afb44) | KEY |
| lock_released | IS | 1:386 | PAGE |
| lock_released | IS | | OBJECT |

***Figure 3-7.*** *Shared (S) locks' behavior in REPEATABLE READ mode*

In the SERIALIZABLE isolation level, shared (S) locks are also held until the end of the transaction. However, SQL Server uses another variation of the locks called *range locks*. Range locks (both shared and exclusive) protect index-key ranges rather than individual rows.

Consider a situation where a Delivery.Orders table has just two rows with OrderId of 1 and 10. In the REPEATABLE READ isolation level, the SELECT statement would acquire two row-level locks. Other sessions would not be able to modify those rows, but they could still insert the new row with OrderId in between those values. In the SERIALIZABLE isolation level, the SELECT statement would acquire a range shared (RangeS-S) lock, preventing other sessions from inserting any rows in between OrderId of 1 and 10.

Figure 3-8 illustrates how SQL Server acquires and releases locks in the SERIALIZABLE isolation level.

| name | mode | resource_descri... | resource_type |
|------|------|--------------------|---------------|
| lock_acquired | IS | | OBJECT |
| lock_acquired | IS | 1:386 | PAGE |
| lock_acquired | RS_S | (bbd62f3afb44) | KEY |
| lock_acquired | RS_S | (a2ae6a22daf4) | KEY |
| lock_released | RS_S | (a2ae6a22daf4) | KEY |
| lock_released | RS_S | (bbd62f3afb44) | KEY |
| lock_released | IS | 1:386 | PAGE |
| lock_released | IS | | OBJECT |

*Figure 3-8.* Shared (S) locks' behavior in SERIALIZABLE isolation level

Optimistic isolation levels—READ COMMITTED SNAPSHOT and SNAPSHOT—do not acquire shared (S) locks. When readers (SELECT queries) encounter a row with an exclusive (X) lock held, they read the old (previously committed) version of this row from the version store in tempdb. Writers and uncommitted data modifications do not block readers in the system.

From the blocking and concurrency standpoints, READ COMMITTED SNAPSHOT has the same behavior as READ UNCOMMITTED. Both isolation levels remove the issue of readers/writers' blocking in the system. READ COMMITTED SNAPSHOT, however, provides better data consistency by eliminating access to uncommitted data and dirty reads. In the vast majority of cases, you should not use READ UNCOMMITTED, and should switch to using READ COMMITTED SNAPSHOT instead.

---

**Note**   We will discuss optimistic isolation levels in greater depth in Chapter 6.

---

Table 3-4 summarizes how SQL Server works with shared (S) locks based on transaction isolation levels.

**Table 3-4.** *Transaction Isolation Levels and Shared (S) Locks' Behavior*

| Transaction Isolation Level | Table Hint | Shared Lock Behavior |
|---|---|---|
| READ UNCOMMITTED | (NOLOCK) | (S) locks not acquired |
| READ COMMITTED (default) | (READCOMMITTED) | (S) locks acquired and released immediately |
| REPEATABLE READ | (REPEATABLEREAD) | (S) locks acquired and held till end of transaction |
| SERIALIZABLE | (SERIALIZABLE) or (HOLDLOCK) | Range locks acquired and held till end of transaction |
| READ COMMITTED SNAPSHOT | N/A | (S) locks not acquired |
| SNAPSHOT | N/A | (S) locks not acquired |

You can control isolation levels and locking behavior on the transaction level by using a SET TRANSACTION ISOLATION LEVEL statement or on the table level with a table locking hint.

It is possible to use different isolation levels in the same query on a per-table basis, as is shown in Listing 3-4.

**Listing 3-4.** Controlling locking behavior with table hints

```
select c.CustomerName, sum(o.Total) as [Total]
from
    dbo.Customers c with (READCOMMITTED) join
        dbo.Orders o with (SERIALIZABLE) on
            o.CustomerId = c.CustomerId
group by
    c.CustomerName;
```

**Note**   The famous NOLOCK hint is just a synonym for READ UNCOMMITTED table access.

Finally, I would like to reiterate that all transaction isolation levels except SNAPSHOT behave in the same way and use update (U) locks during update scans and exclusive (X) locks during data modifications. This leads to writers/writers blocking in the system.

The SNAPSHOT isolation level also uses exclusive (X) locks during data modifications. However, it does not use update (U) locks during update scans, reading the old versions of the rows from the version store in tempdb. This eliminates writers/writers blocking unless multiple sessions are trying to update the same rows simultaneously.

# Transaction Isolation Levels and Data Consistency

As already mentioned in the previous chapter, we may experience several concurrency phenomena in the system. Let's analyze why those phenomena are possible based on the locking behavior of transaction isolation levels.

**Dirty Reads**: This issue arises when transaction reads uncommitted (dirty) data from other uncommitted transactions. It is unknown if those active transactions will be committed or rolled back or if the data is logically consistent.

From the locking perspective, this phenomenon could occur in the READ UNCOMMITTED isolation level when sessions do not acquire shared (S) locks and ignore exclusive (X) locks from the other sessions. All other isolation levels are immune from dirty reads. Pessimistic isolation levels use shared (S) locks and are blocked when trying to access uncommitted rows with exclusive (X) locks held on them. Optimistic isolation levels, on the other hand, read old (previously) committed versions of the rows from the version store.

**Non-Repeatable Reads**: Subsequent attempts to read the same data from within the same transaction return different results. This data inconsistency issue arises when the other transactions modified or even deleted data between reads. Consider a situation where you render a report that displays a list of the orders for a specific customer along with some aggregated information (for example, total amount spent by customer on a monthly basis). If another session modifies or perhaps deletes the orders in between those queries, the result sets will be inconsistent.

From the locking standpoint, such a phenomenon could occur when sessions don't protect/lock the data in between reads. This could happen in the READ UNCOMMITTED and READ COMMITTED SNAPSHOT isolation levels, which do not use shared (S) locks, as well as in the READ COMMITTED isolation level when sessions acquire and release shared (S) locks immediately. REPEATABLE READ and SERIALIZABLE isolation levels hold the shared (S) locks until the end of the transaction, which prevents data modifications once data is read.

The SNAPSHOT isolation level is also immune from this phenomenon as it works with a *snapshot* of the data at the time when the transaction started. We will discuss it in depth in Chapter 6.

**Phantom Reads**: This phenomenon occurs when subsequent reads within the same transaction return new rows (ones that the transaction did not read before). Think about the previous example when another session inserted a new order in between queries' execution. Only the SERIALIZABLE and SNAPSHOT isolation levels are free from such phenomenon. SERIALIZABLE uses range locks while SNAPSHOT accesses a snapshot of the data at the time when the transaction starts.

Two other phenomena are related to data movement due to the change of the index-key value. Neither of them occur with optimistic isolation levels.

**Duplicated Reads**: This issue occurs when a query returns the same row multiple times. Think about a query that returns a list of orders for a specific time interval, scanning the index on the OrderDate column during execution. If another query changes the OrderDate value, moving the row from the processed (scanned) to non-processed part of the index, such a row will be read twice.

This condition is similar to non-repeatable reads and can occur when readers do not hold shared (S) locks after rows are read in READ UNCOMMITTED and READ COMMITTED isolation levels.

**Skipped Rows:** This phenomenon occurs when queries do not return some of the rows. It could occur in a similar condition with duplicated reads as just described if rows have been moved from the non-processed to the processed part of the index. The SERIALIZABLE isolation level, which locks the index-key range interval, and optimistic isolation levels—READ COMMITTED SNAPSHOT and SNAPSHOT—are free from such phenomenon.

Table 3-5 summarizes data inconsistency issues within the different transaction isolation levels.

***Table 3-5.*** *Transaction Isolation Levels and Data Inconsistency Anomalies*

|  | Dirty Reads | Non-Repeatable Reads | Duplicated Reads | Phantom Reads | Skipped Rows |
|---|---|---|---|---|---|
| READ UNCOMMITTED | Yes | Yes | Yes | Yes | Yes |
| READ COMMITTED | No | Yes | Yes | Yes | Yes |
| REPEATABLE READ | No | No | No | Yes | Yes |
| SERIALIZABLE | No | No | No | No | No |
| READ COMMITTED SNAPSHOT | No | Yes | No | Yes | No |
| SNAPSHOT | No | No | No | No | No |

SERIALIZABLE and SNAPSHOT are the only transaction isolation levels that protect you from data inconsistency issues. Both of them have downsides, however. SERIALIZABLE may introduce major blocking issues and deadlocks due to excessive locking in systems with volatile data. SNAPSHOT, on the other hand, may lead to significant tempdb load along with the write/write conflict errors. Use them with care!

# Locking-Related Table Hints

There are several other locking-related table hints in addition to the isolation level–related hints we have already covered.

You can control the type of lock acquired by readers with (UPDLOCK) and (XLOCK) table hints. These hints force SELECT queries to use update (U) and exclusive (X) locks, respectively, rather than shared (S) locks. This can be useful when you need to prevent multiple SELECT queries from reading the same rows simultaneously.

Listing 3-5 demonstrates one such example, implementing custom counters in the system. The SELECT statement uses an update (U) lock, which will block other sessions from reading the same counter row until the transaction is committed.

---

**Note**   This code is shown for demonstration purposes only and does not handle situations where a specific counter does not exist in the table. It is better to use a SEQUENCE object instead.

---

*Listing 3-5.* Counters table management

```
begin tran
    select @Value = Value
    from dbo.Counters with (UPDLOCK)
    where CounterName = @CounterName;

    update dbo.Counters
    set Value += @ReserveCount
    where CounterName = @CounterName;
commit
```

There are several hints that can help you to control lock granularity. The (TABLOCK) and (TABLOCKX) hints force SQL Server to acquire shared (S) or exclusive (X) table-level locks. With the (TABLOCK) hint, the type of the lock depends on the statement—readers acquire shared (S) and writers acquire exclusive (X) locks. The (TABLOCKX) hint, on the other hand, always acquires an exclusive (X) lock on the table, even with readers.

As I already mentioned, SQL Server may decide to use lower-granularity locks in some cases. For example, during the scans, SQL Server may decide to use full (non-intent) page locks instead of acquiring row-level locks on every row from the page. This behavior, however, is not guaranteed, but can be controlled, to a degree, with (PAGLOCK) and (ROWLOCK) hints.

The (PAGLOCK) hint forces SQL Server to use full locks on the page level rather than on the row level. Alternatively, the (ROWLOCK) hint prevents SQL Server from using full page-level locks, forcing it to use row-level locking instead. As usual, both approaches have benefits and downsides, and in the vast majority of cases it is better to allow SQL Server to choose the proper locking strategy rather than using those hints.

The (READPAST) hint allows sessions to skip rows with incompatible locks held on them rather than being blocked. You will see one example where such a hint is useful in Chapter 10. Alternatively, the (NOWAIT) hint triggers an error as soon as SQL Server encounters an incompatible row- or page-level lock from other sessions.

You can combine multiple locking hints together as long as they do not conflict with each other. Listing 3-6 shows such an example. The first SELECT statement would use page-level exclusive (X) locks. The second SELECT statement would use row-level locking, keeping shared (S) locks held until the end of the transaction due to the REPEATABLEREAD hint skipping the rows with incompatible lock types held. Finally, the third statement would fail due to a conflicting locking hint combination.

***Listing 3-6.*** Combining locking hints

```
select OrderId, OrderDate
from Delivery.Orders with (PAGLOCK XLOCK)
where CustomerId = @CustomerId;

select OrderId, OrderDate
from Delivery.Orders with (ROWLOCK REPEATABLEREAD READPAST)
where CustomerId = @CustomerId;

select OrderId, OrderDate
from Delivery.Orders with (NOLOCK TABLOCK)
where CustomerId = @CustomerId;
```

---

**Note**   For more information about table hints, go to https://docs.microsoft.com/en-us/sql/t-sql/queries/hints-transact-sql-table.

---

Finally, there is the SET LOCK_TIMEOUT option, which can be used on the session level to control how long the session should wait for a lock request to be granted. SQL Server generates an error when a request cannot be granted within the specified interval. A value of -1 indicates no timeout and a value of 0 indicates immediate timeout, similar to the (NOWAIT) hint.

SQL Server treats lock timeout errors similarly to other errors in the system. The error would not terminate the batch nor would it make an explicit transaction uncommittable unless you have the XACT_ABORT option set to ON. You need to factor this behavior into the error-handling strategy, as we discussed in the previous chapter.

Also, remember that SET LOCK_TIMEOUT does not override the SQL Client CommandTimeout value. The client call would fail when the statement execution time exceeds CommandTimeout regardless of the root cause of the wait.

# Conversion Locks

*Conversion locks* are another group of lock types you can encounter in production. They are a combination of full and intent locks and may be acquired on page and object levels. SQL Server uses them when it needs to *extend* already acquired full locks with an additional intent lock or, alternatively, already acquired intent locks with a full lock of a different type. You can think about them as internal optimization, which allows the session to avoid holding multiple locks on the same resource.

Let's look at the example and run the code from Listing 3-7. As the first step, we will run a SELECT statement in the active transaction using (REPEATABLEREAD TABLOCK) hints. These hints will force the statement to acquire an object-level lock and hold it for the duration of the transaction.

***Listing 3-7.*** Conversion locks: Running SELECT statement

```
begin tran
    select top 10 OrderId, Amount
    from Delivery.Orders with (REPEATABLEREAD TABLOCK)
    order by OrderId;

select
    l.resource_type
    ,case
```

```
            when l.resource_type = 'OBJECT'
            then
                object_name
                  (
                        l.resource_associated_entity_id
                        ,l.resource_database_id
                  )
                else ''
        end as [table]
        ,l.resource_description
        ,l.request_type
        ,l.request_mode
        ,l.request_status
    from
        sys.dm_tran_locks l
    where
        l.request_session_id = @@spid;
```

Figure 3-9 illustrates the locks acquired by the statement. You can see the object-level shared (S) lock in place.

| | resource_type | table | resource_description | request_type | request_mode | request_status |
|---|---|---|---|---|---|---|
| 1 | DATABASE | | | LOCK | S | GRANT |
| 2 | OBJECT | Orders | | LOCK | S | GRANT |

***Figure 3-9.*** *Conversion locks: Locks held by SELECT statement*

Now, let's run another query that updates one of the rows in the same active transaction, as shown in Listing 3-8.

***Listing 3-8.*** Conversion locks: Running UPDATE statement

```
update Delivery.Orders
set Amount *= 0.95
where OrderId = 100;
```

This operation requires SQL Server to obtain an exclusive (X) lock on the row and intent exclusive (IX) locks on the page and object levels. The table, however, already has a full shared (S) lock held, and SQL Server replaces it with a *shared intent exclusive (SIX)* lock, as shown in Figure 3-10.

| | resource_type | table | resource_description | request_type | request_mode | request_status |
|---|---|---|---|---|---|---|
| 1 | DATABASE | | | LOCK | S | GRANT |
| 2 | PAGE | | 3:11 | LOCK | IX | GRANT |
| 3 | KEY | | (931e04457546) | LOCK | X | GRANT |
| 4 | OBJECT | Orders | | LOCK | SIX | GRANT |

*Figure 3-10.* *Conversion locks: Locks held after UPDATE statement*

There are two other types of conversion locks besides (SIX):

*Shared intent update (SIU)* locks are acquired during update scans when SQL Server needs to acquire an intent update (IU) lock on the same resource on which the shared (S) lock is held.

*Update intent exclusive (UIX)* locks may be acquired when SQL Server needs to acquire an intent exclusive (IX) lock on a resource that already has an update (U) lock held on it. This lock type is usually used on data pages during update scans when SQL Server uses page-level rather than row-level locking. In this mode, SQL Server acquires a page-level update (U) lock first, changing it to an update intent exclusive (UIX) lock if some of the rows on the page need to be updated. It is worth noting that SQL Server does not replace page-level (UIX) locks with intent exclusive (IX) locks afterward, keeping (UIX) locks until the end of transaction.

Conversion locks, in a nutshell, consist of two different lock types. Other locks need to be compatible with both of them in order to be granted. For example, intent shared (IS) locks are compatible with shared intent exclusive (SIX) locks because (IS) locks are compatible with both (S) and (IX) locks. Intent exclusive (IX) locks, on the other hand, are incompatible with (SIX) due to (IX) and (S) locks' incompatibility.

---

**Note**   Table 3-2 in this chapter shows the lock compatibility matrix for regular locks.

---

# Summary

SQL Server uses locking to support data isolation and consistency rules, using row-level locking as the highest degree of granularity.

Exclusive (X) locks are acquired by writers when data is modified. Exclusive (X) locks are always acquired and held until the end of the transaction regardless of the isolation level. Update (U) locks are acquired when writers evaluate if data needs to be modified. Those locks are converted into exclusive (X) locks if data needs to be updated and are released otherwise. Intent (I*) locks are acquired on the object and page levels and indicate the existence of child row-level locks of the same type.

With the exception of the READ UNCOMMITTED isolation level, SQL Server acquires shared (S) locks while reading data in pessimistic isolation levels. Transaction isolation level controls when shared (S) locks are released. In the READ COMMITTED isolation level, these locks are released immediately after the row has been read. In REPEATABLE READ and SERIALIZABLE isolation levels, shared (S) locks are held until the end of the transaction. Moreover, in the SERIALIZABLE isolation level, SQL Server uses range locks to lock the ranges of the index keys rather than individual rows.

Optimistic isolation levels rely on row versioning and read old (previously committed) versions of the rows from the version store in tempdb. READ COMMMITTED SNAPSHOT has the same blocking behavior as READ UNCOMMITTED; however, it provides better data consistency by preventing access to dirty uncommitted data. You should use READ COMMITTED SNAPSHOT instead of READ UNCOMMITTED.

You can control transaction isolation levels with the SET TRANSACTION ISOLATION LEVEL statement on the transaction level or with table locking hints on the table level in the individual queries.

# CHAPTER 4

# Blocking in the System

Blocking is, perhaps, one of the most common concurrency problems encountered in the systems. When blocking occurs, multiple queries block each other, which increases the execution time of queries and introduces timeouts. All of that negatively affects the user experience with the system.

This chapter will show how you can troubleshoot blocking issues in a system. It will illustrate how you can analyze blocking conditions in real time and collect information for further analysis.

## General Troubleshooting Approach

Blocking occurs when multiple sessions compete for the same resource. In some cases, this is the correct and expected behavior; for example, multiple sessions cannot update the same row simultaneously. However, in many cases blocking is unexpected and occurs because queries were trying to acquire unnecessary locks.

Some degree of blocking always exists in systems, and it is completely normal. What is not normal, however, is excessive blocking. From the end user's standpoint, excessive blocking masks itself as a general performance problem. The system is slow, queries are timing out, and often there are deadlocks.

Apart from deadlocks, system slowness is not necessarily a sign of blocking issues— many other factors can negatively impact performance. However, blocking issues can definitely contribute to a general system slowdown.

During the initial phase of performance troubleshooting, you should take a holistic view of the system and find the most critical issues to address. As you can guess, blocking and concurrency issues may or may not be present in this list. We will discuss how to perform that holistic analysis in Chapter 12, focusing on general blocking troubleshooting in this chapter.

© Dmitri Korotkevitch 2018
D. Korotkevitch, *Expert SQL Server Transactions and Locking*, https://doi.org/10.1007/978-1-4842-3957-5_4

In a nutshell, to troubleshoot blocking issues, you must follow these steps:

1. Detect the queries involved in the blocking.

2. Find out why blocking occurs.

3. Fix the root cause of the issue.

SQL Server provides you with several tools that can help you with these tasks. These tools can be separated into two different categories. The first category consists of dynamic management views that you can use to troubleshoot what is happening in the system at present. These tools are useful when you have access to the system at the time of blocking and want to perform real-time troubleshooting.

The second category of tools allows you to collect information about blocking problems in the system and retain it for further analysis. Let's look at both categories in detail.

# Troubleshooting Blocking Issues in Real Time

The key tool for troubleshooting real-time blocking is the `sys.dm_tran_locks` dynamic management view, which provides information about currently active lock requests in the system. It returns you a list of lock requests and their type, status of request (GRANT or WAIT), information about the resources on which the locks were requested, and several other useful attributes.

Table 4-1 shows you the code that leads to the blocking condition.

***Table 4-1.*** *Code That Leads to the Blocking Condition*

| Session 1 (SPID=52) | Session 2 (SPID=53) | Comments |
| --- | --- | --- |
| `begin tran`<br>`    delete from`<br>`Delivery.Orders`<br>`    where OrderId = 95` | | Session 1 acquires exclusive (X) lock on the row with OrderId=95 |
| | `select OrderId, Amount`<br>`from Delivery.Orders`<br>`    with (readcommitted)`<br>`where OrderNum = '1000'` | Session 2 is blocked trying to acquire shared (S) lock on the row with OrderId=95 |
| `rollback` | | |

Figure 4-1 shows the partial output from the sys.dm_tran_locks, sys.dm_os_ waiting_tasks, and sys.dm_exec_requests views at the time the blocking occurred. As you can see, Session 53 is waiting for a shared (S) lock on the row with the exclusive (X) lock held by Session 52. The LCK_M_S wait type in the outputs indicates the shared (S) lock wait. We will discuss wait types in more detail in Chapter 12.

| | request_session_id | resource_type | resource_description | request_mode | request_type | request_status |
|---|---|---|---|---|---|---|
| 1 | 53 | DATABASE | | S | LOCK | GRANT |
| 2 | 52 | DATABASE | | S | LOCK | GRANT |
| 3 | 53 | PAGE | 1:377 | IS | LOCK | GRANT |
| 4 | 52 | PAGE | 1:377 | IX | LOCK | GRANT |
| 5 | 52 | KEY | (5be201b53ff8) | X | LOCK | GRANT |
| 6 | 53 | KEY | (5be201b53ff8) | S | LOCK | WAIT |
| 7 | 53 | OBJECT | | IS | LOCK | GRANT |
| 8 | 52 | OBJECT | | IX | LOCK | GRANT |

| | session_id | wait_duration_ms | wait_type | blocking_session_id | resource_description |
|---|---|---|---|---|---|
| 1 | 53 | 157064 | LCK_M_S | 52 | keylock hobtid=72057594067025920 dbi... |

| | session_id | status | wait_type | wait_time | wait_resource | command |
|---|---|---|---|---|---|---|
| 1 | 53 | suspended | LCK_M_S | 157064 | KEY: 13:72057594067025920 (5be201b53ff8) | SELECT |

***Figure 4-1.*** *Output from the system views at time of blocking*

---

**Note**    It is possible that you will get page-level blocking when you run the code in your system. Session 53 needs to scan all rows from the page, and SQL Server may decide to obtain a page-level shared (S) lock instead of row-level locks. Nevertheless, the session will be blocked due to (S) / (IX) lock incompatibility at the page level.

---

The information provided by the sys.dm_tran_locks view is a bit too cryptic to troubleshoot, and you often need to join it with other dynamic management views, such as sys.dm_exec_requests and sys.dm_os_waiting_tasks, to gain a clearer picture. Listing 4-1 provides the required code.

***Listing 4-1.*** Getting more information about blocked and blocking sessions

```
select
    tl.resource_type as [Resource Type]
    ,db_name(tl.resource_database_id) as [DB Name]
    ,case tl.resource_type
```

```
        when 'OBJECT' then
            object_name
                (
                    tl.resource_associated_entity_id
                    ,tl.resource_database_id
                )
        when 'DATABASE' then 'DB'
        else
            case when tl.resource_database_id = db_id()
                then
                    ( select object_name(object_id, tl.resource_database_id)
                        from sys.partitions
                        where hobt_id = tl.resource_associated_entity_id )
                else '(Run under DB context)'
            end
    end as [Object]
    ,tl.resource_description as [Resource]
    ,tl.request_session_id as [Session]
    ,tl.request_mode as [Mode]
    ,tl.request_status as [Status]
    ,wt.wait_duration_ms as [Wait (ms)]
    ,qi.sql
    ,qi.query_plan
from
    sys.dm_tran_locks tl with (nolock) left outer join
            sys.dm_os_waiting_tasks wt with (nolock) on
                tl.lock_owner_address = wt.resource_address and
                tl.request_status = 'WAIT'
    outer apply
    (
        select
            substring(s.text, (er.statement_start_offset / 2) + 1,
                (( case er.statement_end_offset
                        when -1
                        then datalength(s.text)
```

```
                        else er.statement_end_offset
                    end - er.statement_start_offset) / 2) + 1) as sql
            , qp.query_plan
        from
            sys.dm_exec_requests er with (nolock)
                cross apply sys.dm_exec_sql_text(er.sql_handle) s
                cross apply sys.dm_exec_query_plan(er.plan_handle) qp
        where
            tl.request_session_id = er.session_id
    ) qi
where
    tl.request_session_id <> @@spid
order by
    tl.request_session_id
option (recompile)
```

Figure 4-2 shows the results of the query. As you can see, it is much easier to understand, and it provides you with more useful information, including currently running batches and their execution plans. Keep in mind that the execution plans obtained from the `sys.dm_exec_requests` and `sys.dm_exec_query_stats` DMVs do not include the actual execution statistics metrics, such as the actual number of rows returned by operators and the number of their executions. Also, for the sessions in which lock requests were granted, the SQL statement and query plan represent the *currently executing batch* (`NULL` if session is sleeping), rather than the batch that acquired the original lock.

| | Resource Type | DB Name | Object | Resource | Session | Mode | Status | Wait (ms) | sql | query_plan |
|---|---|---|---|---|---|---|---|---|---|---|
| 1 | DATABASE | SQLServerInternals | DB | | 52 | S | GRANT | NULL | NULL | NULL |
| 2 | OBJECT | SQLServerInternals | Orders | | 52 | IX | GRANT | NULL | NULL | NULL |
| 3 | PAGE | SQLServerInternals | Orders | 1:377 | 52 | IX | GRANT | NULL | NULL | NULL |
| 4 | KEY | SQLServerInternals | Orders | (5be201b53ff8) | 52 | X | GRANT | NULL | NULL | NULL |
| 5 | KEY | SQLServerInternals | Orders | (5be201b53ff8) | 53 | S | WAIT | 486032 | select OrderId, Amount fro... | <ShowPlanXML xmlns="h... |
| 6 | DATABASE | SQLServerInternals | DB | | 53 | S | GRANT | NULL | select OrderId, Amount fro... | <ShowPlanXML xmlns="h... |
| 7 | PAGE | SQLServerInternals | Orders | 1:377 | 53 | IS | GRANT | NULL | select OrderId, Amount fro... | <ShowPlanXML xmlns="h... |
| 8 | OBJECT | SQLServerInternals | Orders | | 53 | IS | GRANT | NULL | select OrderId, Amount fro... | <ShowPlanXML xmlns="h... |

***Figure 4-2.*** *Joining sys.dm_os_tran_locks with other DMVs*

You need to run the query in the context of the database involved in the blocking to correctly resolve the object names. Also of importance, the `OBJECT_NAME()` function used in the code obtains a schema stability (Sch-S) lock on the object, and the statement would be blocked if you tried to resolve the name of the object with an active schema modification (Sch-M) lock held. SQL Server obtains those locks during schema alteration; we will discuss them in depth in Chapter 8.

The sys.dm_tran_locks view returns one row for each active lock request in the system, which can lead to very large result sets when you run it on busy servers. You can reduce the amount of information and perform a self-join of this view based on the resource_description and resource_associated_entity_id columns, and you can identify the sessions that compete for the same resources, as shown in Listing 4-2. Such an approach allows you to filter out the results and only see the sessions that are involved in the active blocking conditions.

*Listing 4-2.* Filtering out blocked and blocking session information

```
select
    tl1.resource_type as [Resource Type]
    ,db_name(tl1.resource_database_id) as [DB Name]
    ,case tl1.resource_type
        when 'OBJECT' then
            object_name
            (
                tl1.resource_associated_entity_id
                ,tl1.resource_database_id
            )
        when 'DATABASE' then 'DB'
        else
            case when tl1.resource_database_id = db_id()
                then
                (
                    select
                        object_name(object_id, tl1.resource_database_id)
                    from sys.partitions
                    where hobt_id = tl1.resource_associated_entity_id
                )
                else '(Run under DB context)'
            end
```

```
    end as [Object]
    ,tl1.resource_description as [Resource]
    ,tl1.request_session_id as [Session]
    ,tl1.request_mode as [Mode]
    ,tl1.request_status as [Status]
    ,wt.wait_duration_ms as [Wait (ms)]
    ,qi.sql
    ,qi.query_plan
from
    sys.dm_tran_locks tl1 with (nolock) join
        sys.dm_tran_locks tl2 with (nolock) on
            tl1.resource_associated_entity_id = tl2.resource_associated_
            entity_id
    left outer join sys.dm_os_waiting_tasks wt with (nolock) on
        tl1.lock_owner_address = wt.resource_address and
        tl1.request_status = 'WAIT'
    outer apply
    (
        select
            substring(s.text, (er.statement_start_offset / 2) + 1,
                ((  case er.statement_end_offset
                        when -1
                        then datalength(s.text)
                        else er.statement_end_offset
                    end - er.statement_start_offset) / 2) + 1) as sql
            , qp.query_plan
        from
            sys.dm_exec_requests er with (nolock)
                cross apply sys.dm_exec_sql_text(er.sql_handle) s
                cross apply sys.dm_exec_query_plan(er.plan_handle) qp
        where
            tl1.request_session_id = er.session_id
    ) qi
```

```
where
    tl1.request_status <> tl2.request_status and
    (
        tl1.resource_description = tl2.resource_description or
        (
            tl1.resource_description is null and
            tl2.resource_description is null
        )
    )
option (recompile)
```

Figure 4-3 illustrates the output of this code. As you can see, this approach significantly reduces the size of the output and simplifies analysis.

| | Resource Type | DB Name | Object | Resource | Session | Mode | Status | Wait (ms) | sql | query_plan |
|---|---|---|---|---|---|---|---|---|---|---|
| 1 | KEY | SQLServerInternals | Orders | (5be201b53ff8) | 52 | X | GRANT | NULL | NULL | NULL |
| 2 | KEY | SQLServerInternals | Orders | (5be201b53ff8) | 53 | S | WAIT | 486154 | select OrderId, Amount  fr... | <ShowPlanXML xmlns="htt... |

***Figure 4-3.*** *Blocked and blocking sessions*

As you already know, blocking occurs when two or more sessions are competing for the same resource. You need to answer two questions during troubleshooting:

1.  Why does the *blocking* session hold the lock on the resource?

2.  Why does the *blocked* session acquire the lock on the resource?

Both questions are equally important; however, there are a couple of challenges you may encounter when analyzing the *blocking* session data. First, as I already mentioned, the *blocking* session data would show the queries that are currently executing rather than those that caused the blocking.

As an example, consider a situation where the session runs several data modification statements in a single transaction. As you remember, SQL Server would acquire and hold exclusive (X) locks on the updated rows until the end of the transaction. The blocking may occur over any of the previously updated rows with exclusive (X) locks held, which may or may not be acquired by the currently executing statement from the session.

The second challenge is related to the *blocking chains* when the blocking session is also blocked by another session. This usually happens in busy OLTP systems and is often related to object-level locks acquired during schema alteration, index maintenance, or in a few other cases.

Consider a situation where you have a Session 1 that holds an intent lock on the table. This intent lock would block Session 2, which may want to obtain a full table lock; for example, during an offline index rebuild. The blocked Session 2, in turn, will block all other sessions that may try to obtain intent locks on the table.

---

**Note**   We will discuss this and other situations that may lead to blocking chains later in the book. For now, however, remember that you need to rewind the blocking chains and include the root blocking session in your analysis when you encounter such a condition.

---

These challenges may lead to the situation where it is easier to start troubleshooting by looking at the *blocked* session, where you have the blocked statement and its execution plan available. In many cases, you can identify the root cause of the blocking by analyzing its execution plan, which you can obtain from the dynamic management views (as was demonstrated earlier) or by rerunning the query.

Figure 4-4 shows the execution plan of the blocked query from our example.

*Figure 4-4.* *Execution plan for the blocked query*

As you can see from the execution plan, the blocked query is scanning the entire table looking for orders with the predicate on the OrderNum column. The query uses a READ COMMITTED transaction isolation level, and it acquires a shared (S) lock on every row in the table. As a result, at some point the query is blocked by the first DELETE query, which holds an exclusive (X) lock on one of the rows. It is worth noting that the query would be blocked even if the row with the exclusive (X) lock held did not have OrderNum='1000'. SQL Server cannot evaluate the predicate until the shared (S) lock is acquired and the row is read.

You can resolve this problem by optimizing the query and adding the index on the `OrderNum` column, which will replace the *Clustered Index Scan* with the *Nonclustered Index Seek* operator in the execution plan. This will significantly reduce the number of locks the statement acquires and eliminate lock collision and blocking as long as the queries do not delete and select the same rows.

Even though in many instances you can detect and resolve the root cause of the blocking by analyzing and optimizing the *blocked* query, this is not always the case. Consider the situation where you have a session that is updating a large number of rows in a table and thus acquires and holds a large number of exclusive (X) locks on those rows. Other sessions that need to access those rows would be blocked, even in the case of efficient execution plans that do not perform unnecessary scans. The root cause of the blocking in this case is the *blocking* rather than *blocked* session.

As we have already discussed, you cannot always rely on the blocked statements returned by data management views. In many cases, you need to analyze what code in the blocking session has caused the blocking. You can use the `sys.dm_exec_sessions` view to obtain information about the host and application of the blocking session. When you know which statement the blocking session is currently executing, you can analyze the client and T-SQL code to locate the transaction to which this statement belongs. One of the previously executed statements in that transaction would be the one that caused the blocking condition.

The *blocked process report*, which we are about to discuss, can also help during such troubleshooting.

# Collecting Blocking Information for Further Analysis

Although DMVs can be very useful in providing information about the current state of the system, they are only helpful if you run them at the exact same time the blocking occurs. Fortunately, SQL Server helps capture blocking information automatically via the *blocked process report*. This report provides information about the blocking condition, which you may retain for further analysis. It is also incredibly useful when you need to deal with blocking chains and complex blocking cases.

There is a configuration setting called *blocked process threshold*, which specifies how often SQL Server checks for blocking in the system and generates a report (it is disabled by default). Listing 4-3 shows the code that sets the threshold to ten seconds.

***Listing 4-3.*** Specifying blocking process threshold

```
sp_configure 'show advanced options', 1;
go
reconfigure;
go
sp_configure 'blocked process threshold', 10; -- in seconds
go
reconfigure;
go
```

You need to fine-tune the value of the blocked process threshold in production. It is important to avoid false positives and, at the same time, capture the problems. Microsoft suggests not going below five seconds as the minimum value, and you obviously need to set the value to less than the query timeout. I usually use either five or ten seconds, depending on the amount of blocking in the system and phase of the troubleshooting.

There are a few ways to capture that report in the system. You can use SQL Trace; there is a "Blocked process report" event in the "Errors and "Warnings" section, as shown in Figure 4-5.

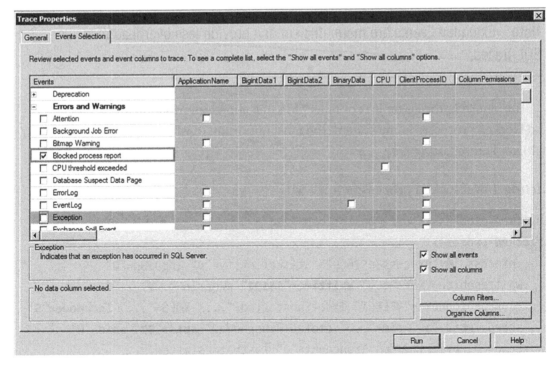

***Figure 4-5.*** *"Blocked process report" event in SQL Trace*

Alternatively, you can create an Extended Event session using a `blocked_process_report` event, as shown in Figure 4-6. This session will provide you with several additional attributes than those offered in SQL Trace.

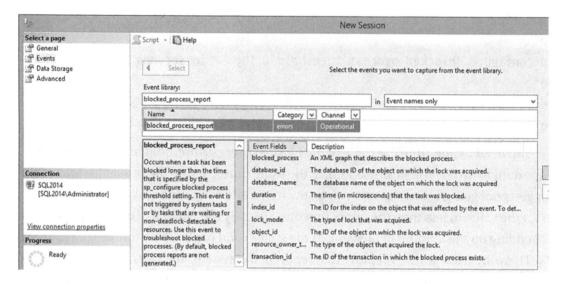

***Figure 4-6.*** *Capturing blocked process report with Extended Events*

---

**Note** Extended Events are more efficient and provide less overhead than SQL Traces.

---

The blocked process report contains XML that shows information about blocking and blocked processes in the system (the most important of which are highlighted in boldface within Listing 4-4).

***Listing 4-4.*** Blocked process report XML

```
<blocked-process-report monitorLoop="224">
<blocked-process>
    <process id="process3e576c928" taskpriority="0" logused="0"
    waitresource="KEY: ..." waittime="14102" ownerId="..."
    transactionname="SELECT" lasttranstarted="..." XDES="..." lockMode="S"
    schedulerid="1" kpid="..." status="suspended" spid="53" sbid="0"
    ecid="0" priority="0" trancount="0" lastbatchstarted="..."
```

```
        lastbatchcompleted="..." lastattention="..." clientapp="..."
        hostname="..." hostpid="..." loginname="..." isolationlevel="read
        committed (2)" xactid="..." currentdb="14" lockTimeout="..."
        clientoption1="..." clientoption2="...">
            <executionStack>
                <frame line="3" stmtstart="46" sqlhandle="..."/>
                <frame line="3" stmtstart="100" sqlhandle="..."/>
            </executionStack>
            <inputbuf>
set transaction isolation level read committed
select OrderId, Amount
from Delivery.Orders
where OrderNum = '1000'
            </inputbuf>
        </process>
</blocked-process>
<blocking-process>
    <process status="sleeping" spid="54" sbid="0" ecid="0" priority="0"
    trancount="1" lastbatchstarted="..." lastbatchcompleted="..."
    lastattention="..." clientapp="..." hostname="..." hostpid="..."
    loginname="..." isolationlevel="read uncommitted (1)"
    xactid="..." currentdb="14" lockTimeout="..." clientoption1="..."
    clientoption2="...">
            <executionStack/>
            <inputbuf>
set transaction isolation level read uncommitted
begin tran
    delete from Delivery.Orders
    where OrderId = 95
        </inputbuf>
    </process>
</blocking-process>
</blocked-process-report>
```

As with real-time troubleshooting, you should analyze both blocking and blocked processes and find the root cause of the problem. From the blocked process standpoint, the most important information is the following:

- `waittime`: The length of time the query is waiting, in milliseconds

- `lockMode`: The type of lock being waited for

- `isolationlevel`: The transaction isolation level

- `executionStack` and `inputBuf`: The query and/or the execution stack. You will see how to obtain the actual SQL statement involved in blocking in Listing 4-5.

From the blocking process standpoint, you must look at the following:

- `status`: It indicates whether the process is *running, sleeping,* or *suspended*. When the process is sleeping, there is an uncommitted transaction. When the process is suspended, that process either waits for the non-locking related resource (for example, a page from the disk) or is also blocked by the other session and so there is a blocking chain condition.

- `trancount`: A value greater than 1 indicates nested transactions. If the process status is *sleeping* at the same time, then there is a chance that the client did not commit the nested transactions correctly (for example, the number of `commit` statements is less than the number of `begin tran` statements in the code).

- `executionStack` and `inputBuf`: As we already discussed, in some cases you need to analyze what happens in the blocking process. Some common issues include runaway transactions (for example, missing `commit` statements in the nested transactions); long-running transactions with perhaps some UI involved; and excessive scans (for example, a missing index on the referencing column in the detail table leads to scans during a referential integrity check). Information about queries from the blocking session could be useful here. Remember that in the case of a blocked process, `executionStack` and `inputBuf` would correspond to the queries that were running at the moment when the blocked process report was generated rather than to the time of the blocking.

In many cases, blocking occurs because of unnecessary scans resulting from nonoptimized queries. Those queries acquire an unnecessarily large number of locks, which lead to lock collision and blocking. You can detect such cases by looking at the blocked queries' execution plans and seeing the inefficiencies there.

You can either run the query and check the execution plan, or use DMVs and obtain an execution plan from sys.dm_exec_query_stats based on the sql_handle, stmtStart, and stmtEnd elements from the execution stack. Listing 4-5 shows the code that achieves that.

***Listing 4-5.*** Obtaining query text and execution plan by SQL handle

```
declare
    @H varbinary(max) = /* Insert sql_handle from the top line of the
    execution stack */
    ,@S int = /* Insert stmtStart from the top line of the execution stack */
    ,@E int = /* Insert stmtEnd from the top line of the execution stack */

select
    substring(qt.text, (qs.statement_start_offset / 2) + 1,
        (( case qs.statement_end_offset
                when -1 then datalength(qt.text)
                else qs.statement_end_offset
            end - qs.statement_start_offset) / 2) + 1) as sql
    ,qp.query_plan
    ,qs.creation_time
    ,qs.last_execution_time
from
    sys.dm_exec_query_stats qs with (nolock)
        cross apply sys.dm_exec_sql_text(qs.sql_handle) qt
        cross apply sys.dm_exec_query_plan(qs.plan_handle) qp
where
    qs.sql_handle = @H and
    qs.statement_start_offset = @S
    and qs.statement_end_offset = @E
option (recompile)
```

Figure 4-7 shows the query output.

| | SQL | query_plan |
|---|---|---|
| 1 | SELECT [OrderId],[Amount] FR... | <ShowPlanXML xmlns="http://schema... |

***Figure 4-7.*** *Getting information from sys.dm_exec_query_stats*

There are a couple of potential problems with the sys.dm_exec_query_stats view of which you should be aware. First, this view relies on the execution plan cache. You will not be able to get the execution plan if it is not in the cache; for example, if a query used statement-level recompile with an option (recompile) clause.

Second, there is a chance that you will have more than one cached plan returned. In some cases, SQL Server keeps the execution statistics even after recompilation occurs, which could produce multiple rows in the result set. Moreover, you may have multiple cached plans when sessions use different SET options. There are two columns—creation_time and last_execution_time—that can help pinpoint the right plan.

This dependency on the plan cache during troubleshooting is the biggest downside of the blocked process report. SQL Server eventually removes old plans from the plan cache after queries are recompiled and/or plans are not reused. Therefore, the longer you wait to do the troubleshooting, the less likely it is that the plan will be present in the cache.

Microsoft Azure SQL Databases and SQL Server 2016 and above allow you to collect and persist information about running queries and their execution plans and statistics in the *Query Store*. The Query Store does not rely on the plan cache and is extremely useful during system troubleshooting.

---

**Note**    You can read about the Query Store at https://docs.microsoft.com/
en-us/sql/relational-databases/performance/monitoring-
performance-by-using-the-query-store.

---

# Blocking Monitoring with Event Notifications

Even though the blocked process report allows you to collect and persist blocking information for further analysis, you often need to access the plan cache to get the text and execution plans of the queries involved in the blocking. Unfortunately, the plan cache changes over time, and longer you wait, the less likely it is that the data you seek will be present there.

You can address this issue by building a monitoring solution based on SQL Server Event Notifications. Event Notifications is a Service Broker–based technology that allows you to capture information about specific SQL Server and DDL events and post a message about them into the Service Broker queue. Furthermore, you can define the activation procedure on the queue and react to an event—in our case, parse a blocked process report—nearly in real time.

---

**Note**    You can read about Event Notifications at `https://docs.microsoft.com/` `en-us/sql/relational-databases/service-broker/event-notifications`.

---

Let's look at the implementation. In my environments, I prefer to persist the blocking information in a separate database. Listing 4-6 creates the database and corresponding Service Broker and Event Notifications objects. Remember: You need to have the blocked process threshold set for the events to be fired.

***Listing 4-6.*** Setting up event notifications objects

```
use master
go

create database DBA;

exec sp_executesql
    N'alter database DBA set enable_broker;
    alter database DBA set recovery simple;';
go

use DBA
go

create queue dbo.BlockedProcessNotificationQueue
with status = on;
go
```

```
create service BlockedProcessNotificationService
on queue dbo.BlockedProcessNotificationQueue
([http://schemas.microsoft.com/SQL/Notifications/PostEventNotification]);
go

create event notification BlockedProcessNotificationEvent
on server
for BLOCKED_PROCESS_REPORT
to service
    'BlockedProcessNotificationService',
    'current database';
```

In the next step, shown in Listing 4-7, we need to create an activation stored procedure that would parse the blocked process report, as well as a table to persist blocking information.

You can enable or disable the collection of execution plans by setting the @collectPlan variable in the stored procedure. While execution plans are extremely useful during troubleshooting, sys.dm_exec_query_plan calls are CPU-intensive and may introduce noticeable CPU overhead in the system, along with a large amount of blocking. You need to consider this and disable plan collection when your servers are CPU-bound.

*Listing 4-7.* Creating a table and an activation stored procedure

```
create table dbo.BlockedProcessesInfo
(
    ID int not null identity(1,1),
    EventDate datetime not null,
    -- ID of the database where locking occurs
    DatabaseID smallint not null,
    -- Blocking resource
    [Resource] varchar(64) null,
    -- Wait time in MS
    WaitTime int not null,
    -- Raw blocked process report
    BlockedProcessReport xml not null,
    -- SPID of the blocked process
```

```
BlockedSPID smallint not null,
-- XACTID of the blocked process
BlockedXactId bigint null,
-- Blocked Lock Request Mode
BlockedLockMode varchar(16) null,
-- Transaction isolation level for blocked session
BlockedIsolationLevel varchar(32) null,
-- Top SQL Handle from execution stack
BlockedSQLHandle varbinary(64) null,
-- Blocked SQL Statement Start offset
BlockedStmtStart int null,
-- Blocked SQL Statement End offset
BlockedStmtEnd int null,
-- Blocked Query Hash
BlockedQueryHash binary(8) null,
-- Blocked Query Plan Hash
BlockedPlanHash binary(8) null,
-- Blocked SQL based on SQL Handle
BlockedSql nvarchar(max) null,
-- Blocked InputBuf from the report
BlockedInputBuf nvarchar(max) null,
-- Blocked Plan based on SQL Handle
BlockedQueryPlan xml null,
-- SPID of the blocking process
BlockingSPID smallint null,
-- Blocking Process status
BlockingStatus varchar(16) null,
-- Blocking Process Transaction Count
BlockingTranCount int null,
-- Blocking InputBuf from the report
BlockingInputBuf nvarchar(max) null,
-- Blocked SQL based on SQL Handle
BlockingSql nvarchar(max) null,
-- Blocking Plan based on SQL Handle
BlockingQueryPlan xml null
);
```

```
create unique clustered index IDX_BlockedProcessInfo_EventDate_ID
on dbo.BlockedProcessesInfo(EventDate, ID);
go

create function dbo.fnGetSqlText
(
    @SqlHandle varbinary(64)
    , @StmtStart int
    ,@StmtEnd int
)
returns table
/********************************************************************
Function: dbo.fnGetSqlText
Author: Dmitri V. Korotkevitch
Purpose:
    Returns sql text based on sql_handle and statement start/end offsets
    Includes several safeguards to avoid exceptions

Returns: 1-column table with SQL text
********************************************************************/
as
return
(
    select
        substring(
            t.text
            ,@StmtStart / 2 + 1
            ,((
                case
                    when @StmtEnd = -1
                    then datalength(t.text)
                    else @StmtEnd
                end - @StmtStart) / 2) + 1
        ) as [SQL]
```

```
    from sys.dm_exec_sql_text(nullif(@SqlHandle,0x)) t
    where
        isnulL(@SqlHandle,0x) <> 0x and
        -- In some rare cases, SQL Server may return empty or
        -- incorrect sql text
        isnull(t.text,'') <> '' and
        (
            case when @StmtEnd = -1
                then datalength(t.text)
                else @StmtEnd
            end > @StmtStart
        )
)
go

create function dbo.fnGetQueryInfoFromExecRequests
(
    @collectPlan bit
    ,@SPID smallint
    ,@SqlHandle varbinary(64)
    ,@StmtStart int
    ,@StmtEnd int
)
/*********************************************************************
Function: dbo. fnGetQueryInfoFromExecRequests
Author: Dmitri V. Korotkevitch
Purpose:
    Returns Returns query and plan hashes, and optional query plan
    from sys.dm_exec_requests based on @@spid, sql_handle and
    statement start/end offsets
*********************************************************************/
returns table
as
return
```

```
(
    select
        1 as DataExists
        ,er.query_plan_hash as plan_hash
        ,er.query_hash
        ,case
            when @collectPlan = 1
            then
            (
                select qp.query_plan
                from sys.dm_exec_query_plan(er.plan_handle) qp
            )
            else null
        end as query_plan
        from
            sys.dm_exec_requests er
        where
            er.session_id = @SPID and
            er.sql_handle = @SqlHandle and
            er.statement_start_offset = @StmtStart and
            er.statement_end_offset = @StmtEnd
)
go

create function dbo.fnGetQueryInfoFromQueryStats
(
    @collectPlan bit
    ,@SqlHandle varbinary(64)
    ,@StmtStart int
    ,@StmtEnd int
    ,@EventDate datetime
    ,@LastExecTimeBuffer int
)
```

```
/*******************************************************************
Function: dbo. fnGetQueryInfoFromQueryStats
Author: Dmitri V. Korotkevitch
Purpose:
    Returns Returns query and plan hashes, and optional query plan
    from sys.dm_exec_query_stats based on @@spid, sql_handle and
    statement start/end offsets
*******************************************************************/
returns table
as
return
(
    select top 1
        qs.query_plan_hash as plan_hash
        ,qs.query_hash
        ,case
            when @collectPlan = 1
            then
            (
                select qp.query_plan
                from sys.dm_exec_query_plan(qs.plan_handle) qp
            )
            else null
        end as query_plan
    from
        sys.dm_exec_query_stats qs with (nolock)
    where
        qs.sql_handle = @SqlHandle and
        qs.statement_start_offset = @StmtStart and
        qs.statement_end_offset = @StmtEnd and
        @EventDate between qs.creation_time and
            dateadd(second,@LastExecTimeBuffer,qs.last_execution_time)
    order by
        qs.last_execution_time desc
)
go
```

```
create procedure [dbo].[SB_BlockedProcessReport_Activation]
with execute as owner
/********************************************************************
Proc: dbo.SB_BlockedProcessReport_Activation
Author: Dmitri V. Korotkevitch
Purpose:
   Activation stored procedure for Blocked Processes Event Notification
********************************************************************/
as
begin
  set nocount on

  declare
    @Msg varbinary(max)
    ,@ch uniqueidentifier
    ,@MsgType sysname
    ,@Report xml
    ,@EventDate datetime
    ,@DBID smallint
    ,@EventType varchar(128)
    ,@blockedSPID int
    ,@blockedXactID bigint
    ,@resource varchar(64)
    ,@blockingSPID int
    ,@blockedSqlHandle varbinary(64)
    ,@blockedStmtStart int
    ,@blockedStmtEnd int
    ,@waitTime int
    ,@blockedXML xml
    ,@blockingXML xml
    ,@collectPlan bit = 1 -- Controls if we collect execution plans

  while 1 = 1
  begin
    begin try
      begin tran
        waitfor
```

```
(
  receive top (1)
    @ch = conversation_handle
    ,@Msg = message_body
    ,@MsgType = message_type_name
  from dbo.BlockedProcessNotificationQueue
), timeout 10000

if @@ROWCOUNT = 0
begin
  rollback;
  break;
end

if @MsgType = N'http://schemas.microsoft.com/SQL/Notifications/
EventNotification'
begin
  select
    @Report = convert(xml,@Msg)

  select
    @EventDate = @Report
      .value('(/EVENT_INSTANCE/StartTime/text())[1]','datetime')
    ,@DBID = @Report
      .value('(/EVENT_INSTANCE/DatabaseID/text())[1]','smallint')
    ,@EventType = @Report
      .value('(/EVENT_INSTANCE/EventType/text())[1]','varchar(128)');

  IF @EventType = 'BLOCKED_PROCESS_REPORT'
  begin
    select
      @Report = @Report
        .query('/EVENT_INSTANCE/TextData/*');

    select
      @blockedXML = @Report
        .query('/blocked-process-report/blocked-process/*')
```

```
select
  @resource = @blockedXML
    .value('/process[1]/@waitresource','varchar(64)')
  ,@blockedXactID = @blockedXML
    .value('/process[1]/@xactid','bigint')
  ,@waitTime = @blockedXML
    .value('/process[1]/@waittime','int')
  ,@blockedSPID = @blockedXML
    .value('process[1]/@spid','smallint')
  ,@blockingSPID = @Report
    .value ('/blocked-process-report[1]/blocking-process[1]/
    process[1]/@spid','smallint')
  ,@blockedSqlHandle = @blockedXML
    .value ('xs:hexBinary(substring((/process[1]/executionStack[1]/
    frame[1]/@sqlhandle)[1],3))','varbinary(max)')
  ,@blockedStmtStart = isnull(@blockedXML
    .value('/process[1]/executionStack[1]/frame[1]/
    @stmtstart','int'), 0)
  ,@blockedStmtEnd = isnull(@blockedXML
    .value('/process[1]/executionStack[1]/frame[1]/
    @stmtend','int'), -1);

update t
set t.WaitTime =
    case when t.WaitTime < @waitTime
      then @waitTime
      else t.WaitTime
    end
from [dbo].[BlockedProcessesInfo] t
where
  t.BlockedSPID = @blockedSPID and
  IsNull(t.BlockedXactId,-1) = isnull(@blockedXactID,-1) and
  isnull(t.[Resource],'aaa') = isnull(@resource,'aaa') and
  t.BlockingSPID = @blockingSPID and
```

```
      t.BlockedSQLHandle = @blockedSqlHandle and
      t.BlockedStmtStart = @blockedStmtStart and
      t.BlockedStmtEnd = @blockedStmtEnd and
      t.EventDate >=
        dateadd(millisecond,-@waitTime - 100, @EventDate);

IF @@rowcount = 0
begin
  select
    @blockingXML = @Report
      .query('/blocked-process-report/blocking-process/*');

  ;with Source
  as
  (
    select
      repData.BlockedLockMode
      ,repData.BlockedIsolationLevel
      ,repData.BlockingStmtStart
      ,repData.BlockingStmtEnd
      ,repData.BlockedInputBuf
      ,repData.BlockingStatus
      ,repData.BlockingTranCount
      ,BlockedSQLText.SQL as BlockedSQL
      ,coalesce(
        blockedERPlan.query_plan
        ,blockedQSPlan.query_plan
      ) AS BlockedQueryPlan
      ,coalesce(
        blockedERPlan.query_hash
        ,blockedQSPlan.query_hash
      ) AS BlockedQueryHash
      ,coalesce(
        blockedERPlan.plan_hash
        ,blockedQSPlan.plan_hash
      ) AS BlockedPlanHash
```

99

```
    ,BlockingSQLText.SQL as BlockingSQL
    ,repData.BlockingInputBuf
    ,coalesce(
      blockingERPlan.query_plan
      ,blockingQSPlan.query_plan
    ) AS BlockingQueryPlan
from
  -- Parsing report XML
  (
    select
      @blockedXML
        .value('/process[1]/@lockMode','varchar(16)')
          as BlockedLockMode
      ,@blockedXML
        .value('/process[1]/@isolationlevel','varchar(32)')
          as BlockedIsolationLevel
      ,isnull(@blockingXML
        .value('/process[1]/executionStack[1]/frame[1]/
        @stmtstart'
        ,'int') , 0) as BlockingStmtStart
      ,isnull(@blockingXML
        .value('/process[1]/executionStack[1]/frame[1]/
        @stmtend'
        ,'int'), -1) as BlockingStmtEnd
      ,@blockedXML
        .value('(/process[1]/inputbuf/text())[1]',
        'nvarchar(max)')
          as BlockedInputBuf
      ,@blockingXML
        .value('/process[1]/@status','varchar(16)')
          as BlockingStatus
      ,@blockingXML
        .value('/process[1]/@trancount','smallint')
          as BlockingTranCount
```

```
    ,@blockingXML
      .value('(/process[1]/inputbuf/text())[1]',
      'nvarchar(max)')
        as BlockingInputBuf
    ,@blockingXML
      .value('xs:hexBinary(substring((/process[1]/
      executionStack[1]/frame[1]/@sqlhandle)[1],3))'
          ,'varbinary(max)')
        as BlockingSQLHandle
) as repData
-- Getting Query Text
outer apply
  dbo.fnGetSqlText
  (
      @blockedSqlHandle
      ,@blockedStmtStart
      ,@blockedStmtEnd
  ) BlockedSQLText
outer apply
  dbo.fnGetSqlText
  (
      repData.BlockingSQLHandle
      ,repData.BlockingStmtStart
      ,repData.BlockingStmtEnd
  ) BlockingSQLText
-- Check if statement is still blocked in
   sys.dm_exec_requests
outer apply
  dbo.fnGetQueryInfoFromExecRequests
  (
      @collectPlan
      ,@blockedSPID
      ,@blockedSqlHandle
      ,@blockedStmtStart
      ,@blockedStmtEnd
  ) blockedERPlan
```

```
-- if there is no plan handle
-- let's try sys.dm_exec_query_stats
outer apply
(
  select plan_hash, query_hash, query_plan
  from
      dbo.fnGetQueryInfoFromQueryStats
        (
            @collectPlan
            ,@blockedSqlHandle
            ,@blockedStmtStart
            ,@blockedStmtEnd
            ,@EventDate
            ,60
        )
  where
    blockedERPlan.DataExists is null
) blockedQSPlan
outer apply
  dbo.fnGetQueryInfoFromExecRequests
  (
    @collectPlan
    ,@blockingSPID
    ,repData.BlockingSQLHandle
    ,repData.BlockingStmtStart
    ,repData.BlockingStmtEnd
  ) blockingERPlan
-- if there is no plan handle
-- let's try sys.dm_exec_query_stats
outer apply
(
  select query_plan
  from dbo.fnGetQueryInfoFromQueryStats
  (
    @collectPlan
    ,repData.BlockingSQLHandle
```

```
                ,repData.BlockingStmtStart
                ,repData.BlockingStmtEnd
                 ,@EventDate
                 ,60
              )
              where blockingERPlan.DataExists is null
           ) blockingQSPlan
      )
      insert into [dbo].[BlockedProcessesInfo]
      (
        EventDate,DatabaseID,[Resource]
        ,WaitTime,BlockedProcessReport
        ,BlockedSPID,BlockedXactId
        ,BlockedLockMode,BlockedIsolationLevel
        ,BlockedSQLHandle,BlockedStmtStart
        ,BlockedStmtEnd,BlockedSql
        ,BlockedInputBuf,BlockedQueryPlan
        ,BlockingSPID,BlockingStatus,BlockingTranCount
        ,BlockingSql,BlockingInputBuf,BlockingQueryPlan
        ,BlockedQueryHash,BlockedPlanHash
      )
      select
        @EventDate,@DBID,@resource
        ,@waitTime,@Report,@blockedSPID
        ,@blockedXactID,BlockedLockMode
        ,BlockedIsolationLevel,@blockedSqlHandle
        ,@blockedStmtStart,@blockedStmtEnd
        ,BlockedSQL,BlockedInputBuf,BlockedQueryPlan
        ,@blockingSPID,BlockingStatus,BlockingTranCount
        ,BlockingSQL,BlockingInputBuf,BlockingQueryPlan
        ,BlockedQueryHash,BlockedPlanHash
        from Source
      option (maxdop 1);
   end
end -- @EventType = BLOCKED_PROCESS_REPORT
```

```
    end -- @MsgType = http://schemas.microsoft.com/SQL/Notifications/
    EventNotification
    else if @MsgType = N'http://schemas.microsoft.com/SQL/
    ServiceBroker/EndDialog'
      end conversation @ch;
    -- else handle errors here
  commit
end try
begin catch
  -- capture info about error message here
  if @@trancount > 0
    rollback;

  declare
    @Recipient VARCHAR(255) = 'DBA@mycompany.com',
    @Subject NVARCHAR(255) = + @@SERVERNAME +
      ': SB_BlockedProcessReport_Activation - Error',
    @Body NVARCHAR(MAX) = 'LINE: ' +
      convert(nvarchar(16), error_line()) +
      char(13) + char(10) + 'ERROR:' + error_message()

  exec msdb.dbo.sp_send_dbmail
    @recipients = @Recipient,
    @subject = @Subject,
    @body = @Body;
  throw;
end catch
end
end
```

As the next step, we need to grant enough permissions to the stored procedure to execute and access data management views. We can either sign the stored procedure with a certificate, as shown in Listing 4-8, or mark the database as trustworthy by using an ALTER DATABASE DBA SET TRUSTWORTHY ON statement. Remember: Marking a database as trustworthy violates security best practices and generally is not recommended.

***Listing 4-8.*** Signing stored procedure with certificate

```
use DBA
go

create master key encryption by password = 'StrOngPas$word1';
go

create certificate BMFrameworkCert
with subject = 'Cert for event monitoring',
expiry_date = '20301031';
go

add signature to dbo.SB_BlockedProcessReport_Activation
by certificate BMFrameworkCert;
go

backup certificate BMFrameworkCert
to file='BMFrameworkCert.cer';
go

use master
go

create certificate BMFrameworkCert
from file='BMFrameworkCert.cer';
go

create login BMFrameworkLogin
from certificate BMFrameworkCert;
go

grant view server state, authenticate server to BMFrameworkLogin;
```

As the final step, we need to enable an activation on dbo.BlockedProcess NotificationQueue, as shown in Listing 4-9.

***Listing 4-9.*** Enable an activation on the queue

```
use DBA
go

alter queue dbo.BlockedProcessNotificationQueue
with
    status = on,
    retention = off,
    activation
    (
        status = on,
        procedure_name = dbo.SB_BlockedProcessReport_Activation,
        max_queue_readers = 1,
        execute as owner
    );
```

Now, if we repeat the blocking condition with the code from Table 4-1, the blocked process report would be captured and parsed, and data would be saved in the dbo.BlockedProcessInfo table, as shown in Figure 4-8.

| | ID | EventDate | DatabaseID | Resource | WaitTime | BlockedProcessReport | BlockedSPID | BlockedXactId | BlockedLockMode |
|---|----|-----------|-----------|----------|----------|---------------------|-------------|---------------|-----------------|
| 1 | 1 | 2018-01-29 05:34:54.863 | 5 | KEY (5be201b53f8) | 2148450 | \<blocked-process-repor... | 53 | 39116 | S |

| BlockedIsolationLevel | BlockedSQLHandle | BlockedStmtStart | BlockedStmtEnd | BlockedSql | BlockedInputBuf | BlockedQueryPlan |
|----------------------|------------------|------------------|----------------|-----------|-----------------|------------------|
| read committed (2) | 0x0200000081CA5... | 36 | 174 | SELECT [OrderId],[Amou... | set transaction isol... | \<ShowPlanXML.xml... |

| BlockingSPID | BlockingTranCount | BlockingInputBuf | | BlockingSql | BlockingQueryPlan |
|--------------|-------------------|------------------|---|-------------|-------------------|
| 52 | 1 | set transaction isolation level read uncommitted begin tran  delete from Delivery.Orders  ... | | NULL | NULL |

***Figure 4-8.*** *Captured blocking information*

Setting up blocking monitoring with Event Notifications is extremely useful during concurrency-issue troubleshooting. I usually have it enabled as part of the regular monitoring framework on all my servers.

---

**Note**  The source code is included in the companion materials of the book. The latest version is also available for download from my blog at http:// aboutsqlserver.com/bmframework.

---

# Summary

Blocking occurs when multiple sessions compete for the same resources using incompatible lock types. The process of troubleshooting requires you to detect queries involved in the blocking, find the root cause of the problem, and address the issue.

The `sys.dm_tran_locks` data management view provides you with information about all active lock requests in the system. It can help you detect blocking conditions in real time. You can join this view with other DMVs, such as `sys.dm_exec_requests`, `sys.dm_exec_query_stats`, `sys.dm_exec_sessions`, and `sys.dm_os_waiting_tasks`, to obtain more information about the sessions and queries involved in the blocking conditions.

SQL Server can generate a blocked process report that provides you with information about blocking, which you can collect and retain for further analysis. You can use SQL Traces, Extended Events, and Event Notifications to capture it.

In a large number of cases, blocking occurs as a result of excessive scans introduced by nonoptimized queries. You should analyze the execution plans of both blocking and blocked queries to detect and optimize inefficiencies.

Another common issue that results in blocking is incorrect transaction management in the code, which includes runaway transactions and interactions with users in the middle of open transactions, among other things.

# CHAPTER 5

# Deadlocks

A deadlock is a special blocking case that occurs when multiple sessions—or sometimes multiple execution threads within a single session—block each other. When it happens, SQL Server terminates one of the sessions, allowing the others to continue.

This chapter will demonstrate why deadlocks occur in the system and explain how to troubleshoot and resolve them.

## Classic Deadlock

A classic deadlock occurs when two or more sessions are competing for the same set of resources. Let's look at a by-the-book example and assume that you have two sessions updating two rows in the table in the opposite order.

As the first step, session 1 updates the row *R1* and session 2 updates the row *R2*. You know that at this point both sessions acquire and hold exclusive (X) locks on the rows. You can see this happening in Figure 5-1.

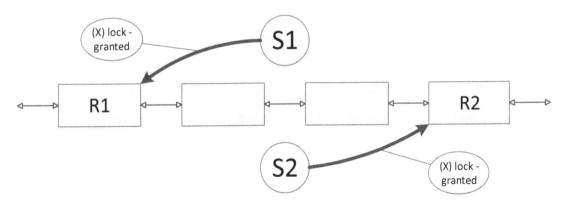

***Figure 5-1.*** *Classic deadlock: Step 1*

© Dmitri Korotkevitch 2018

D. Korotkevitch, *Expert SQL Server Transactions and Locking*, https://doi.org/10.1007/978-1-4842-3957-5_5

Next, let's assume that session 1 wants to update the row *R2*. It will try to acquire an exclusive (X) lock on *R2* and would be blocked because of the exclusive (X) lock already held by session 2. If session 2 wanted to update R1, the same thing would happen—it would be blocked because of the exclusive (X) lock held by session 1. As you can see, at this point both sessions wait on each other and cannot continue the execution. This represents the *classic* or *cycle* deadlock, shown in Figure 5-2.

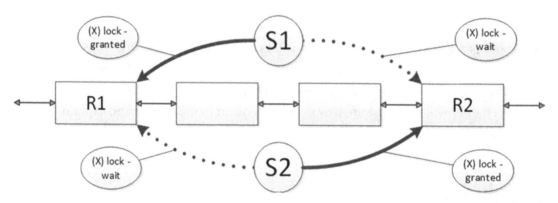

***Figure 5-2.*** *Classic deadlock: Step 2*

The system task *Deadlock Monitor* wakes up every five seconds and checks if there are any deadlocks in the system. When a deadlock is detected, SQL Server rolls back one of the transactions with the error 1205. That releases all locks held in that transaction and allows the other sessions to continue.

---

**Note**    The Deadlock Monitor wake-up interval goes down if there are deadlocks in the system. In some cases, it could wake up as often as ten times per second.

---

The decision as to which session is chosen as the deadlock victim depends on a few things. By default, SQL Server rolls back the session that uses less log space for the transaction. You can control it, up to a degree, by setting a deadlock priority for the session with the SET DEADLOCK_PRIORITY option.

# Deadlock Due to Non-Optimized Queries

While the classic deadlock often happens when the data is highly volatile and the same rows are updated by multiple sessions, there is another common reason for deadlocks. They happen as a result of the scans introduced by non-optimized queries. Let's look at an example and assume that you have a process that updates an order row in `Delivery.Orders` table and, as a next step, queries how many orders the customer has. Let's see what happens when two such sessions are running in parallel using the `READ COMMITTED` transaction isolation level.

As the first step, two sessions run two `UPDATE` statements. Both statements run fine without blocking involved—as you remember, the table has the clustered index on the `OrderId` column, so you will have *Clustered Index Seek* operators in the execution plan. Figure 5-3 illustrates this step.

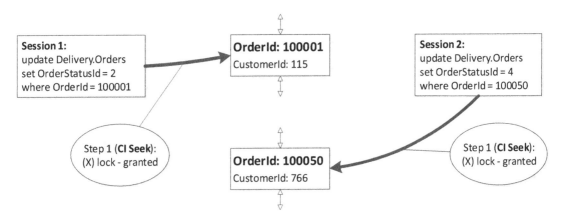

***Figure 5-3.*** *Deadlock due to the scans: Step 1*

At this point, both sessions hold exclusive (X) locks on the updated rows. As the second step, sessions run the `SELECT` statements based on the `CustomerId` filter. There are no nonclustered indexes on the table, and the execution plan will have the *Clustered Index Scan* operation. In the `READ COMMITTED` isolation level, SQL Server acquires shared (S) locks when reading the data, and as a result both sessions are blocked as soon as they try to read the row with exclusive (X) locks held on it. Figure 5-4 illustrates that.

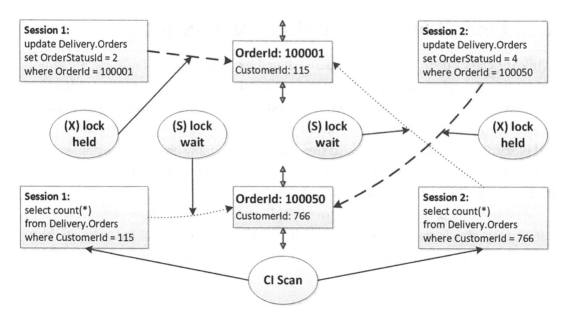

***Figure 5-4.*** *Deadlock due to the scans: Step 2*

If you ran the query shown in Listing 5-1 at the time when both sessions were blocked and before the Deadlock Monitor task woke up, you would see that both sessions block each other.

***Listing 5-1.*** Lock requests at the time when both sessions were blocked

```
select
    tl.request_session_id as [SPID]
    ,tl.resource_type as [Resouce Type]
    ,tl.resource_description as [Resource]
    ,tl.request_mode as [Mode]
    ,tl.request_status as [Status]
    ,wt.blocking_session_id as [Blocked By]
from
    sys.dm_tran_locks tl with (nolock) left outer join
        sys.dm_os_waiting_tasks wt with (nolock) on
            tl.lock_owner_address = wt.resource_address and
            tl.request_status = 'WAIT'
```

```
where
    tl.request_session_id <> @@SPID and tl.resource_type = 'KEY'
order by
    tl.request_session_id
```

Figure 5-5 shows the output of the query. As you can see, both sessions block each other. It does not matter that the sessions were not going to include those rows in the count calculation. SQL Server is unable to evaluate the CustomerId predicate until the shared (S) locks are acquired and rows are read.

| | SPID | Resouce Type | Resource | Mode | Status | Blocked By |
|---|------|--------------|----------|------|--------|------------|
| 1 | 51 | KEY | (2fe59e02884b) | S | WAIT | 52 |
| 2 | 51 | KEY | (74a07545ba5b) | X | GRANT | NULL |
| 3 | 52 | KEY | (74a07545ba5b) | S | WAIT | 51 |
| 4 | 52 | KEY | (2fe59e02884b) | X | GRANT | NULL |

***Figure 5-5.*** *Lock requests at the time of the deadlock*

You will have deadlocks like these in any transaction isolation level where readers acquire shared (S) locks. It would not deadlock in the READ UNCOMMITTED, READ COMMITTED SNAPSHOT, or SNAPSHOT isolation levels, where shared (S) locks are not used.

Nevertheless, you can still have deadlocks in the READ UNCOMMITTED and READ COMMITTED SNAPSHOT isolation levels as a result of the writers' collision. You can trigger it by replacing the SELECT statement with the UPDATE that introduces the scan operation in the previous example. The SNAPSHOT isolation level, on the other hand, does not have writer/writer blocking unless you are updating the same rows, and it would not deadlock, even with UPDATE statements.

Query optimization helps to fix deadlocks caused by scans and non-optimized queries. In the preceding case, you can solve the problem by adding a nonclustered index on the CustomerId column. This would change the execution plan of SELECT statement replacing *Clustered Index Scan* with *Nonclustered Index Seek*. As a result, the session would not need to read the rows that were modified by another session and have incompatible locks held.

113

# Key Lookup Deadlock

In some cases, you can have a deadlock when multiple sessions are trying to read and update the same row simultaneously.

Let's assume that you have a nonclustered index on the table, and one session wants to read the row using this index. If the index is not covering and the session needs some data from the clustered index, SQL Server may generate the execution plan with the Nonclustered Index Seek and Key Lookup operations. The session would acquire a shared (S) lock on the nonclustered index row first, and then on the clustered index row.

Meanwhile, if you have another session that updates one of the columns that is part of the nonclustered index using the clustered key value as the query predicate, that session would acquire exclusive (X) locks in the opposite order; that is, on the clustered index row first and on the nonclustered index row after that.

Figure 5-6 shows what happens after the first step, when both sessions successfully acquire locks on the rows in the clustered and nonclustered indexes.

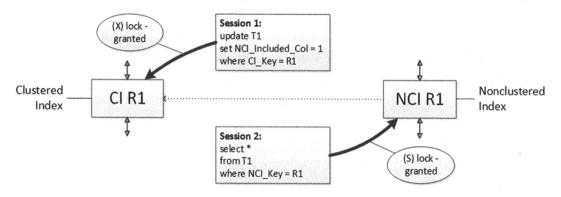

***Figure 5-6.***  *Key Lookup deadlock: Step 1*

In the next step, both sessions try to acquire locks on the rows in the other indexes, and they are blocked, as shown in Figure 5-7.

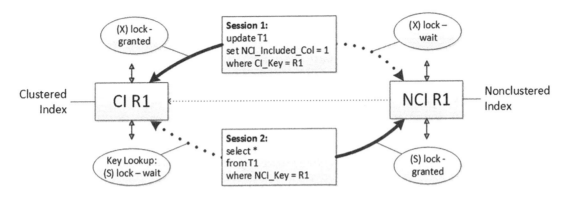

**Figure 5-7.** *Key Lookup deadlock: Step 2*

If it happens in the same moment, you would have a deadlock, and the session that reads the data would be chosen as the deadlock victim. This is an example of the classic cycle deadlock we saw earlier. Despite the fact that both sessions are working with a single table row, SQL Server internally deals with two rows—one each in the clustered and nonclustered indexes.

You can address this type of deadlock by making nonclustered indexes covering and avoiding the Key Lookup operation. Unfortunately, that solution would increase the size of the leaf rows in the nonclustered index and introduce additional overhead during data modification and index maintenance. Alternatively, you can use optimistic isolation levels and switch to READ COMMITTED SNAPSHOT mode, where readers do not acquire shared (S) locks.

# Deadlock Due to Multiple Updates of the Same Row

A deadlock pattern that is similar to the previous can be introduced by having multiple updates of the same row when updates access or change columns in different indexes. This could lead to a deadlock situation—similar to the Key Lookup deadlock—where another session places a lock on the nonclustered index row in between the updates. One of the common scenarios where it happens is with AFTER UPDATE triggers that update the same row.

Let's look at a situation where you have a table with both clustered and nonclustered indexes and the AFTER UPDATE trigger defined. Let's have session 1 update a column that does not belong to the nonclustered index. This step is shown in Figure 5-8. It acquires an exclusive (X) lock on the row from the clustered index only.

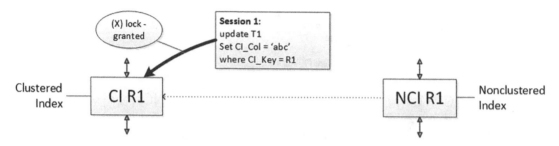

***Figure 5-8.*** *Deadlock due to multiple updates of the same row: Step 1*

The update fires the AFTER UPDATE trigger. Meanwhile, let's assume that another session is trying to select the same row using the nonclustered index. This session successfully acquires a shared (S) lock on the nonclustered index row during the Nonclustered Index Seek operation. However, it would be blocked when trying to obtain a shared (S) lock on the clustered index row during the Key Lookup, as shown in Figure 5-9.

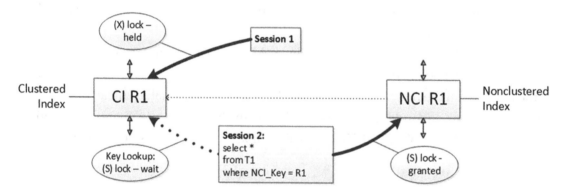

***Figure 5-9.*** *Deadlock due to the multiple updates of the same row: Step 2*

Finally, if session 1 trigger tries to update the same row again, modifying the column that exists in the nonclustered index, it would be blocked by the shared (S) lock held by session 2. Figure 5-10 illustrates this situation.

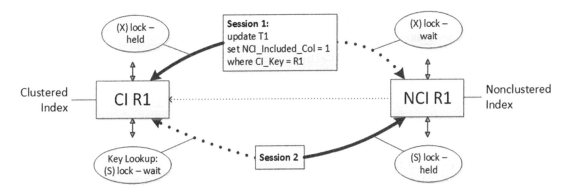

***Figure 5-10.*** *Deadlock due to multiple updates of the same row*

Let's prove that with the code shown in Listing 5-2.

***Listing 5-2.*** Multiple updates of the same row

```
create table dbo.T1
(
    CI_Key int not null,
    NCI_Key int not null,
    CI_Col varchar(32),
    NCI_Included_Col int
);

create unique clustered index IDX_T1_CI on dbo.T1(CI_Key);

create nonclustered index IDX_T1_NCI
on dbo.T1(NCI_Key)
include (NCI_Included_Col);

insert into dbo.T1(CI_Key,NCI_Key,CI_Col,NCI_Included_Col)
values(1,1,'a',0), (2,2,'b',0), (3,3,'c',0), (4,4,'d',0);

begin tran
    update dbo.T1 set CI_Col = 'abc' where CI_Key = 1;

    select
        l.request_session_id as [SPID]
        ,object_name(p.object_id) as [Object]
        ,i.name as [Index]
        ,l.resource_type as [Lock Type]
```

```
        ,l.resource_description as [Resource]
        ,l.request_mode as [Mode]
        ,l.request_status as [Status]
        ,wt.blocking_session_id as [Blocked By]
    from
        sys.dm_tran_locks l join sys.partitions p on
            p.hobt_id = l.resource_associated_entity_id
        join sys.indexes i on
            p.object_id = i.object_id and p.index_id = i.index_id
        left outer join sys.dm_os_waiting_tasks wt with (nolock) on
            l.lock_owner_address = wt.resource_address and
            l.request_status = 'WAIT'
    where
        resource_type = 'KEY' and request_session_id = @@SPID;

    update dbo.T1 set NCI_Included_Col = 1 where NCI_Key = 1
    select
        l.request_session_id as [SPID]
        ,object_name(p.object_id) as [Object]
        ,i.name as [Index]
        ,l.resource_type as [Lock Type]
        ,l.resource_description as [Resource]
        ,l.request_mode as [Mode]
        ,l.request_status as [Status]
        ,wt.blocking_session_id as [Blocked By]
    from
        sys.dm_tran_locks l join sys.partitions p on
            p.hobt_id = l.resource_associated_entity_id
        join sys.indexes i on
            p.object_id = i.object_id and p.index_id = i.index_id
        left outer join sys.dm_os_waiting_tasks wt with (nolock) on
            l.lock_owner_address = wt.resource_address and
            l.request_status = 'WAIT'
    where
        resource_type = 'KEY' and request_session_id = @@SPID;
commit
```

The code in Listing 5-2 updates the row twice. If you look at the row-level locks held after the first update, you see only one lock held on the clustered index, as shown in Figure 5-11.

| | SPID | Object | Index | Lock Type | Resource | Mode | Status | Blocked By |
|---|---|---|---|---|---|---|---|---|
| 1 | 56 | T1 | IDX_T1_CI | KEY | (8194443284a0) | X | GRANT | NULL |

**Figure 5-11.** *Row-level locks after the first update*

The second update, which updates the column that exists in the nonclustered index, places another exclusive (X) there, as shown in Figure 5-12. This proves that the lock on the nonclustered index row is not acquired unless the index columns are actually updated.

| | SPID | Object | Index | Lock Type | Resource | Mode | Status | Blocked By |
|---|---|---|---|---|---|---|---|---|
| 1 | 56 | T1 | IDX_T1_CI | KEY | (8194443284a0) | X | GRANT | NULL |
| 2 | 56 | T1 | IDX_T1_NCI | KEY | (e2338e2f4a9f) | X | GRANT | NULL |

**Figure 5-12.** *Row-level locks after the second update*

Now, let's look at another session with SPID = 55 running the SELECT shown in Listing 5-3 in between two updates, at a time when you have just one row-level lock held.

**Listing 5-3.** The code that leads to the deadlock

```
select CI_Key, CI_Col
from dbo.T1 with (index = IDX_T1_NCI)
where NCI_Key = 1
```

As you can see in Figure 5-13, the query successfully acquires the shared (S) lock on the nonclustered index row and is blocked by trying to acquire the lock on the clustered index row.

| | SPID | Object | Index | Lock Ty... | Resource | Mode | Status | Blocked By |
|---|---|---|---|---|---|---|---|---|
| 1 | 56 | T1 | IDX_T1_CI | KEY | (8194443284a0) | X | GRANT | NULL |
| 2 | 55 | T1 | IDX_T1_CI | KEY | (8194443284a0) | S | WAIT | 56 |
| 3 | 55 | T1 | IDX_T1_NCI | KEY | (e2338e2f4a9f) | S | GRANT | NULL |

***Figure 5-13.*** *Row-level locks when SELECT query is blocked*

If you ran the second update in the original session with SPID = 56, it would try to acquire an exclusive (X) lock on the nonclustered index, and it would be blocked by the second (SELECT) session, as shown in Figure 5-14. That leads to the deadlock condition.

| | SPID | Object | Index | Lock Ty... | Resource | Mode | Status | Blocked By |
|---|---|---|---|---|---|---|---|---|
| 1 | 56 | T1 | IDX_T1_CI | KEY | (8194443284a0) | X | GRANT | NULL |
| 2 | 55 | T1 | IDX_T1_CI | KEY | (8194443284a0) | S | WAIT | 56 |
| 3 | 55 | T1 | IDX_T1_NCI | KEY | (e2338e2f4a9f) | S | GRANT | NULL |
| 4 | 56 | T1 | IDX_T1_NCI | KEY | (e2338e2f4a9f) | X | WAIT | 55 |

***Figure 5-14.*** *Row-level locks when second update is running (deadlock)*

The best method to avoid such problems is to eliminate multiple updates of the same rows. You can use variables or temporary tables to store preliminary data and run the single UPDATE statement close to the end of the transaction. Alternatively, you can change the code and assign some temporary value to NCI_Included_Col as part of the first UPDATE statement, which would acquire exclusive (X) locks on both of the indexes. The SELECT from the second session would be unable to acquire the lock on the nonclustered index, and the second update would run just fine.

As a last resort, you could read the row using a plan that requires both indexes to use an (XLOCK) locking hint, which would place exclusive (X) locks on both rows, as shown in Listing 5-4 and Figure 5-15. Obviously, you need to consider the overhead this would introduce.

***Listing 5-4.*** Obtaining exclusive (X) locks on the rows in both indexes

```
begin tran
    declare
        @Dummy varchar(32)

    select @Dummy = CI_Col
    from dbo.T1 with (XLOCK index=IDX_T1_NCI)
    where NCI_Key = 1;
```

```
select
    l.request_session_id as [SPID]
    ,object_name(p.object_id) as [Object]
    ,i.name as [Index]
    ,l.resource_type as [Lock Type]
    ,l.resource_description as [Resource]
    ,l.request_mode as [Mode]
    ,l.request_status as [Status]
    ,wt.blocking_session_id as [Blocked By]
from
    sys.dm_tran_locks l join sys.partitions p on
        p.hobt_id = l.resource_associated_entity_id
    join sys.indexes i on
        p.object_id = i.object_id and p.index_id = i.index_id
    left outer join sys.dm_os_waiting_tasks wt with (nolock) on
        l.lock_owner_address = wt.resource_address and
        l.request_status = 'WAIT'
where
    resource_type = 'KEY' and request_session_id = @@SPID;

update dbo.T1 set CI_Col = 'abc' where CI_Key = 1;

/* some code */

update dbo.T1 set NCI_Included_Col = 1 where NCI_Key = 1;
commit
```

| | SPID | Object | Index | Lock Type | Resource | Mode | Status |
|---|------|--------|-------|-----------|----------|------|--------|
| 1 | 56 | T1 | IDX_T1_CI | KEY | (8194443284a0) | X | GRANT |
| 2 | 56 | T1 | IDX_T1_NCI | KEY | (e2338e2f4a9f) | X | GRANT |

*Figure 5-15.* Row-level locks after SELECT statement with (XLOCK) hint

# Deadlock Troubleshooting

In a nutshell, deadlock troubleshooting is very similar to the blocking troubleshooting we discussed in the previous chapter. You need to analyze the processes and queries involved in the deadlock, identify the root cause of the problem, and, finally, fix it.

Similar to the *blocked process report*, there is the *deadlock graph*, which provides you with information about the deadlock in an XML format. There are plenty of ways to obtain the deadlock graph:

- `xml_deadlock_report` Extended Event

- Starting with SQL Server 2008, every system has a `system_health` Extended Event session enabled by default in every SQL Server installation. That session captures basic server health information, including `xml_deadlock_report` events.

- Trace Flag 1222: This trace flag saves deadlock information to the SQL Server Error Log. You can enable it for all sessions with the `DBCC TRACEON(1222,-1)` command or by using startup parameter `T1222`. It is a perfectly safe method to use in production; however, nowadays, it may be redundant because of the `system_health` session.

- `Deadlock graph` SQL Trace event. It is worth noting that SQL Profiler displays the graphic representation of the deadlock. The "Extract Event Data" action from the event context menu (right mouse click) allows you to extract an XML deadlock graph.

With the `system_health` xEvent session, `xml_deadlock_graph` is captured by default. You may have the data for troubleshooting even if you did not explicitly enable any other collection methods. In SQL Server 2012 and above, you can access `system_health` session data from the *Management* node in Management Studio, as shown in Figure 5-16. You could analyze the *target data*, searching for an `xml_deadlock_report` event.

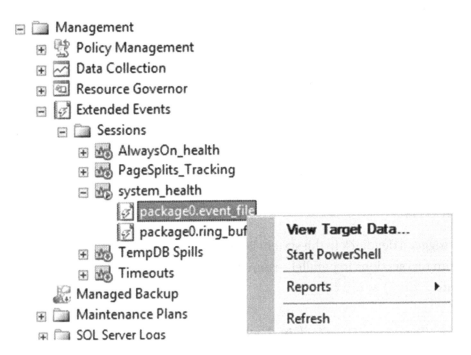

***Figure 5-16.*** *Accessing system_health xEvents session*

The XML representation of the deadlock graph contains two different sections, as shown in Listing 5-5. The sections <process-list> and <resource-list> contain information about the processes and resources involved in the deadlock, respectively.

***Listing 5-5.*** Deadlock graph format

```
<deadlock-list>
     <deadlock victim="...">
          <process-list>
               <process id="...">
                    ...
               </process>
               <process id="...">
                    ...
               </process>
          </process-list>
```

```
    <resource-list>
        <information about resource involved in the deadlock>
            ...
        </ information about resource involved in the deadlock>
        <information about resource involved in the deadlock>
            ...
        </ information about resource involved in the deadlock>
    </resource-list>
    </deadlock>
</deadlock-list>
```

Let's trigger a deadlock in the system by using the code shown in Table 5-1. You need to run two sessions in parallel—running UPDATE statements first and then SELECT statements.

***Table 5-1.*** *Triggering Deadlock in the System*

| Session 1 | Session 2 |
| --- | --- |
| begin tran | begin tran |
|    update Delivery.Orders |    update Delivery.Orders |
|    set OrderStatusId = 1 |    set OrderStatusId = 1 |
|    where OrderId = 10001; |    where OrderId = 10050; |
|    select count(*) as [Cnt] |    select count(*) as [Cnt] |
|    from Delivery.Orders with |    from Delivery.Orders with |
|    (READCOMMITTED) |    (READCOMMITTED) |
|    where CustomerId = 317; |    where CustomerId = 766; |
| commit | commit |

Each <process> node in the deadlock graph shows details for a specific process, as shown in Listing 5-6. I removed the values from some of the attributes to make it easier to read. I also have highlighted the ones that I've found especially helpful during troubleshooting.

*Listing 5-6.* Deadlock graph: <Process> node

```
<process id="process3e4b29868" taskpriority="0" logused="264"
waitresource="KEY: ..." waittime="..." ownerId="..." transactionname="... "
lasttranstarted="..." XDES="..." lockMode="S" schedulerid="..." kpid="..."
status="suspended" spid="55" sbid="..." ecid="..." priority="0"
trancount="1" lastbatchstarted="..." lastbatchcompleted="..."
lastattention="..." clientapp="..." hostname="..." hostpid="..."
loginname="..." isolationlevel="read committed (2)" xactid="..."
currentdb="..." lockTimeout="..." clientoption1="..." clientoption2="...">
    <executionStack>
        <frame procname="adhoc" line="1" stmtstart="26" sqlhandle="...">
            SELECT COUNT(*) [Cnt] FROM [Delivery].[Orders] with
            (REACOMMITTED) WHERE [CustomerId]=@1
        </frame>
    </executionStack>
    <inputbuf>
            select count(*) as [Cnt]
            from Delivery.Orders with (REACOMMITTED)
            where CustomerId = 766
        commit
    </inputbuf>
</process>
```

The id attribute uniquely identifies the process. Waitresource and lockMode provide information about the lock type and the resource for which the process is waiting. In our example, you can see that the process is waiting for the shared (S) lock on one of the rows (keys).

The Isolationlevel attribute shows you the current transaction isolation level. Finally, executionStack and inputBuf allow you to find the SQL statement that was executed when the deadlock occurred. As the opposite of the *blocked process report*, executionStack in the deadlock graph usually provides you with information about the query and module involved in the deadlock. However, in some cases, you would need to use the sys.dm_exec_sql_text function to get the SQL statements in the same way as we did in Listing 4-5 in the previous chapter.

The `<resource-list>` section of the deadlock graph contains information about the resources involved in the deadlock. It is shown in Listing 5-7.

***Listing 5-7.*** Deadlock graph: <Resource-list> node

```
<resource-list>
    <keylock hobtid="72057594039500800" dbid="14"
    objectname="SqlServerInternals.Delivery.Orders" indexname="PK_Orders"
    id="lock3e98b5d00" mode="X" associatedObjectId="72057594039500800">
        <owner-list>
            <owner id="process3e6a890c8" mode="X"/>
        </owner-list>
        <waiter-list>
            <waiter id="process3e4b29868" mode="S" requestType="wait"/>
        </waiter-list>
    </keylock>
    <keylock hobtid="72057594039500800" dbid="14"
    objectname="SqlServerInternals.Delivery.Orders" indexname="PK_Orders"
    id="lock3e98ba500" mode="X" associatedObjectId="72057594039500800">
        <owner-list>
            <owner id="process3e4b29868" mode="X"/>
        </owner-list>
        <waiter-list>
            <waiter id="process3e6a890c8" mode="S" requestType="wait"/>
        </waiter-list>
    </keylock>
</resource-list>
```

The name of the XML element identifies the type of resource. Keylock, pagelock, and objectlock stand for the row-level, page, and object locks, respectively. You can also see to what objects and indexes those locks belong. Finally, owner-list and waiter-list nodes provide information about the processes that own and wait for the locks, along with the types of locks acquired and requested. You can correlate this information with the data from the process-list section of the graph.

As you have probably already guessed, the next steps are very similar to the blocked process troubleshooting; that is, you need to pinpoint the queries involved in the deadlock and find out why the deadlock occurs.

There is one important factor to consider, however. In most cases, a deadlock involves more than one statement per session running in the same transaction. The deadlock graph provides you with information about the last statement only—the one that triggered the deadlock.

You can see the *signs* of the other statements in the resource-list node. It shows you the locks held by the transaction, but it does not tell you about the statements that acquired them. It is very useful to identify those statements while analyzing the root cause of the problem.

In our example, when you look at the code shown in Table 5-1, you see the two statements. The UPDATE statement updates a single row—it acquires and holds an exclusive (X) lock there. You can see that both processes own those exclusive (X) locks in the resource-list node of the deadlock graph.

In the next step, you need to understand why SELECT queries are trying to obtain shared (S) locks on the rows with exclusive (X) locks held. You can look at the execution plans for SELECT statements from the process nodes by either running the queries or using sys.dm_exec_query_stats DMV, as was shown in Listing 4-5 in the previous chapter. As a result, you will get the execution plans shown in Figure 5-17. The figure also shows the number of locks acquired during query execution.

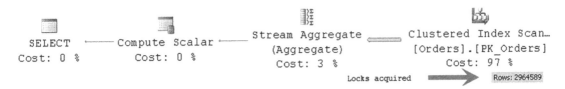

***Figure 5-17.*** *Execution plan for the query*

---

**Tip**   You can obtain cached execution plans for the stored procedures using the sys.dm_exec_procedure_stats view.

---

As you can see, there is a *Clustered Index Scan* in the plan, which gives you enough data for analysis. SELECT queries scanned the entire table. Because both processes were using the READ COMMITTED isolation level, the queries tried to acquire shared (S) locks on every row from the table and were blocked by the exclusive (X) locks held by another session. It did not matter that those rows did not have the CustomerId that the queries were looking for. In order to evaluate this predicate, queries had to read those rows, which required acquiring shared (S) locks on them.

You can solve this deadlock situation by adding a nonclustered index on the CustomerID column. This would eliminate the *Clustered Index Scan* and replace it with an *Index Seek* operator, as shown in Figure 5-18.

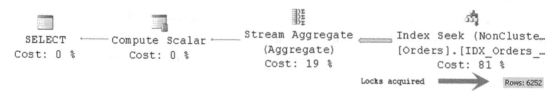

```
  SELECT    ──────  Compute Scalar  ──────  Stream Aggregate  _____  Index Seek (NonCluste...
Cost: 0 %             Cost: 0 %              (Aggregate)                [Orders].[IDX_Orders_...
                                             Cost: 19 %                       Cost: 81 %

                                                            Locks acquired  ══════════▶   Rows: 6252
```

***Figure 5-18.*** *Execution plan for the query with nonclustered index*

Instead of acquiring a shared (S) lock on every row of the table, the query would read only the rows that belong to a specific customer. This would dramatically reduce the number of shared (S) locks to be acquired, and it would prevent the query from being blocked by exclusive (X) locks on rows that belong to different customers.

Unfortunately, deadlock troubleshooting has the same dependency on the plan cache as blocking troubleshooting does. You often need to obtain the text and execution plans of the statements involved in deadlocks from there. The data in the plan cache changes over time, and the longer you wait, the less likely it is that required information will be present.

You can address this by implementing a monitoring solution based on Event Notifications, similar to what we did in the previous chapter. The code is included to companion materials of the book as part of Blocking Monitoring Framework code and also available for download from my blog at: http://aboutsqlserver.com/bmframework.

Finally, in some cases you can have intra-query parallelism deadlocks—when a query with a parallel execution plan deadlocks itself. Fortunately, such cases are rare and are usually introduced by a bug in SQL Server rather than application or database issues. You can detect such cases when a deadlock graph has more than two processes with the same SPID and the resource-list has exchangeEvent and/or threadPoll listed as the resources, without any lock resources associated with them. When it happens, you can work around the problem by reducing or even completely removing parallelism for the query with the MAXDOP hint. There is also a great chance that the issue has already been fixed in the latest service pack or cumulative update.

# Deadlock Due to IGNORE_DUP_KEY Index Option

There is one very particular type of deadlock that is extremely confusing and hard to explain. At first glance, it seems that this deadlock violates the SQL Server Concurrency Model by using range locks in non-SERIALIZABLE isolation levels. However, there is a simple explanation.

As you remember, SQL Server uses range locks to protect a range of the index keys, thus avoiding phantom and non-repeatable reads phenomena. Such locks guarantee that queries executed in a transaction will always work with the same set of data and would be unaffected by any modifications from the other sessions.

There is another case, however, when SQL Server uses the range locks. They are used during data modification of nonclustered indexes that have the IGNORE_DUP_KEY option set to ON. When this is the case, SQL Server ignores the rows with duplicated values of the key rather than raising an exception.

Let's look at the example and create a table, as shown in Listing 5-8.

***Listing 5-8.*** IGNORE_DUP_KEY deadlock: Table creation

```
create table dbo.IgnoreDupKeysDeadlock
(
    CICol int not null,
    NCICol int not null
);

create unique clustered index IDX_IgnoreDupKeysDeadlock_CICol
on dbo.IgnoreDupKeysDeadlock(CICol);

create unique nonclustered index IDX_IgnoreDupKeysDeadlock_NCICol
on dbo.IgnoreDupKeysDeadlock(NCICol)
with (ignore_dup_key = on);

insert into dbo.IgnoreDupKeysDeadlock(CICol, NCICol)
values(0,0),(5,5),(10,10),(20,20);
```

Now, let's start the transaction by using the READ UNCOMMITTED isolation level and then insert a row into the table, checking the locks acquired by the session. The code is shown in Listing 5-9.

***Listing 5-9.*** IGNORE_DUP_KEY deadlock: Inserting a row into the table

```
set transaction isolation level read uncommitted
begin tran
    insert into dbo.IgnoreDupKeysDeadlock(CICol,NCICol)
    values(1,1);

    select request_session_id, resource_type, resource_description
            ,resource_associated_entity_id, request_mode, request_type,
            request_status
    from sys.dm_tran_locks
    where request_session_id = @@SPID;
```

Figure 5-19 illustrates the output from the sys.dm_tran_locks view. As you can see, the session acquired two exclusive (X) locks on the rows in the clustered and nonclustered indexes. It also acquired a range (RangeS-U) lock on the nonclustered index. This lock type means that the existing keys are protected with shared (S) locks, and the interval itself is protected with an update (U) lock.

| | request_session_id | resource_type | resource_description | resource_associated_entity_id | request_mode | request_type | request_status |
|---|---|---|---|---|---|---|---|
| 1 | 55 | PAGE | 3:56 | 72057594046447616 | IX | LOCK | GRANT |
| 2 | 55 | PAGE | 3:88 | 72057594046513152 | IX | LOCK | GRANT |
| 3 | 55 | KEY | (8194443284a0) | 72057594046447616 | X | LOCK | GRANT |
| 4 | 55 | KEY | (8194443284a0) | 72057594046513152 | X | LOCK | GRANT |
| 5 | 55 | KEY | (59855d342c69) | 72057594046513152 | RangeS-U | LOCK | GRANT |
| 6 | 55 | OBJECT | | 766625774 | IX | LOCK | GRANT |

***Figure 5-19.*** *Locks acquired by the first session*

In this scenario, the range lock is required because of the way SQL Server handles data modifications. As we have already discussed, the data is modified in the clustered index first, followed by nonclustered indexes. With IGNORE_DUP_KEY=ON, SQL Server needs to prevent the situation where duplicated keys are inserted into nonclustered indexes simultaneously after the clustered index inserts, and therefore some inserts need to be rolled back. Thus, it locks the range of the keys in the nonclustered index, preventing other sessions from inserting any rows there.

We can confirm it by looking at the lock_acquired Extended Event as shown in Figure 5-20. As you can see, the range lock was acquired before exclusive (X) locks in both indexes.

| name | resource_type | mode | resource_0 |
|------|--------------|------|-----------|
| lock_acquired | OBJECT | IX | 766625774 |
| lock_acquired | PAGE | IU | 88 |
| lock_acquired | KEY | RS_U | 131 |
| lock_acquired | PAGE | IX | 56 |
| lock_acquired | KEY | X | 130 |
| lock_acquired | PAGE | IX | 88 |
| lock_acquired | KEY | X | 131 |

**Figure 5-20.** *lock_acquired Extended Events*

The key problem here, however, is that range locks behave the same way as they do in the SERIALIZABLE isolation level. They are held until the end of the transaction regardless of the isolation level in use. This behavior greatly increases the chance of deadlocks.

Let's run the code from Listing 5-10 in another session. The first statement would succeed, while the second would be blocked.

**Listing 5-10.** IGNORE_DUP_KEY deadlock: Second session code

```
set transaction isolation level read uncommitted
begin tran
    -- Success
    insert into dbo.IgnoreDupKeysDeadlock(CICol,NCICol)
    values(12,12);

    -- Statement is blocked
    insert into dbo.IgnoreDupKeysDeadlock(CICol,NCICol)
    values(2,2);
commit;
```

Now, if we look at the locks held by both sessions, we would see the picture shown in Figure 5-21. The range (RangeS-U) lock from the first session protects the interval of 0..5 and blocks the second session, which is trying to acquire a range lock in the same interval.

| | request_session_id | resource_type | resource_description | resource_associated_entity_id | request_mode | request_type | request_status |
|---|---|---|---|---|---|---|---|
| 1 | 57 | PAGE | 3:56 | 72057594046447616 | IX | LOCK | GRANT |
| 2 | 55 | PAGE | 3:56 | 72057594046447616 | IX | LOCK | GRANT |
| 3 | 57 | PAGE | 3:88 | 72057594046513152 | IX | LOCK | GRANT |
| 4 | 55 | PAGE | 3:88 | 72057594046513152 | IX | LOCK | GRANT |
| 5 | 55 | KEY | (8194443284a0) | 72057594046447616 | X | LOCK | GRANT |
| 6 | 55 | KEY | (8194443284a0) | 72057594046513152 | X | LOCK | GRANT |
| 7 | 57 | KEY | (286fc18d83ea) | 72057594046513152 | RangeS-U | LOCK | GRANT |
| 8 | 55 | KEY | (59855d342c69) | 72057594046513152 | RangeS-U | LOCK | GRANT |
| 9 | 57 | KEY | (59855d342c69) | 72057594046513152 | RangeS-U | LOCK | WAIT |
| 10 | 57 | OBJECT | | 766625774 | IX | LOCK | GRANT |
| 11 | 55 | OBJECT | | 766625774 | IX | LOCK | GRANT |
| 12 | 57 | KEY | (11ea04af99f6) | 72057594046447616 | X | LOCK | GRANT |
| 13 | 57 | KEY | (11ea04af99f6) | 72057594046513152 | X | LOCK | GRANT |

***Figure 5-21.*** *Lock requests at time of blocking*

The second session, in turn, is holding a range lock (RangeS-U) on the interval of 10..20. If the first session tries to insert another row into that interval with the code from Listing 5-11, it would be blocked, which would lead to the classic deadlock situation.

***Listing 5-11.*** IGNORE_DUP_KEY deadlock: Second insert from the first session

```
insert into dbo.IgnoreDupKeysDeadlock(CICol,NCICol)
values(11,11);
```

Figure 5-22 shows the partial output from the deadlock graph. As you can see, this particular pattern is clearly identifiable by the presence of range locks in non-SERIALIZABLE isolation levels.

```
<deadlock>
    <victim-list>
        <victimProcess id="process3123b79848" />
    </victim-list>
    <process-list>
        <process id="process3123b79848" waitresource="KEY: 5:72057594046513152 (11ea04af99f6)"
            lockMode="RangeS-U" spid="55" isolationlevel="read uncommitted (1)">

        </process>
        <process id="process3123b78108" waitresource="KEY: 5:72057594046513152 (59855d342c69)"
            lockMode="RangeS-U" spid="57" isolationlevel="read uncommitted (1)">
        </process>
</process-list>
<resource-list>
    <keylock hobtid="72057594046513152" objectname="SQLServerInternals.dbo.IgnoreDupKeysDeadlock"
            indexname="IDX_IgnoreDupKeysDeadlock_NCICol" >
        <owner-list>
            <owner id="process3123b78108" mode="X" />
        </owner-list>
        <waiter-list>
            <waiter id="process3123b79848" mode="RangeS-U" requestType="wait" />
        </waiter-list>
    </keylock>
    <keylock hobtid="72057594046513152" objectname="SQLServerInternals.dbo.IgnoreDupKeysDeadlock"
            indexname="IDX_IgnoreDupKeysDeadlock_NCICol" >
        <owner-list>
            <owner id="process3123b79848" mode="RangeS-U" />
        </owner-list>
        <waiter-list>
            <waiter id="process3123b78108" mode="RangeS-U" requestType="wait" />
        </waiter-list>
    </keylock>
 </resource-list>
</deadlock>
```

***Figure 5-22.*** *Deadlock graph*

There is very little you can do about this problem besides removing the IGNORE_DUP_
KEY index option. Fortunately, this option is rarely required, and in many cases the issue
can be solved by using the NOT EXISTS predicate and/or with staging tables.

Finally, it is important to note that SQL Server does not use range locks to enforce
the IGNORE_DUP_KEY=ON setting in clustered indexes. The data is inserted or modified in
the clustered indexes first, and SQL Server does not need to use range locks to avoid race
conditions.

# Reducing the Chance of Deadlocks

Finally, there are several practical bits of advice I can provide toward helping to reduce the chance of deadlocks in the system:

1. Optimize the queries. Scans introduced by non-optimized queries are the most common causes of deadlocks. The right indexes not only improve the performance of the queries, but also reduce the number of rows that need to be read and locks that need to be acquired, thus reducing the chance of lock collisions with the other sessions.

2. Keep locks as short as possible. As you will recall, all exclusive (X) locks are held until the end of the transaction. Make transactions short and try to update data as close to the end of the transaction as possible to reduce the chance of lock collision. In our example from Table 5-1, you can change the code and swap around the SELECT and UPDATE statements. This would solve the particular deadlock problem because the transactions do not have any statements that can be blocked after exclusive (X) locks are acquired.

3. Consider using optimistic isolation levels such as READ COMMITTED SNAPSHOT or SNAPSHOT. When it is impossible, use the lowest transaction isolation level that provides the required data consistency. This reduces the time shared (S) locks are held. Even if you swapped the SELECT and UPDATE statements in the previous example, you would still have the deadlock in the REPEATABLE READ or SERIALIZABLE isolation levels. With those isolation levels, shared (S) locks are held until the end of the transaction, and they would block UPDATE statements. In READ COMMITTED mode, shared (S) locks are released after a row is read, and UPDATE statements would not be blocked.

4. Avoid updating a row multiple times within the same transaction when multiple indexes are involved. As you saw earlier in this chapter, SQL Server does not place exclusive (X) locks on nonclustered index rows when index columns are not updated. Other sessions can place incompatible locks there and block subsequent updates, which would lead to deadlocks.

5.  Use retry logic. Wrap critical code into TRY..CATCH blocks and retry the action if deadlock occurs. The error number for the exception caused by the deadlock is 1205. The code in Listing 5-12 shows how you can implement that.

***Listing 5-12.*** Using TRY..CATCH block to retry the operation in case of deadlock

```
-- Declare and set variable to track number of retries to try before
exiting.
declare
    @retry tinyint = 5

-- Keep trying to update table if this task is selected as the deadlock
victim.
while (@retry > 0)
begin
    begin try
        begin tran
            -- some code that can lead to the deadlock
        commit
    end try
    begin catch
        -- Check error number. If deadlock victim error, then reduce
        retry count
        -- for next update retry. If some other error occurred, then exit
        WHILE loop.
            if (error_number() = 1205)
                set @retry = @retry - 1;
            else
                set @retry = 0;

            if @@trancount > 0
                rollback;
    end catch
end
```

# Summary

With the exception of intra-query parallelism deadlocks, which are considered to be a bug in the SQL Server code, deadlocks occur when multiple sessions compete for the same set of resources.

The key element in deadlock troubleshooting is the deadlock graph, which provides information about the processes and resources involved in the deadlock. You can collect the deadlock graph by enabling trace flag T1222, capturing xml_deadlock_report Extended Event and Deadlock graph SQL Trace event, or setting up a deadlock event notification in the system. In SQL Server 2008 and above, the xml_deadlock_report event is included in the system_health Extended Event session, which is enabled by default on every SQL Server installation.

The deadlock graph will provide you with information about the queries that triggered the deadlock. You should remember, however, that in the majority of cases, a deadlock involves multiple statements that acquired and held the locks within the same transaction and you may need to analyze all of them to address the problem.

Even though deadlocks can happen for many reasons, more often than not they happen because of excessive locking during scans in non-optimized queries. Query optimization can help to address them.

# CHAPTER 6

# Optimistic Isolation Levels

Optimistic transaction isolation levels were introduced in SQL Server 2005 as a new way to deal with blocking problems and address concurrency phenomena in a system. With optimistic transaction isolation levels, queries read "old" committed versions of rows while accessing data modified by the other sessions, rather than being blocked by the incompatibility of shared (S) and exclusive (X) locks.

This chapter will explain how optimistic isolation levels are implemented and how they affect the locking behavior of the system.

## Row Versioning Overview

With optimistic transaction isolation levels, when updates occur, SQL Server stores the old versions of the rows in a special part of `tempdb` called the *version store*. The original rows in the database reference them with 14-byte version pointers, which SQL Server adds to modified (updated and deleted) rows. Depending on the situation, you can have more than one version record stored in the version store for the row. Figure 6-1 illustrates this behavior.

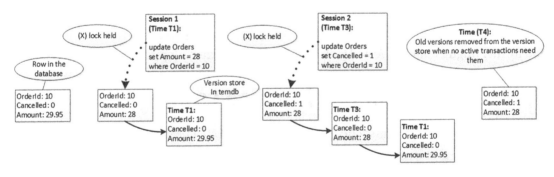

***Figure 6-1.*** *Version store*

© Dmitri Korotkevitch 2018

D. Korotkevitch, *Expert SQL Server Transactions and Locking*, https://doi.org/10.1007/978-1-4842-3957-5_6

Now, when readers (and sometimes writers) access a row that holds an exclusive (X) lock, they read the old version from the version store rather than being blocked, as shown in Figure 6-2.

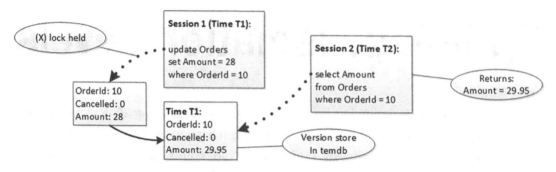

***Figure 6-2.*** *Readers and version store*

As you can guess, while optimistic isolation levels help reduce blocking, there are some tradeoffs. Most significant among these is that they contribute to tempdb load. Using optimistic isolation levels on highly volatile systems can lead to very heavy tempdb activity and can significantly increase tempdb size. We will look at this issue in greater detail later in this chapter.

There is overhead during data modification and retrieval. SQL Server needs to copy the data to tempdb as well as maintain a linked list of the version records. Similarly, it needs to traverse that list when reading data. This adds additional CPU, memory, and I/O load. You need to remember these tradeoffs, especially when you host the system in the cloud, where I/O performance is often less efficient than that of modern high-end disk arrays you can find on-premises.

Finally, optimistic isolation levels contribute to index fragmentation. When a row is modified, SQL Server increases the row size by 14 bytes due to the version pointer. If a page is tightly packed and a new version of the row does not fit into the page, it will lead to a page split and further fragmentation. We will look at this behavior in more depth later in the chapter.

# Optimistic Transaction Isolation Levels

There are two optimistic transaction isolation levels: READ COMMITTED SNAPSHOT and SNAPSHOT. To be precise, SNAPSHOT is a separate transaction isolation level, while READ COMMITTED SNAPSHOT is a database option that changes the behavior of the readers in the READ COMMITTED transaction isolation level.

Let's examine these levels in depth.

# READ COMMITTED SNAPSHOT Isolation Level

Both optimistic isolation levels need to be enabled on the database level. You can enable READ COMMITTED SNAPSHOT (RCSI) with the ALTER DATABASE SET READ_COMMITTED_ SNAPSHOT ON command. That statement acquires an exclusive (X) database lock to change the database option, and it will be blocked if there are other users connected to the database. You can address that by running the ALTER DATABASE SET READ_ COMMITTED_SNAPSHOT ON WITH ROLLBACK AFTER X SECONDS command. This will roll back all active transactions and terminate existing database connections, which allows the changing of the database option.

---

**Note**   READ COMMITTED SNAPSHOT is enabled by default in Microsoft Azure SQL Databases.

---

As already mentioned, RCSI changes the behavior of the readers in READ COMMITTED mode. It does not affect the behavior of the writers, however.

As you can see in Figure 6-3, instead of acquiring shared (S) locks and being blocked by any exclusive (X) locks held on the row, readers use the old version from the version store. Writers still acquire update (U) and exclusive (X) locks in the same way as in pessimistic isolation levels. Again, as you can see, blocking between writers from different sessions still exists, although writers do not block readers similar to READ UNCOMMITTED mode.

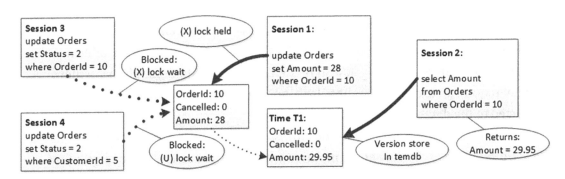

***Figure 6-3.*** *READ COMMITTED SNAPSHOT isolation level behavior*

There is a major difference between the READ UNCOMMITTED and READ COMMITTED SNAPSHOT isolation levels, however. READ UNCOMMITTED removes the blocking at the expense of data consistency. Many consistency anomalies are possible, including reading uncommitted data, duplicated reads, and missed rows. On the other hand, the READ COMMITTED SNAPSHOT isolation level provides you with full *statement-level consistency*. Statements running in this isolation level do not access uncommitted data nor data committed after the statement started.

As the obvious conclusion, you should avoid using the (NOLOCK) hint in the queries when READ COMMITTED SNAPSHOT isolation level is enabled. While using (NOLOCK) and READ UNCOMMITTED is a bad practice by itself, it is completely useless when READ COMMITTED SNAPSHOT provides you with similar non-blocking behavior without losing data consistency for the queries.

---

**Tip**    Switching a database to the READ COMMITTED SNAPSHOT isolation level can be a great emergency technique when the system is suffering from blocking issues. It removes writers/readers blocking without any code changes, assuming that readers are running in the READ COMMITTED isolation level. Obviously, this is only a temporary solution, and you need to detect and eliminate the root cause of the blocking.

---

# SNAPSHOT Isolation Level

SNAPSHOT is a separate transaction isolation level, and it needs to be set explicitly in the code with a SET TRANSACTION ISOLATION LEVEL SNAPSHOT statement.

By default, using the SNAPSHOT isolation level is prohibited. You must enable it with an ALTER DATABASE SET ALLOW_SNAPSHOT_ISOLATION ON statement. This statement does not require an exclusive database lock, and it can be executed with other users connected to the database.

The SNAPSHOT isolation level provides *transaction-level consistency*. Transactions will see a *snapshot* of the data at the moment when the transaction started regardless of how long the transaction is active and how many data changes were made in other transactions during that time.

---

**Note**    SQL Server starts an explicit transaction at the time when it accesses the data for the first time rather than at the time of the BEGIN TRAN statement.

---

In the example shown in Figure 6-4, we have a session 1 that starts the transaction and reads the row at time *T1*. At time *T2*, we have a session 2 that modifies the row in an autocommitted transaction. At this moment, the old (original) version of the row moved to the version store in tempdb.

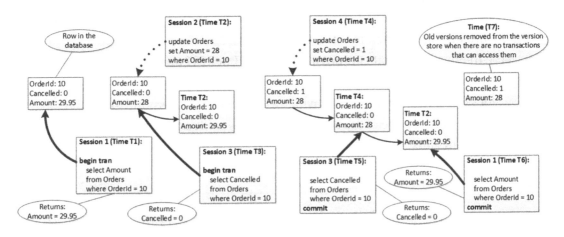

***Figure 6-4.*** *Snapshot isolation level and readers behavior*

In the next step, we have a session 3 that starts another transaction and reads the same row at time *T3*. It sees the version of the row as modified and committed by session 2 (at time *T2*). At time *T4*, we have a session 4 that modifies the row in the autocommitted transaction again. At this time, we have two versions of the rows in the version store—one that existed between *T2* and *T4*, and the original version that existed before *T2*. Now, if session 3 runs the SELECT again, it would use the version that existed between *T2* and *T4* because this version was committed at the time that the session 3 transaction started. Similarly, session 1 would use the original version of the row that existed before *T2*. At some point, after session 1 and session 3 are committed, the *version store clean-up task* would remove both records from the version store, assuming, of course, that there are no other transactions that need them.

The SERIALIZABLE and SNAPSHOT isolation levels provide the same level of protection against data inconsistency issues; however, there is a subtle difference in their behavior. A SNAPSHOT isolation level transaction sees data as of the beginning of a transaction.

With the SERIALIZABLE isolation level, the transaction sees data as of the time when the data was accessed for the first time and locks were acquired. Consider a situation where a session is reading data from a table in the middle of a transaction. If another session changed the data in that table after the transaction started but before data was read, the transaction in the SERIALIZABLE isolation level would see the changes while the SNAPSHOT transaction would not.

Optimistic transaction isolation levels provide statement- or transaction-level data consistency reducing or even eliminating the blocking, although they could generate an enormous amount of data in the tempdb. If you have a session that deletes millions of rows from the table, all of those rows would need to be copied to the version store, even if the original DELETE statement were running in a pessimistic isolation level, just to preserve the state of the data for possible SNAPSHOT or RCSI transactions. You will see such an example later in the chapter.

Now, let's examine the writers' behavior. Let's assume that session 1 starts the transaction and updates one of the rows. That session holds an exclusive (X) lock there, as shown in Figure 6-5.

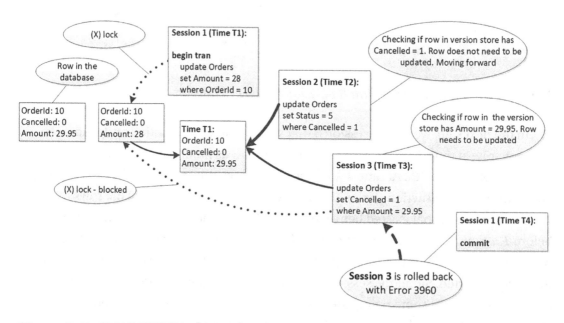

***Figure 6-5.*** *SNAPSHOT isolation level and writers' behavior*

Session 2 wants to update all rows where Cancelled = 1. It starts to scan the table, and when it needs to read the data for OrderId = 10, it reads the row from the version store; that is, the last committed version before the session 2 transaction started. This version is the original (non-updated) version of the row, and it has `Cancelled = 0`, so session 2 does not need to update it. Session 2 continues scanning the rows without being blocked by update (U) and exclusive (X) lock incompatibility.

Similarly, session 3 wants to update all rows with `Amount = 29.95`. When it reads the version of the row from the version store, it determines that the row needs to be updated. Again, it does not matter that session 1 also changes the amount for the same row. At this point, a "new version" of the row has not been committed and is invisible to the other sessions. Now, session 3 wants to update the row in the database, tries to acquire an exclusive (X) lock, and is blocked because session 1 already has an exclusive (X) lock there.

Now, if session 1 commits the transaction, session 3 would be rolled back with Error 3960, as shown in Figure 6-6, which indicates a write/write conflict. This is different behavior than any other isolation level, in which session 3 would successfully overwrite the changes from session 1 as soon as the session 1 exclusive (X) lock was released.

```
Msg 3960, Level 16, State 2, Line 1
Snapshot isolation transaction aborted due to update conflict. You cannot use snapshot isolation
to access table 'Delivery.Orders' directly or indirectly in database 'SqlServerInternals' to
update, delete, or insert the row that has been modified or deleted by another transaction. Retry
the transaction or change the isolation level for the update/delete statement.
```

***Figure 6-6.*** *Error 3960*

A write/write conflict occurs when a `SNAPSHOT` transaction is trying to update data that has been modified after the transaction started. In our example, this would happen even if session 1 committed before session 3's `UPDATE` statement, as long as this commit occurred after session 3's transaction started.

---

**Tip**   You can implement retry logic with `TRY..CATCH` statements to handle the 3960 errors if business requirements allow that.

---

You need to keep this behavior in mind when you are updating data in the `SNAPSHOT` isolation level in a system with volatile data. If other sessions update the rows that you are modifying after the transaction is started, you would end up with Error 3960, even if you did not access those rows before the update. One of the possible workarounds is using `(READCOMMITTED)` or other non-optimistic isolation level table hints as part of the `UPDATE` statement, as shown in Listing 6-1.

**Listing 6-1.** Using READCOMMITTED hint to prevent 3960 error

```
set transaction isolation level snapshot
begin tran
    select count(*) from Delivery.Drivers;

    update Delivery.Orders with (readcommitted)
    set Cancelled = 1
    where OrderId = 10;
commit
```

SNAPSHOT isolation levels can change the behavior of the system. Let's assume there is a table dbo.Colors with two rows: *Black* and *White*. The code that creates the table is shown in Listing 6-2.

**Listing 6-2.** SNAPSHOT isolation level update behavior: Table creation

```
create table dbo.Colors
(
    Id int not null,
    Color char(5) not null
);

insert into dbo.Colors(Id, Color) values(1,'Black'),(2,'White')
```

Now, let's run two sessions simultaneously. In the first session, we run the update that sets the color to *white* for the rows where the color is currently *black* using the UPDATE dbo.Colors SET Color='White' WHERE Color='Black' statement. In the second session, let's perform the opposite operation, using the UPDATE dbo.Colors SET Color='Black' WHERE Color='White' statement.

Let's run both sessions simultaneously in READ COMMITTED or any other pessimistic transaction isolation level. In the first step, as shown in Figure 6-7, we have the race condition. One of the sessions places exclusive (X) locks on the row it updated, while the other session is blocked when trying to acquire an update (U) lock on the same row.

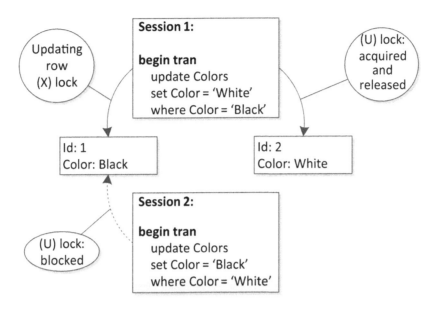

**Figure 6-7.** *Pessimistic locking behavior: Step 1*

When the first session commits the transaction, the exclusive (X) lock is released. At this point, the row has a Color value updated by the first session, so the second session updates two rows rather than one, as shown in Figure 6-8. In the end, both rows in the table will be in either black or white depending on which session acquires the lock first.

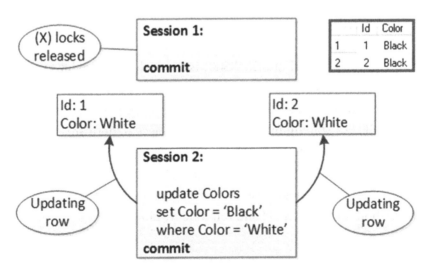

**Figure 6-8.** *Pessimistic locking behavior: Step 2*

With the SNAPSHOT isolation level, however, this works a bit differently, as shown in Figure 6-9. When the session updates the row, it moves the old version of the row to the version store. Another session will read the row from there, rather than being blocked and vice versa. As a result, the colors will be swapped.

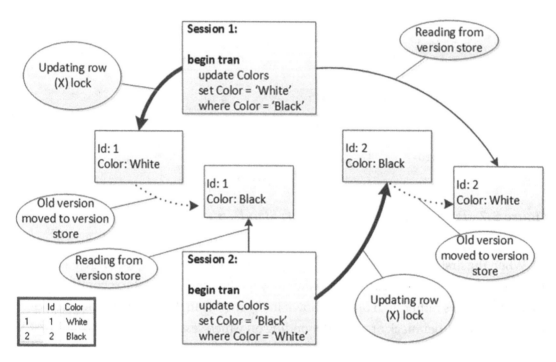

***Figure 6-9.*** *SNAPSHOT isolation level locking behavior*

You need to be aware of RCSI and SNAPSHOT isolation level behavior, especially if you have code that relies on blocking. One example is a trigger-based implementation of referential integrity. You can have an ON DELETE trigger on the referenced table where you are running a SELECT statement; this trigger will check if there are any rows in another table referencing the deleted rows. With an optimistic isolation level, the trigger can skip the rows that were inserted after the transaction started. The solution here again is a (READCOMMITTED) or other pessimistic isolation level table hint as part of the SELECT in the triggers on both the referenced and referencing tables.

**Note**   SQL Server uses a READ COMMITTED isolation level when validating foreign key constraints. This means that you can still have blocking between writers and readers even with optimistic isolation levels, especially if there are no indexes on the referencing column that leads to a table scan of the referencing table.

# Version Store Behavior and Monitoring

As already mentioned, you need to monitor how optimistic isolation levels affect tempdb in your system. For example, let's run the code from Listing 6-3, which deletes all rows from the Delivery.Orders table using the READ UNCOMMITTED transaction isolation level.

*Listing 6-3.* Deleting data from Delivery.Orders table

```
set transaction isolation level read uncommitted
begin tran
        delete from Delivery.Orders;
commit
```

Even if there are no other transactions using optimistic isolation levels at the time when DELETE statement started, there is still a possibility that one might start before the transaction commits. As a result, SQL Server needs to maintain the version store, regardless of whether there are any active transactions that use optimistic isolation levels.

Figure 6-10 shows tempdb free space and version store size. As you can see, as soon as the deletion starts, the version store grows and takes up all of the free space in tempdb.

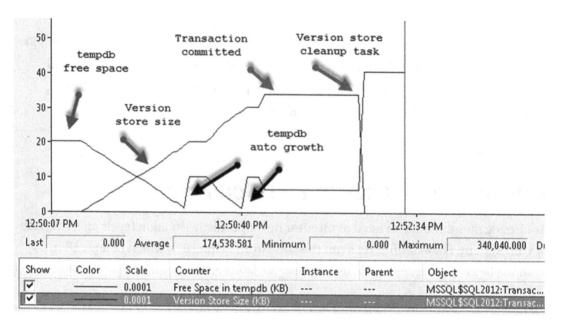

**Figure 6-10.** *tempdb free space and version store size*

In Figure 6-11, you can see the version store generation and cleanup rate. The generation rate remains more or less the same during execution, while the cleanup task cleans the version store after the transaction is committed. By default, the cleanup task runs once per minute as well as before any auto-growth event, in case tempdb is full.

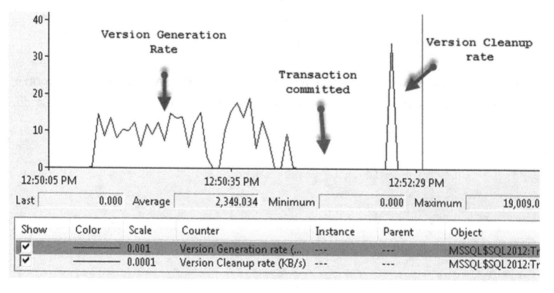

**Figure 6-11.** *Version generation and cleanup rates*

As you can see, the version store adds overhead to the system. Do not enable optimistic isolation levels in the database unless you are planning to use them. This is especially true for SNAPSHOT isolation, which requires you to explicitly set it in the code. While many systems could benefit from READ COMMITTED SNAPSHOT without any code changes, this would not happen with the SNAPSHOT isolation level.

There are three other performance counters related to optimistic isolation levels that may be helpful during version store monitoring:

1. *Snapshot Transactions.* This shows the total number of active snapshot transactions. You can analyze this counter to determine if applications use the SNAPSHOT isolation level when it is enabled in the system.

2. *Update Conflict Ratio.* This shows the ratio of the number of update conflicts to the total number of update snapshot transactions.

3. *Longest Transaction Running Time.* This shows the duration in seconds of the oldest active transaction that is using row versioning. A high value for this counter may explain the large version store size in the system.

There are also a few dynamic management views (DMVs) that can be useful in troubleshooting various issues related to the version store and transactions in general.

The sys.dm_db_file_space_usage view returns space usage information for every file in the database. One of the columns in the view, version_store_reserved_page_count, returns the number of pages used by the version store. Listing 6-4 illustrates this view in action.

***Listing 6-4.*** Using sys.dm_db_file_space_usage view

```
select
    sum(user_object_reserved_page_count) * 8
            as [User Objects (KB)]
    ,sum(internal_object_reserved_page_count) * 8
            as [Internal Objects (KB)]
    ,sum(version_store_reserved_page_count) * 8
            as [Version Store (KB)]
```

```
    ,sum(unallocated_extent_page_count) * 8
            as [Free Space (KB)]
from
    tempdb.sys.dm_db_file_space_usage;
```

You can track version store usage on a per-database basis using the `sys.dm_tran_version_store` view, as shown in Listing 6-5. This view returns information about every row from the version store, and it can be extremely inefficient when the version store is large. It also does not include information about reserved but not used space.

*Listing 6-5.*  Using sys.dm_tran_version_store view

```
select
    db_name(database_id) as [database]
    ,database_id
    ,sum(record_length_first_part_in_bytes + record_length_second_part_in_
    bytes) / 1024
            as [version store (KB)]
from
    sys.dm_tran_version_store
group by
    database_id
```

In SQL Server 2017, you can obtain the same information with the `sys.dm_tran_version_store_space_usage` view. This view is more efficient than `sys.dm_tran_version_store`, and it also returns information about reserved space, as shown in Listing 6-6.

*Listing 6-6.*  Using sys.dm_tran_version_store_space_usage view

```
select
    db_name(database_id) as [database]
    ,database_id
    ,reserved_page_count
    ,reserved_space_kb
from
    sys.dm_tran_version_store_space_usage
```

When the version store becomes very large, you need to identify active transactions that prevent its cleanup. Remember: When optimistic isolation levels are enabled, row versioning is used regardless of the isolation level of the transaction that performed the data modification.

Listing 6-7 shows how to identify the five oldest user transactions in the system. Long-running transactions are the most common reason why the version store is not cleaning up. They may also introduce other issues in the system; for example, preventing the truncation of the transaction log.

---

**Important**   Some SQL Server features, such as Online Index Rebuild, AFTER UPDATE and AFTER DELETE triggers, and MARS, use the version store regardless if optimistic isolation levels are enabled. Moreover, the row versioning is also used in the systems that have AlwaysOn Availability Groups with readable secondaries enabled. We will discuss it in greater details in chapter 12.

---

*Listing 6-7.* Identifying oldest active transactions in the system

```
select top 5
    at.transaction_id
    ,at.elapsed_time_seconds
    ,at.session_id
    ,s.login_time
    ,s.login_name
    ,s.host_name
    ,s.program_name
    ,s.last_request_start_time
    ,s.last_request_end_time
    ,er.status
    ,er.wait_type
    ,er.blocking_session_id
    ,er.wait_type
    ,substring(
        st.text,
        (er.statement_start_offset / 2) + 1,
```

```
    (case
        er.statement_end_offset
    when -1
        then datalength(st.text)
        else er.statement_end_offset
    end - er.statement_start_offset) / 2 + 1
    ) as [SQL]
from
    sys.dm_tran_active_snapshot_database_transactions at
        join sys.dm_exec_sessions s on
            at.session_id = s.session_id
        left join sys.dm_exec_requests er on
            at.session_id = er.session_id
        outer apply
            sys.dm_exec_sql_text(er.sql_handle) st
order by
    at.elapsed_time_seconds desc
```

---

**Note**    There are several other useful transaction-related dynamic management views. You can read about them at `https://docs.microsoft.com/en-us/ sql/relational-databases/system-dynamic-management-views/ transaction-related-dynamic-management-views-and-functions- transact-sql`.

---

Finally, it is worth noting that SQL Server exposes the information if `READ COMMITTED SNAPSHOT` and `SNAPSHOT` isolation levels are enabled in `sys.databases` view. The `is_read_committed_snapshot` column indicates if RCSI is enabled. The `snapshot_ isolation_state` and `snapshot_isolation_state_desc` columns indicate whether `SNAPSHOT` transactions are allowed and/or if the database is in a transition state after you run the `ALTER DATABASE SET ALLOW_SNAPSHOT_ISOLATION` statement, respectively.

# Row Versioning and Index Fragmentation

Optimistic isolation levels rely on row versioning. During updates, the old versions of the rows are copied to the version store in `tempdb`. The rows in the database reference them through 14-byte version store pointers that are added during update operations.

The same thing happens during deletions. In SQL Server, a `DELETE` statement does not remove the rows from the table, but rather marks them as *deleted*, reclaiming the space in the background after the transaction is committed. With optimistic isolation levels, deletions also copy the rows to the version store, expanding the deleted rows with version store pointers.

The version store pointer increases the row size by 14 bytes, which may lead to the situation where the data page does not have enough free space to accommodate the new version of the row. This would trigger a *page split* and increase index fragmentation.

Let's look at an example. As the first step, we will disable optimistic isolation levels and rebuild the index on the `Delivery.Orders` table using `FILLFACTOR=100`. This forces SQL Server to fully populate the data pages without reserving any free space on them. The code is shown in Listing 6-8.

***Listing 6-8.*** Optimistic isolation levels and fragmentation: Index rebuild

```
alter database SQLServerInternals
set read_committed_snapshot off
with rollback immediate;
go

alter database SQLServerInternals
set allow_snapshot_isolation off;
go

alter index PK_Orders on Delivery.Orders rebuild
with (fillfactor = 100);
```

Listing 6-9 shows the code that analyzes the index fragmentation of the clustered index in the `Delivery.Orders` table.

153

**Listing 6-9.**  Optimistic isolation levels and fragmentation: Analyzing fragmentation

```
select
    alloc_unit_type_desc as [alloc_unit]
    ,index_level
    ,page_count
    ,convert(decimal(4,2),avg_page_space_used_in_percent)
            as [space_used]
    ,convert(decimal(4,2),avg_fragmentation_in_percent)
            as [frag %]
    ,min_record_size_in_bytes as [min_size]
    ,max_record_size_in_bytes as [max_size]
    ,avg_record_size_in_bytes as [avg_size]
from
    sys.dm_db_index_physical_stats(db_id()
            ,object_id(N'Delivery.Orders'),1,null,'DETAILED');
```

As you can see in Figure 6-12, the index is using 1,392 pages and does not have any fragmentation.

| | alloc_unit | index_level | page_count | space_used | frag % | min_size | max_size | avg_size |
|---|---|---|---|---|---|---|---|---|
| 1 | IN_ROW_DATA | 0 | 1392 | 98.18 | 0.22 | 163 | 201 | 166.831 |
| 2 | IN_ROW_DATA | 1 | 4 | 55.87 | 50.00 | 11 | 11 | 11 |
| 3 | IN_ROW_DATA | 2 | 1 | 0.62 | 0.00 | 11 | 11 | 11 |

**Figure 6-12.**  *Index statistics with FILLFACTOR = 100*

Now, let's run the code from Listing 6-10 and delete 50 percent of the rows from the table. Note that we rolled back the transaction to reset the environment before the next test.

**Listing 6-10.**  Optimistic isolation levels and fragmentation: Deleting 50 percent of the rows

```
begin tran
    delete from Delivery.Orders where OrderId % 2 = 0;
    -- update Delivery.Orders set Pieces += 1;

    select
```

```
    alloc_unit_type_desc as [alloc_unit]
    ,index_level
    ,page_count
    ,convert(decimal(4,2),avg_page_space_used_in_percent)
            as [space_used]
    ,convert(decimal(4,2),avg_fragmentation_in_percent)
            as [frag %]
    ,min_record_size_in_bytes as [min_size]
    ,max_record_size_in_bytes as [max_size]
    ,avg_record_size_in_bytes as [avg_size]
from
    sys.dm_db_index_physical_stats(db_id()
            ,object_id(N'Delivery.Orders'),1,null,'DETAILED');
rollback
```

Figure 6-13 shows the output of this code. As you can see, this operation does not increase the number of pages in the index. The same will happen if you update a value of any fixed-length column. This update would not change the size of the rows, and therefore it would not trigger any page splits.

| | alloc_unit | index_level | page_count | space_used | frag % | min_size | max_size | avg_size |
|---|---|---|---|---|---|---|---|---|
| 1 | IN_ROW_DATA | 0 | 1392 | 98.18 | 0.22 | 163 | 201 | 166.831 |
| 2 | IN_ROW_DATA | 1 | 4 | 55.87 | 50.00 | 11 | 11 | 11 |
| 3 | IN_ROW_DATA | 2 | 1 | 0.62 | 0.00 | 11 | 11 | 11 |

*Figure 6-13.* *Index statistics after DELETE statement*

Now, let's enable the READ COMMITTED SNAPSHOT isolation level and repeat our test. Listing 6-11 shows the code to do that.

*Listing 6-11.* Optimistic isolation levels and fragmentation: Repeating the test with RCSI enabled

```
alter database SQLServerInternals
set read_committed_snapshot on
with rollback immediate;
go
```

```
set transaction isolation level read uncommitted
begin tran
    delete from Delivery.Orders where OrderId % 2 = 0;
    -- update Delivery.Orders set Pieces += 1;
rollback
```

Figure 6-14 shows index statistics after the operation. Note that we were using the READ UNCOMMITTED isolation level and rolling back the transaction. Nevertheless, row versioning is used, which introduces page splits during data deletion.

| | alloc_unit | index_level | page_count | space_used | frag % | min_size | max_size | avg_size |
|---|---|---|---|---|---|---|---|---|
| 1 | IN_ROW_DATA | 0 | 2780 | 49.15 | 98.74 | 163 | 201 | 166.831 |
| 2 | IN_ROW_DATA | 1 | 8 | 55.79 | 100.00 | 11 | 11 | 11 |
| 3 | IN_ROW_DATA | 2 | 1 | 1.26 | 0.00 | 11 | 11 | 11 |

*Figure 6-14.* *Index statistics after DELETE statement with RCSI enabled*

After being added, the 14-byte version store pointers stay in the rows, even after the records are removed from the version store. You can reclaim this space by performing an index rebuild.

You need to remember this behavior and factor it into your index maintenance strategy. It is best not to use FILLFACTOR = 100 if optimistic isolation levels are enabled. The same applies to indexes defined on tables that have AFTER UPDATE and AFTER DELETE triggers defined. Those triggers rely on row versioning and will also use the version store internally.

# Summary

SQL Server uses a row-versioning model with optimistic isolation levels. Queries access "old" committed versions of rows rather than being blocked by the incompatibility of shared (S), update (U), and exclusive (X) locks. There are two optimistic transaction isolation levels available: READ COMMITTED SNAPSHOT and SNAPSHOT.

READ COMMITTED SNAPSHOT is a database option that changes the behavior of readers in READ COMMITTED mode. It does not change the behavior of writers—there is still blocking due to (U)/(U) and (U)/(X) locks' incompatibility. READ COMMITTED SNAPSHOT does not require any code changes, and it can be used as an emergency technique when a system is experiencing blocking issues.

READ COMMITTED SNAPSHOT provides statement-level consistency; that is, the query reads a snapshot of the data at the time the statement started.

The SNAPSHOT isolation level is a separate transaction isolation level that needs to be explicitly specified in the code. This level provides transaction-level consistency; that is, the query accesses a snapshot of the data at the time the transaction started.

With the SNAPSHOT isolation level, writers do not block each other, with the exception of the situation where both sessions are updating the same rows. That situation leads either to blocking or to a 3960 error.

While optimistic isolation levels reduce blocking, they can significantly increase tempdb load, especially in OLTP systems where data is constantly changing. They also contribute to index fragmentation by adding 14-byte pointers to the data rows. You should consider the tradeoffs of using them at the implementation stage, perform tempdb optimization, and monitor the system to make sure that the version store is not abused.

# CHAPTER 7

# Lock Escalation

Although row-level locking is great from a concurrency standpoint, it is expensive. In memory, a lock structure uses 64 bytes in 32-bit and 128 bytes in 64-bit operating systems. Keeping information about millions of row- and page-level locks would use gigabytes of memory.

SQL Server reduces the number of locks held in memory with a technique called *lock escalation*, which we will discuss in this chapter.

## Lock Escalation Overview

SQL Server tries to reduce memory consumption and the overhead of lock management by using the simple technique called lock escalation. Once a statement acquires at least 5,000 row- and page-level locks on the same object, SQL Server tries to escalate—or perhaps better said, replace—those locks with a single table- or, if enabled, partition-level lock. The operation succeeds if no other sessions hold incompatible locks on the object or partition.

When an operation succeeds, SQL Server releases all row- and page-level locks held by the transaction on the object (or partition), keeping the object- (or partition-) level lock only. If an operation fails, SQL Server continues to use row-level locking and repeats escalation attempts after about every 1,250 new locks acquired. In addition to reacting to the number of locks taken, SQL Server can escalate locks when the total number of locks in the instance exceeds memory or configuration thresholds.

---

**Note**   The number of locks thresholds of 5,000/1,250 is an approximation. The actual number of acquired locks that triggers lock escalation may vary and is usually slightly bigger than that threshold.

---

Let's look at the example and run a SELECT statement that counts the number of rows in the Delivery.Orders table in a transaction with a REPEATABLE READ isolation level. As you will remember, in this isolation level, SQL Server keeps shared (S) locks until the end of the transaction.

159

© Dmitri Korotkevitch 2018
D. Korotkevitch, *Expert SQL Server Transactions and Locking*, https://doi.org/10.1007/978-1-4842-3957-5_7

Let's disable lock escalation for this table with the ALTER TABLE SET (LOCK_
ESCALATION=DISABLE) command (more about this later) and look at the number of
locks SQL Server acquires, as well as at the memory required to store them. We will use
a (ROWLOCK) hint to prevent the situation in which SQL Server *optimizes* the locking by
acquiring page-level shared (S) locks instead of row-level locks. In addition, while the
transaction is still active, let's insert another row from a different session to demonstrate
how lock escalation affects concurrency in the system.

Table 7-1 shows the code of both sessions along with the output from the dynamic
management views.

***Table 7-1.*** *Test Code with Lock Escalation Disabled*

| Session 1 | Session 2 |
|---|---|
| alter table Delivery.Orders<br>set (lock_escalation=disable);<br><br>set transaction isolation level<br>repeatable read<br><br>begin tran<br>   select count(*)<br>   from Delivery.Orders<br>     with (rowlock); | |
| | -- Success<br>insert into Delivery.Orders<br>   (OrderDate,OrderNum,CustomerId)<br>values(getUTCDate(),'99999',100); |
| -- Result: 10,212,326<br>select count(*) as [Lock Count]<br>from sys.dm_tran_locks;<br><br>-- Result: 1,940,272 KB<br>select sum(pages_kb) as [Memory, KB]<br>from sys.dm_os_memory_clerks<br>where type =<br>   'OBJECTSTORE_LOCK_MANAGER';<br>commit | |

Figure 7-1 shows the *Lock Memory (KB)* system performance counter while the transaction is active.

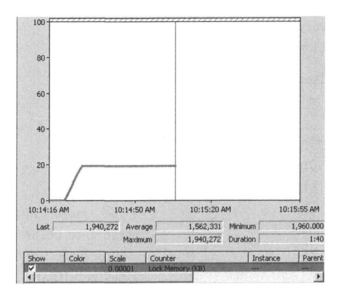

**Figure 7-1.**  *Lock Memory (KB) system performance counter*

As you can see, from a concurrency standpoint, the row-level locking is perfect. Sessions do not block each other as long as they do not compete for the same rows. At the same time, keeping the large number of locks is memory intensive, and memory is one of the most precious resources in SQL Server. In our example, SQL Server needs to keep millions of lock structures, utilizing almost two gigabytes of RAM. This number includes the row-level shared (S) locks, as well as the page-level intent shared (IS) locks. Moreover, there is the overhead of maintaining the locking information and the large number of lock structures in the system.

Let's see what happens if we enable default lock escalation behavior with the ALTER TABLE SET (LOCK_ESCALATION=TABLE) command and run the code shown in Table 7-2.

**Table 7-2.**  *Test Code with Lock Escalation Enabled*

| Session 1 (SPID=57) | Session 2 (SPID=58) |
|---|---|

```
alter table Delivery.Orders
set (lock_escalation=table);

set transaction isolation level
repeatable read
begin tran
   select count(*)
   from Delivery.Orders
     with (rowlock);
```

```
                                    -- The session is blocked
                                    insert into Delivery.Orders
                                       (OrderDate,OrderNum,CustomerId)
                                    values(getUTCDate(),'100000',100);
```

```
   select
     request_session_id as [SPID]
     ,resource_type as [Resource]
     ,request_mode as [Lock Mode]
     ,request_status as [Status]
   from sys.dm_tran_locks;
commit
```

Figure 7-2 shows the output from the sys.dm_tran_locks view.

|   | SPID | Resource | Lock Mo... | Status |
|---|---|---|---|---|
| 1 | 57 | DATABASE | S | GRANT |
| 2 | 58 | DATABASE | S | GRANT |
| 3 | 57 | OBJECT | S | GRANT |
| 4 | 58 | OBJECT | IX | WAIT |

***Figure 7-2.***  *Sys.dm_tran_locks output with lock escalation enabled*

SQL Server replaces the row- and page-level locks with the object shared (S) lock. Although it is great from a memory-usage standpoint—there is just a single lock to maintain—it affects concurrency. As you can see, the second session is blocked—it cannot acquire an intent exclusive (IX) lock on the table because it is incompatible with the full shared (S) lock held by the first session.

The locking granularity hints, such as (ROWLOCK) and (PAGLOCK), do not affect lock-escalation behavior. For example, with the (PAGLOCK) hint, SQL Server uses full page-level rather than row-level locks. This, however, may still trigger lock escalation after the number of acquired locks exceeds the threshold.

Lock escalation is enabled by default and could introduce blocking issues, which can be confusing for developers and database administrators. Let's talk about a few typical cases.

The first case occurs when reporting queries use REPEATABLE READ or SERIALIZABLE isolation levels for data consistency purposes. If reporting queries are reading large amounts of data when there are no sessions updating the data, those queries could escalate shared (S) locks to the table level. Afterward, all writers would be blocked, even when trying to insert new data or modify the data not read by the reporting queries, as you saw earlier in this chapter. One of the ways to address this issue is by switching to optimistic transaction isolation levels, which we discussed in the previous chapter.

The second case is the implementation of the purge process. Let's assume that you need to purge a large amount of old data using a DELETE statement. If the implementation deletes a large number of rows at once, you could have exclusive (X) locks escalated to the table level. This would block access to the table for all writers, as well as for the readers in READ COMMITTED, REPEATABLE READ, or SERIALIZABLE isolation levels, even when those queries are working with a completely different set of data than what you are purging.

Finally, you can think about a process that inserts a large batch of rows with a single INSERT statement. Like the purge process, it could escalate exclusive (X) locks to the table level and block other sessions from accessing it.

All these patterns have one thing in common—they acquire and hold a large number of row- and page-level locks as part of a single statement. That triggers lock escalation, which will succeed if there are no other sessions holding incompatible locks on the table (or partition) level. This will block other sessions from acquiring incompatible intent or full locks on the table (or partition) until the first session has completed the transaction, regardless of whether the blocked sessions are trying to access the data affected by the first session.

It is worth repeating that lock escalation is triggered by the number of locks acquired by the statement, rather than by the transaction. If the separate statements acquire less than 5,000 row- and page-level locks each, lock escalation is not triggered, regardless of the total number of locks the transaction holds. Listing 7-1 shows an example in which multiple UPDATE statements run in a loop within a single transaction.

*Listing 7-1.* Lock escalation and multiple statements

```
declare
    @id int = 1

begin tran
    while @id < 100000
    begin
        update Delivery.Orders
        set OrderStatusId = 1
        where OrderId between @id and @id + 4998;

        select @id += 4999;
    end

    select count(*) as [Lock Count]
    from sys.dm_tran_locks
    where request_session_id = @@SPID;
commit
```

Figure 7-3 shows the output of the SELECT statement from Listing 7-1. Even when the total number of locks the transaction holds is far more than the threshold, lock escalation is not triggered.

| | Total Lock Count |
|---|---|
| 1 | 133870 |

*Figure 7-3.* *Number of locks held by the transaction*

# Lock Escalation Troubleshooting

Lock escalation is completely normal. It helps to reduce locking-management overhead and memory usage, which improves system performance. You should keep it enabled unless it starts to introduce noticeable blocking issues in the system. Unfortunately, it is not always easy to detect if lock escalation contributes to blocking, and you need to analyze individual blocking cases to understand it.

One sign of potential lock escalation blocking is a high percentage of intent-lock waits (LCK_M_I*) in the wait statistics. Lock escalation, however, is not the only reason for such waits, and you need to look at other metrics during analysis.

---

**Note**   We will talk about wait statistics analysis in Chapter 12.

---

The lock escalation event leads to a full table-level lock. You would see this in the sys.dm_tran_locks view output and in the blocked process report. Figure 7-4 illustrates the output of Listing 3-2 from Chapter 3 if you were to run it at a time when blocking is occurring. As you can see, the blocked session is trying to acquire an intent lock on the object, while the blocking session—the one that triggered lock escalation—holds an incompatible full lock.

| | Resource Type | DB Name | Object | Resource | Session | Mode | Status | Wait (ms) | sql | query_plan |
|---|---|---|---|---|---|---|---|---|---|---|
| 1 | OBJECT | SqlServerInternals | Orders | | 62 | S | GRANT | NULL | NULL | NULL |
| 2 | OBJECT | SqlServerInternals | Orders | | 63 | IX | WAIT | 3455 | INSERT INTO [Deli... | <ShowPlan... |

***Figure 7-4.***  *Listing 3-2 output (sys.dm_tran_locks view) during lock escalation*

If you look at the blocked process report, you will see that the blocked process is waiting on the intent lock on the object, as shown in Listing 7-2.

***Listing 7-2.***  Blocked process report (partial)

```
<blocked-process-report>
 <blocked-process>
  <process id="..." taskpriority="0" logused="0" waitresource="OBJECT:
  ..." waittime="..." ownerId="..." transactionname="user_transaction"
  lasttranstarted="..." XDES="..." lockMode="IX" schedulerid="..."  ...>
```

Again, keep in mind that there could be other reasons for sessions to acquire full object locks or be blocked while waiting for an intent lock on the table. You must correlate information from other venues to confirm that the blocking occurred because of lock escalation.

You can capture lock escalation events with SQL Traces. Figure 7-5 illustrates the output in the *Profiler* application.

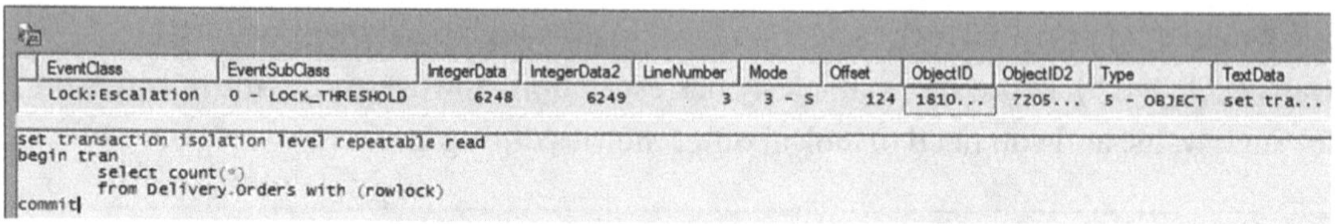

**Figure 7-5.**  *Lock escalation event shown in SQL Server Profiler*

SQL Traces provide the following attributes:

- `EventSubClass` indicates what triggered lock escalation—number of locks or memory threshold.

- `IntegerData` and `IntegerData2` show the number of locks that existed at the time of the escalation and how many locks were converted during the escalation process. It is worth noting that in our example lock escalation occurred when the statement acquired 6,248 rather than 5,000 locks.

- `Mode` tells what kind of lock was escalated.

- `ObjectID` is the `object_id` of the table for which lock escalation was triggered.

- `ObjectID2` is the *HoBT* ID for which lock escalation was triggered.

- `Type` represents lock escalation granularity.

- `TextData`, `LineNumber`, and `Offset` provide information on the batch and statement that triggered lock escalation.

Another, and better, way of capturing lock escalation occurences is by using Extended Events. Figure 7-6 illustrates a `lock_escalation` event and some of the available event fields. This event is available in SQL Server 2012 and above.

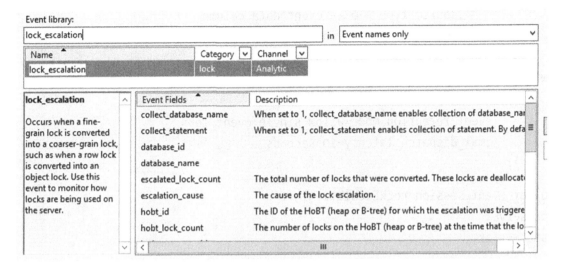

**Figure 7-6.** *Lock_escalation Extended Event*

The Extended Event is useful to understand which objects triggered lock escalation most often. You can query and aggregate the raw captured data or, alternatively, do the aggregation in an Extended Event session using a `histogram` target.

Listing 7-3 shows the latter approach, grouping the data by `object_id` field. This code would work in SQL Server 2012 and above.

**Listing 7-3.** Capturing number of lock escalation occurences with xEvents

```
create event session LockEscalationInfo
on server
add event
    sqlserver.lock_escalation
    (
        where
            database_id = 5   -- DB_ID()
    )
add target
    package0.histogram
    (
        set
            slots = 1024 -- Based on # of tables in the database
            ,filtering_event_name = 'sqlserver.lock_escalation'
```

```
            ,source_type = 0 -- event data column
            ,source = 'object_id' -- grouping column
    )
with
    (

        event_retention_mode=allow_single_event_loss
        ,max_dispatch_latency=10 seconds
    );

alter event session LockEscalationInfo
on server
state=start;
```

The code from Listing 7-4 queries a session target and returns the number of lock escalations on a per-table basis.

***Listing 7-4.*** Analyzing captured results

```
;with TargetData(Data)
as
(
    select convert(xml,st.target_data) as Data
    from sys.dm_xe_sessions s join sys.dm_xe_session_targets st on
        s.address = st.event_session_address
    where s.name = 'LockEscalationInfo' and st.target_name = 'histogram'
)
,EventInfo([count],object_id)
as
(
    select
        t.e.value('@count','int')
        ,t.e.value('((./value)/text())[1]','int')
    from
        TargetData cross apply
            TargetData.Data.nodes('/HistogramTarget/Slot') as t(e)
)
```

```
select
    e.object_id
    ,s.name + '.' + t.name as [table]
    ,e.[count]
from
    EventInfo e join sys.tables t on
        e.object_id = t.object_id
    join sys.schemas s on
        t.schema_id = s.schema_id
order by
    e.count desc;
```

You should not use this data just for the purpose of disabling lock escalation. It is very useful, however, when you are analyzing blocking cases with object-level blocking involved.

I would like to reiterate that lock escalation is completely normal and is a very useful feature in SQL Server. Even though it can introduce blocking issues, it helps to preserve SQL Server memory. The large number of locks held by the instance reduces the size of the buffer pool. As a result, you have fewer data pages in the cache, which could lead to a higher number of physical I/O operations and degrade the performance of queries.

In addition, SQL Server could terminate the queries with Error 1204 when there is no available memory to store the lock information. Figure 7-7 shows just such an error message.

```
⊞ Results  📄 Messages
Msg 1204, Level 19, State 4, Line 4
The instance of the SQL Server Database Engine cannot obtain a LOCK resource at this time.
Rerun your statement when there are fewer active users. Ask the database administrator to
check the lock and memory configuration for this instance, or to check for long-running
transactions.
```

***Figure 7-7.*** *Error 1204*

In SQL Server 2008 and above, you can control escalation behavior at the table level by using the ALTER TABLE SET LOCK_ESCALATION statement. This option affects lock escalation behavior for all indexes—both clustered and nonclustered—defined on the table. Three options are available:

DISABLE: This option disables lock escalation for a specific table.

TABLE: SQL Server escalates locks to the table level. This is the default option.

AUTO: SQL Server escalates locks to the partition level when the table
is partitioned or to the table level when the table is not partitioned.
Use this option with large partitioned tables, especially when there
are large reporting or purge queries running on the old data.

---

**Note**    The sys.tables catalog view provides information about the table lock
escalation mode in the lock_escalation and lock_escalation_desc columns.

---

Unfortunately, SQL Server 2005 does not support this option, and the only way to
disable lock escalation in this version is by using documented trace flags T1211 or T1224
at the instance or session level. Keep in mind that you need to have sysadmin rights to
call the DBCC TRACEON command and set trace flags at the session level.

- T1211 disables lock escalation, regardless of the memory conditions.

- T1224 disables lock escalation based on the number-of-locks
  threshold, although lock escalation can still be triggered in the case of
  memory pressure.

---

**Note**    You can read more about trace flags T1211 and T1224 at https://
docs.microsoft.com/en-us/sql/t-sql/database-console-commands/
dbcc-traceon-trace-flags-transact-sql.

---

As with the other blocking issues, you should find the root cause of the lock
escalation. You should also think about the pros and cons of disabling lock escalation
on particular tables in the system. Although it could reduce blocking in the system,
SQL Server would use more memory to store lock information. And, of course, you can
consider code refactoring as another option.

If lock escalation is triggered by the writers, you can reduce the batches to the point
where they are acquiring fewer than 5,000 row- and page-level locks per object. You can
still process multiple batches in the same transaction—the 5,000 locks threshold is per
statement. At the same time, you should remember that smaller batches are usually less
effective than larger ones. You need to fine-tune the batch sizes and find the optimal
values. It is normal to have lock escalation triggered if object-level locks are not held for
an excessive period of time and/or do not affect the other sessions.

As for lock escalation triggered by the readers, you should avoid situations in which many shared (S) locks are held. One example is scans due to non-optimized or reporting queries in the REPEATABLE READ or SERIALIZABLE transaction isolation levels, where queries hold shared (S) locks until the end of the transaction. The example shown in Listing 7-5 runs the SELECT from the Delivery.Orders table using the SERIALIZABLE isolation level.

***Listing 7-5.*** Lock escalation triggered by non-optimized query

```
set transaction isolation level serializable
begin tran
    select OrderId, OrderDate, Amount
    from Delivery.Orders with (rowlock)
    where OrderNum = '1';

    select
        resource_type as [Resource Type]
        ,case resource_type
            when 'OBJECT' then
                object_name
                (
                    resource_associated_entity_id
                    ,resource_database_id
                )
            when 'DATABASE' then 'DB'
            else
                (
                    select object_name(object_id, resource_database_id)
                    from sys.partitions
                    where hobt_id = resource_associated_entity_id
                )
        end as [Object]
        ,request_mode as [Mode]
        ,request_status as [Status]
    from sys.dm_tran_locks
    where request_session_id = @@SPID;
commit
```

Figure 7-8 shows the output of the second query from the `sys.dm_tran_locks` view.

|   | OrderId | OrderDate |  | Amount |
|---|---------|-----------|--|--------|
| 1 | 1 | 2017-12-29 13:01:00 |  | 20.00 |

|   | Resource Type | Object | Mode | Status |
|---|---------------|--------|------|--------|
| 1 | DATABASE | DB | S | GRANT |
| 2 | OBJECT | Orders | S | GRANT |

***Figure 7-8.*** *Selecting data in the SERIALIZABLE isolation level*

Even if the query returned just a single row, you see that shared (S) locks have been escalated to the table level. As usual, we need to look at the execution plan, shown in Figure 7-9, to troubleshoot it.

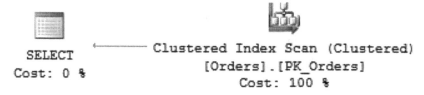

SELECT
Cost: 0 %

Clustered Index Scan (Clustered)
[Orders].[PK_Orders]
Cost: 100 %

***Figure 7-9.*** *Execution plan of the query*

There are no indexes on the `OrderNum` column, and SQL Server uses the *Clustered Index Scan* operator. Even though the query returned just a single row, it acquired and held shared (S) range locks on all the rows it read due to the `SERIALIZABLE` isolation level. As a result, lock escalation was triggered. If you add the index on the `OrderNum` column, it changes the execution plan to *Nonclustered Index Seek*. Only one row is read, very few row- and page-level locks are acquired and held, and lock escalation is not needed.

In some cases, you may consider partitioning the tables and setting the lock escalation option to use partition-level escalation, rather than table level, using the `ALTER TABLE SET (LOCK_ESCALATION=AUTO)` statement. This could help in scenarios in which you must purge old data using the `DELETE` statement or run reporting queries against old data in the `REPEATABLE READ` or `SERIALIZABLE` isolation levels. In those cases, statements would escalate the locks to partitions, rather than tables, and queries that are not accessing those partitions would not be blocked.

In other cases, you can switch to optimistic isolation levels. Finally, you would not have any reader-related blocking issues in the READ UNCOMMITTED transaction isolation level, where shared (S) locks are not acquired, although this method is not recommended because of all the other data consistency issues it introduces.

# Summary

SQL Server escalates locks to the object or partition levels after the statement acquires and holds about 5,000 row- and page-level locks. When escalation succeeds, SQL Server keeps the single object-level lock, blocking other sessions with incompatible lock types from accessing the table. If escalation fails, SQL Server repeats escalation attempts after about every 1,250 new locks are acquired.

Lock escalation fits perfectly into the *"it depends"* category. It reduces the SQL Server Lock Manager memory usage and the overhead of maintaining a large number of locks. At the same time, it could increase blocking in the system because of the object- or partition-level locks held.

You should keep lock escalation enabled, unless you find that it introduces noticeable blocking issues in the system. Even in those cases, however, you should perform a root-cause analysis as to why blocking resulting from lock escalation occurs and evaluate the pros and cons of disabling it. You should also look at the other options available, such as code and database schema refactoring, query tuning, and switching to optimistic transaction isolation levels. Any of these options might be a better choice to solve your blocking problems than disabling lock escalation.

# CHAPTER 8

# Schema and Low-Priority Locks

SQL Server uses two additional lock types called *schema locks* to prevent table and metadata alterations during query execution. This chapter will discuss schema locks in depth along with low-priority locks, which were introduced in SQL Server 2014 to reduce blocking during online index rebuilds and partition switch operations.

## Schema Locks

SQL Server needs to protect database metadata in order to prevent situations where a table's structure is changed in the middle of query execution. The problem is more complicated than it seems. Even though exclusive (X) table locks can, in theory, block access to the table during ALTER TABLE operations, they would not work in READ UNCOMMITTED, READ COMMITTED SNAPSHOT, and SNAPSHOT isolation levels, where readers do not acquire intent shared (IS) table locks.

SQL Server uses two additional lock types to address the problem: schema stability (Sch-S) and schema modification (Sch-M) locks. Schema modification (Sch-M) locks are acquired when any metadata changes occur and during the execution of a TRUNCATE TABLE statement. You can think of this lock type as a "super-lock." It is incompatible with any other lock types, and it completely blocks access to the object.

Like exclusive (X) locks, schema modification (Sch-M) locks are held until the end of the transaction. You need to keep this in mind when you run DDL statements within explicit transactions. While that allows you to roll back all of the schema changes in case of an error, it also prevents any access to the affected objects until the transaction is committed.

© Dmitri Korotkevitch 2018
D. Korotkevitch, *Expert SQL Server Transactions and Locking*, https://doi.org/10.1007/978-1-4842-3957-5_8

**Important**    Many database schema comparison tools use explicit transactions in the alteration script. This could introduce serious blocking when you run the script on live servers while other users are accessing the system.

SQL Server also uses schema modification (Sch-M) locks while altering the partition function. This can seriously affect the availability of the system when such alterations introduce data movement or scans. Access to all partitioned tables that use such a partition function is then blocked until the operation is completed.

Schema stability (Sch-S) locks are used during DML query compilation and execution. SQL Server acquires them regardless of the transaction isolation level, even in READ UNCOMMITTED mode. The only purpose they serve is to protect the table from being altered or dropped while the query accesses it. Schema stability (Sch-S) locks are compatible with any other lock types, except schema modification (Sch-M) locks.

SQL Server can perform some optimizations to reduce the number of locks acquired. While a schema stability (Sch-S) lock is always used during query compilation, SQL Server can replace it with an intent object lock during query execution. Let's look at the example shown in Table 8-1.

***Table 8-1.***  *Schema Locks: Query Compilation*

| Session 1 (SPID=64) | Session 2 (SPID=65) | Session 3 (SPID=66) |
|---|---|---|
| `begin tran`<br>`   alter table`<br>`Delivery.Orders`<br>`   add Dummy int;` | | |
| | `select count(*)`<br>`from Delivery.Orders`<br>`   with (nolock);` | `delete from`<br>`Delivery.Orders`<br>`where OrderId = 1;` |
| `   select`<br>`      request_session_id`<br>`      ,resource_type`<br>`      ,request_type`<br>`      ,request_mode`<br>`      ,request_status`<br>`   from sys.dm_tran_locks`<br>`   where`<br>`      resource_type = 'OBJECT';`<br>`rollback` | | |

The first session starts the transaction and alters the table, acquiring a schema modification (Sch-M) lock there. In the next step, two other sessions run a `SELECT` statement in the `READ UNCOMMITTED` isolation level and a `DELETE` statement, respectively.

As you can see in Figure 8-1, sessions 2 and 3 were blocked while waiting for schema stability (Sch-S) locks that were required for query compilation.

| | request_session_id | resource_type | request_type | request_mode | request_status |
|---|---|---|---|---|---|
| 1 | 64 | OBJECT | LOCK | Sch-M | GRANT |
| 2 | 65 | OBJECT | LOCK | Sch-S | WAIT |
| 3 | 66 | OBJECT | LOCK | IX | WAIT |

***Figure 8-2.***  *Schema locks when execution plans are cached*

If you run that example a second time, when queries are compiled and plans are in the cache, you would see a slightly different picture, as shown in Figure 8-2.

|   | request_session_id | resource_type | request_type | request_mode | request_status |
|---|---|---|---|---|---|
| 1 | 64 | OBJECT | LOCK | Sch-M | GRANT |
| 2 | 65 | OBJECT | LOCK | Sch-S | WAIT |
| 3 | 66 | OBJECT | LOCK | Sch-S | WAIT |

***Figure 8-1.*** *Schema locks during query compilation*

The second session would still wait for the schema stability (Sch-S) lock to be granted. There are no shared (S) locks in the READ UNCOMMITTED mode, and the schema stability (Sch-S) lock is the only way to keep a schema stable during execution. However, the session with the DELETE statement would wait for an intent exclusive (IX) lock instead. That lock type needs to be acquired anyway, and it can replace a schema stability (Sch-S) lock because it is also incompatible with schema modification (Sch-M) locks and prevents the schema from being altered.

Mixing schema modification locks with other lock types in the same transaction increases the possibility of deadlocks. Let's assume that we have two sessions: the first one starts the transaction, and it updates the row in the table. At this point, it holds an exclusive (X) lock on the row and two intent exclusive (IX) locks on the page and table. If another session tries to read (or update) the same row, it would be blocked. At this point, it would wait for the shared (S) lock on the row and have intent shared (IS) locks held on the page and the table. That stage is illustrated in Figure 8-3. (Page-level intent locks are omitted.)

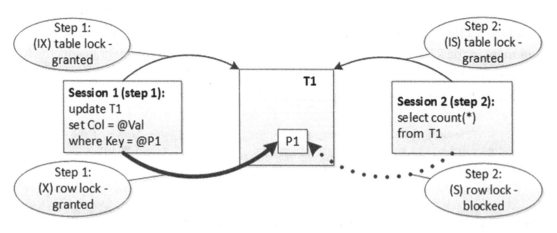

***Figure 8-3.*** *Deadlock due to mixed DDL and DML statements: Steps 1 and 2*

If at this point the first session wanted to alter the table, it would need to acquire a schema modification (Sch-M) lock. That lock type is incompatible with any other lock type, and the session would be blocked by the intent shared (IS) lock held by the second session, which leads to the deadlock condition, as shown in Figure 8-4.

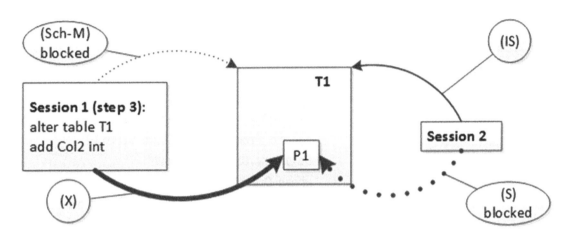

**Figure 8-4.** *Deadlock due to mixed DDL and DML statements: Step 3*

It is worth noting that this particular deadlock pattern may occur with any full table-level locks. However, schema modification (Sch-M) locks increase deadlock possibility due to their incompatibility with all other lock types in the system.

# Lock Queues and Lock Compatibility

Up until now, we have looked at blocking conditions with only two sessions involved and with an incompatible lock type already being held on a resource. In real life, the situation is usually more complicated. In busy systems, it is common to have dozens or even hundreds of sessions accessing the same resource—a table, for example—simultaneously. Let's look at several examples and analyze lock compatibility rules when multiple sessions are involved.

First, let's look at a scenario where multiple sessions are acquiring row-level locks. As you can see in Table 8-2, the first session (SPID=55) holds a shared (S) lock on the row. The second session (SPID=54) is trying to acquire an exclusive (X) lock on the same row, and it is being blocked due to lock incompatibility. The third session (SPID=53) is reading the same row in the READ COMMITTED transaction isolation level. This session has not been blocked.

***Table 8-2.*** *Multiple Sessions and Lock Compatibility: READ COMMITTED Isolation Level*

| Session 1 (SPID=55) | Session 2 (SPID=54) | Session 3 (SPID=53) |
| --- | --- | --- |
| ```
begin tran
    select OrderId, Amount
    from Delivery.Orders
        with (repeatableread)
    where OrderId = 1;
``` | | |
| | ```
-- Blocked
delete from
Delivery.Orders
where OrderId = 1;
``` | ```
-- Success
select OrderId,
Amount
from Delivery.Orders
        with (readcommitted)
where OrderId = 1;
``` |
| ```
    select
        l.request_session_id as
        [SPID]
        ,l.resource_description
        ,l.resource_type
        ,l.request_mode
        ,l.request_status
        ,r.blocking_session_id
    from
        sys.dm_tran_locks l join
sys.dm_exec_requests r on

l.request_session_id =
            r.session_id
    where l.resource_type = 'KEY'
rollback
``` | | |

Figure 8-5 illustrates the row-level locks held on the row with OrderId=1.

| | SPID | resource_description | resource_type | request_mode | request_status | blocking_session_id |
|---|---|---|---|---|---|---|
| 1 | 55 | (8194443284a0) | KEY | S | GRANT | 0 |
| 2 | 54 | (8194443284a0) | KEY | X | WAIT | 55 |

***Figure 8-5.*** *Lock compatibility with more than two sessions: READ COMMITTED*

As you can see in Figure 8-6, the third session (SPID=53) did not even try to acquire a shared (S) lock on the row. There is already a shared (S) lock on the row held by the first session (SPID=55), which guarantees that the row has not been modified by uncommitted transactions. In the READ COMMITTED isolation level, a shared (S) lock releases immediately after a row is read. As a result, session 3 (SPID=53) does not need to hold its own shared (S) lock after reading the row, and it can rely on the lock from session 1.

| EventClass | EventSequence | SPID | Mode | Type | TextData |
|---|---|---|---|---|---|
| Lock:Acquired | 34 | 55 | 6 - IS | 5 - OBJECT | |
| Lock:Acquired | 35 | 55 | 6 - IS | 6 - PAGE | 1:323 |
| Lock:Acquired | 36 | 55 | 3 - S | 7 - KEY | (8194443284a0) |
| Lock:Acquired | 37 | 54 | 8 - IX | 5 - OBJECT | |
| Lock:Acquired | 38 | 54 | 8 - IX | 6 - PAGE | 1:323 |
| Lock:Acquired | 39 | 53 | 6 - IS | 5 - OBJECT | |
| Lock:Acquired | 40 | 53 | 6 - IS | 6 - PAGE | 1:323 |

***Figure 8-6.*** *Locks acquired during the operation*

Let's change our example and see what happens if the third session tries to read the row in a REPEATABLE READ isolation level, where a shared (S) lock needs to be held until the end of the transaction, as shown in Table 8-3. In this case, the third session cannot rely on the shared (S) lock from another session, because it would have a different lifetime. The session will need to acquire its own shared (S) lock, and it will be blocked due to an incompatible exclusive (X) lock from the second session in the queue.

***Table 8-3.*** *Multiple Sessions and Lock Compatibility (REPEATABLE READ Isolation Level)*

| Session 1 (SPID=55) | Session 2 (SPID=54) | Session 3 (SPID=53) |
|---|---|---|
| begin tran<br>  select OrderId, Amount<br>  from Delivery.Orders<br>   with (repeatableread)<br>  where OrderId = 1; | | |
| | -- Blocked<br>delete from<br>Delivery.Orders<br>where OrderId = 1; | -- Blocked<br>select OrderId,<br>Amount<br>from Delivery.Orders<br>      with<br>(repeatableread)<br>where OrderId = 1; |
|   select<br>    l.request_session_id<br>      as [SPID]<br>,l.resource_description<br>   ,l.resource_type<br>   ,l.request_mode<br>   ,l.request_status<br>,r.blocking_session_id<br>  from<br>    sys.dm_tran_locks l join<br>sys.dm_exec_requests r<br>    on<br>l.request_session_id =<br>       r.session_id<br>  where l.resource_type = 'KEY';<br>rollback | | |

Figure 8-7 illustrates the row-level lock requests at this point.

| | SPID | resource_description | resource_type | request_mode | request_status | blocking_session_id |
|---|---|---|---|---|---|---|
| 1 | 55 | (8194443284a0) | KEY | S | GRANT | 0 |
| 2 | 54 | (8194443284a0) | KEY | X | WAIT | 55 |
| 3 | 53 | (8194443284a0) | KEY | S | WAIT | 54 |

*Figure 8-7. Lock compatibility with more than two sessions*

This leads us to a very important conclusion: *In order to be granted, a lock needs to be compatible with all of the lock requests on that resource—granted or not.*

---

**Important**    The first scenario, when the third session ran in READ COMMITTED isolation level and did not acquire the lock on the resource, can be considered an internal optimization, which you should not rely on. In some cases, SQL Server still acquires another shared (S) lock on the resource in READ COMMITTED mode, even if there is another shared (S) lock held. In such a case, the query would be blocked like in the REPEATABLE READ isolation level example.

---

Unfortunately, sessions in SQL Server do not reuse locks from other sessions on the table level. It is impossible to estimate the time for which any table-level lock-intent, full, or schema stability-needs be held. The session will always try to acquire an object-level lock, and it will be blocked if any other incompatible lock types are present in the locking queue.

This behavior may introduce serious blocking issues in the system. One of the most common cases where it occurs is with online index rebuild operations. Even though it holds an intent shared (IS) table lock during the rebuild process, it needs to acquire a shared (S) table lock at the beginning and a schema modification (Sch-M) lock at the final phase of execution. Both locks are held for a very short time; however, they can introduce blocking issues in busy OLTP environments.

Consider a situation where you start an online index rebuild at a time when you have another active transaction modifying data in a table. That transaction will hold an intent exclusive (IX) lock on the table, which prevents the online index rebuild from acquiring a shared (S) table lock. The lock request will wait in the queue and block all other transactions that want to modify data in the table and requesting intent exclusive (IX) locks there. Figure 8-8 illustrates this situation.

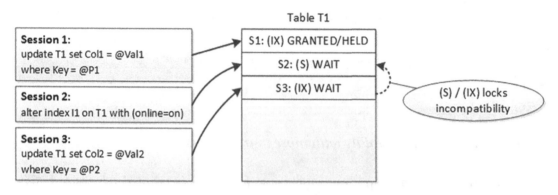

*Figure 8-8.  Blocking during the initial stage of an index rebuild*

This blocking condition will clear only after the first transaction is completed and the online index rebuild acquires and releases a shared (S) table lock. Similarly, more severe blocking could occur in the final stage of an online index rebuild when it needs to acquire a schema modification (Sch-M) lock to replace an index reference in the metadata. Both readers and writers will be blocked while the index rebuild waits for the schema modification (Sch-M) lock to be granted.

Similar blocking may occur during partition switch operations, which also acquire schema modification (Sch-M) locks. Even though a partition switch is done on the metadata level and is very fast, the schema modification (Sch-M) lock would block other sessions while waiting in the queue to be granted.

You need to remember this behavior when you design index maintenance and partition management strategies. There is very little that can be done in non-Enterprise editions of SQL Server or even in Enterprise Edition prior to SQL Server 2014. You can schedule operations to run at a time when the system handles the least activity. Alternatively, you can write the code terminating the operation using the LOCK_TIMEOUT setting.

Listing 8-1 illustrates this approach. You can use it with offline index rebuild and partition switch operations. You would still have blocking during the offline index rebuild while the schema modification (Sch-M) lock is held. However, you would eliminate blocking if this lock could not be acquired within the LOCK_TIMEOUT interval. Remember, with XACT_ABORT set to OFF, the lock timeout error does not roll back the transaction. Use proper transaction management and error handling, as we discussed in Chapter 2.

Also, as another word of caution, do not use LOCK_TIMEOUT with online index rebuilds, because it may terminate and roll back the operation at its final phase while the session is waiting for a schema modification (Sch-M) lock to replace the index definition in the metadata.

***Listing 8-1.*** Reduce blocking during offline index rebuild

```
set xact_abort off
set lock_timeout 100 -- 100 milliseconds
go

declare
    @attempt int = 1
    ,@maxAttempts int = 10

while @attempt <= @maxAttempts
begin
    begin try
        raiserror('Rebuilding index. Attempt %d / %d',0,1,@attempt,
        @maxAttempts) with nowait;

        alter index PK_Orders
        on Delivery.Orders rebuild
        with (online = off);

        break;
    end try
    begin catch
        if ERROR_NUMBER() = 1222 and @attempt < @maxAttempts
        begin
            set @attempt += 1;
            waitfor delay '00:00:15.000';
        end
        else
            throw;
    end catch
end;
```

Fortunately, the Enterprise Edition of SQL Server 2014 and above provides a better way to handle this problem.

# Low-Priority Locks

SQL Server 2014 introduced a new feature—*low-priority locks*–that helps to reduce blocking during online index rebuild and partition switch operations. Conceptually, you can think of low-priority locks as staying in a different locking queue than regular locks. Figure 8-9 illustrates it.

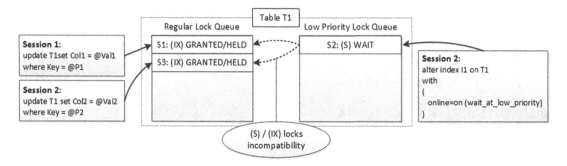

***Figure 8-9.*** *Low-priority locks*

---

**Important**    It is essential to remember that, as soon as a low-priority lock is acquired, it will behave the same as a regular lock, preventing other sessions from acquiring incompatible locks on the resource.

---

Figure 8-10 shows the output of the query from Listing 3-2 in Chapter 3. It demonstrates how low-priority locks are shown in the sys.dm_tran_locks view output. It is worth noting that the view does not provide the wait time of those locks.

| | Resource Type | DB Name | Object | Resource | Session | Mode | Status | Wait (ms) | sql |
|---|---|---|---|---|---|---|---|---|---|
| 1 | OBJECT | Dummy2 | Customers | | 61 | IX | GRANT | NULL | update Delivery.Customers set Name = 'Customer' ... |
| 2 | OBJECT | Dummy2 | Customers | | 62 | S | LOW_PRIORITY_WAIT | NULL | alter index PK_Customers on Delivery.Customers re... |
| 3 | OBJECT | Dummy2 | PK_Customers | | 62 | Sch-S | GRANT | NULL | alter index PK_Customers on Delivery.Customers re... |
| 4 | OBJECT | Dummy2 | Customers | | 62 | IS | GRANT | NULL | alter index PK_Customers on Delivery.Customers re... |

***Figure 8-10.*** *Low-priority locks in the* sys.dm_tran_locks *data management view*

You can specify lock priority with a WAIT_AT_LOW_PRIORITY clause in the ALTER INDEX and ALTER TABLE statements, as shown in Listing 8-2.

***Listing 8-2.*** Specifying lock priority

```
alter index PK_Customers on Delivery.Customers rebuild
with
(
    online=on
    (
        wait_at_low_priority
        (
          max_duration=10 minutes
          ,abort_after_wait=blockers
        )
    )
);

alter table Delivery.Orders
switch partition 1 to Delivery.OrdersTmp
with
(
    wait_at_low_priority
    (
      max_duration=60 minutes
      ,abort_after_wait=self
    )
)
```

As you can see, WAIT_AT_LOW_PRIORITY has two options. The MAX_DURATION setting specifies the lock wait time in minutes. The ABORT_AFTER_WAIT setting defines the session behavior if a lock cannot be obtained within the specified time limit. The possible values are:

- NONE: The low-priority lock is converted to a regular lock. After that, it behaves as a regular lock, blocking other sessions that try to acquire incompatible lock types on the resource. The session continues to wait until the lock is acquired.

- SELF: The operation is aborted if a lock cannot be granted within the time specified by the MAX_DURATION setting.

- BLOCKERS: All sessions that hold locks on the resource are aborted, and the session, which is waiting for a low-priority lock, will be able to acquire it.

---

**Note**   Omitting the `WAIT_AT_LOW_PRIORITY` option works the same way as specifying `WAIT_AT_LOW_PRIORITY(MAX_DURATION=0 MINUTES, ABORT_AFTER_WAIT=NONE)`.

---

Very active OLTP tables always have a large number of concurrent sessions accessing them. Therefore, there is always the possibility that a session will not be able to acquire a low-priority lock, even with a prolonged `MAX_DURATION` specified. You may consider using the `ABORT_AFTER_WAIT=BLOCKERS` option, which will allow the operation to complete, especially when client applications have proper exception handling and retry logic implemented.

Finally, it is worth noting that online index rebuilds are supported only in the Enterprise Edition of SQL Server and in Microsoft Azure SQL Databases. You cannot use low-priority locks during index rebuilds in other editions. Table partitioning, however, is supported in non-Enterprise editions starting with SQL Server 2016 SP1, and you can use low-priority locks in this scenario in any edition of SQL Server.

# Summary

SQL Server uses schema locks to protect metadata from alteration during query compilation and execution. There are two types of schema locks in SQL Server: schema stability (Sch-S) and schema modification (Sch-M) locks.

Schema stability (Sch-S) locks are acquired on objects referenced by queries during query compilation and execution. In some cases, however, SQL Server can replace schema stability (Sch-S) locks with intent table locks, which also protect the table schema. Schema stability (Sch-S) locks are compatible with any other lock type, with the exception of schema modification (Sch-M) locks.

Schema modification (Sch-M) locks are incompatible with any other lock type. SQL Server uses them during DDL operations. If a DDL operation needs to scan or modify the data (for example, adding a trusted foreign key constraint to the table or altering a partition function on a non-empty partition), the schema modification (Sch-M) lock would be held for the duration of the operation. This can take a long time on large tables and cause severe blocking issues in the system. You need to keep this in mind when designing systems with DDL and DML operations running in parallel.

In order to be granted, a lock needs to be compatible with all of the lock requests on that resource—granted or not. This may lead to serious blocking in busy systems when some session requests schema modification (Sch-M) or full object-level locks on the table. You need to remember this behavior when you design index or partition maintenance strategies in the system.

SQL Server 2014 and above support low-priority locks, which can be used to reduce blocking during online index rebuild and partition switch operations. These locks do not block other sessions requesting incompatible lock types at the time when an operation is waiting for a low-priority lock to be acquired.

# CHAPTER 9

# Lock Partitioning

SQL Server, as with other modern database engines, is designed to work on servers with a large number of CPUs. It has many optimizations that help the Engine to scale and efficiently work in such environments.

This chapter will discuss one such optimization: lock partitioning, which is automatically enabled on servers with 16 or more logical CPUs.

## Lock Partitioning Overview

As all of us are aware, hardware costs are dropping over time, allowing us to build more powerful servers. Twenty years ago, database servers used to have just one or very few CPUs. Nowadays, it is very common to work with servers that have dozens or sometimes even hundreds of cores.

The majority of multi-CPU servers are built using *Non-Uniform Memory Access (NUMA)* architecture. In this architecture, physical CPUs are partitioned into groups, called *NUMA nodes*. The memory is also partitioned across the nodes, and each node uses a separate system bus to access it. Each processor can access all memory in the system; however, access to the *local memory* that belongs to a CPU's NUMA node is faster than access to *foreign memory* from different NUMA nodes.

---

**Note** You can read more about NUMA architecture at `https://technet. microsoft.com/en-us/library/ms178144.aspx`.

---

SQL Server natively supports NUMA architecture and has several internal optimizations to take advantage of it. For example, SQL Server always tries to allocate local memory for the thread, and it also has distributed I/O threads on a per-NUMA basis.

191

© Dmitri Korotkevitch 2018
D. Korotkevitch, *Expert SQL Server Transactions and Locking*, https://doi.org/10.1007/978-1-4842-3957-5_9

Moreover, various caches and queues are partitioned on a per-NUMA—and sometimes per-scheduler—basis, which reduces possible contention when multiple schedulers (logical CPUs) access them. This includes lock queues in the system. When a system has 16 or more logical processors, SQL Server starts to use a technique called *lock partitioning*.

When lock partitioning is enabled, SQL Server starts to store information about locks on a per-scheduler basis. In this mode, object-level intent shared (IS), intent exclusive (IX), and schema stability (Sch-S) locks are acquired and stored in a single partition on the CPU (scheduler) where the batch is executing. All other lock types need to be acquired on all partitions.

This does not change anything from a lock-compatibility standpoint. When the session needs to acquire an exclusive (X) table lock, for example, it would go through all lock partitions and would be blocked if any of the partitions held an incompatible intent lock on the table. This, however, may lead to interesting situations where an object-level lock is being granted on a subset of partitions and is being blocked on another partition with an incompatible intent (I*) or schema stability (Sch-S) lock held on it.

Let's look at an example that demonstrates this. As I already mentioned, lock partitioning is enabled automatically on servers with 16 or more logical CPUs. You can change the number of schedulers in your test system using undocumented startup parameter -P. *Do not use this parameter in production!*

Listing 9-1 shows a query that starts a transaction and selects one row from the table in the REPEATABLE READ isolation level, which holds a shared (S) lock until the end of the transaction. As the next step, it obtains information about the locks held by the session using the sys.dm_tran_locks view. I am running this code in my test environment using the -P16 startup parameter, which creates 16 schedulers and enables lock partitioning.

***Listing 9-1.*** Lock partitioning: Updating one row in the table

```
begin tran
    select *
    from Delivery.Orders with (repeatableread)
    where OrderId = 100;

    select
        request_session_id
        ,resource_type
        ,resource_lock_partition
```

```
        ,request_mode
        ,request_status
from sys.dm_tran_locks
where request_session_id = @@SPID;
```

Figure 9-1 illustrates the output of the SELECT statement. The resource_lock_ partition column indicates the partition (scheduler) where the lock is stored (NULL means the lock is not partitioned and has been acquired on all partitions). As you can see, the table-level intent shared (IS) lock is partitioned and stored in partition four. Page- and row-level locks are not partitioned and are stored in all partitions.

| | request_session_id | resource_type | resource_lock_partition | request_mode | request_status |
|---|---|---|---|---|---|
| 1 | 89 | DATABASE | 4 | S | GRANT |
| 2 | 89 | KEY | NULL | S | GRANT |
| 3 | 89 | OBJECT | 4 | IS | GRANT |
| 4 | 89 | PAGE | NULL | IS | GRANT |

***Figure 9-1.*** *Lock requests after update*

Now, let's run the code in another session that wants to perform an index rebuild of the same table, using the ALTER INDEX PK_Orders on Delivery.Orders REBUILD command. This operation needs to acquire a schema modification (Sch-M) lock on the table. This lock type is non-partitioned and needs to be acquired across all partitions in the system.

Figure 9-2 shows the lock requests from both sessions. As you can see, session 2 (SPID=77) was able to successfully acquire schema modification (Sch-M) locks on partitions 0-3 and was blocked by Session 1 (SPID=89), which holds an intent shared (IS) lock on partition 4.

| | request_session_id | resource_type | resource_lock_partition | request_mode | request_status |
|---|---|---|---|---|---|
| 1 | 77 | OBJECT | 4 | Sch-M | WAIT |
| 2 | 77 | OBJECT | 3 | Sch-M | GRANT |
| 3 | 77 | OBJECT | NULL | Sch-M | GRANT |
| 4 | 77 | OBJECT | 2 | Sch-M | GRANT |
| 5 | 77 | OBJECT | 1 | Sch-M | GRANT |
| 6 | 77 | OBJECT | 0 | Sch-M | GRANT |
| 7 | 77 | OBJECT | 2 | Sch-S | GRANT |
| 8 | 89 | KEY | NULL | S | GRANT |
| 9 | 89 | OBJECT | 4 | IS | GRANT |
| 10 | 89 | PAGE | NULL | IS | GRANT |

*Figure 9-2.*  *Lock requests during ALTER INDEX operation*

Now, when other sessions try to access the table and acquire object-level locks, they either get blocked or succeed depending on which scheduler handles their requests.

Figure 9-3 illustrates this condition. As you can see, the request from the session with SPID=53 executes on scheduler 14 and is granted. However, the request from the session with SPID=115 runs on scheduler 1 and is blocked due to an incompatible schema modification (Sch-M) lock from SPID=77 held on this partition.

| | request_session_id | resource_type | (No column name) | (No column name) | request_status |
|---|---|---|---|---|---|
| 1 | 53 | KEY | NULL | S | GRANT |
| 2 | 53 | OBJECT | 14 | IS | GRANT |
| 3 | 53 | PAGE | NULL | IS | GRANT |
| 4 | 77 | OBJECT | 2 | IS | GRANT |
| 5 | 77 | OBJECT | 4 | Sch-M | WAIT |
| 6 | 77 | OBJECT | 3 | Sch-M | GRANT |
| 7 | 77 | OBJECT | NULL | Sch-M | GRANT |
| 8 | 77 | OBJECT | 2 | Sch-M | GRANT |
| 9 | 77 | OBJECT | 1 | Sch-M | GRANT |
| 10 | 77 | OBJECT | 0 | Sch-M | GRANT |
| 11 | 89 | PAGE | NULL | IS | GRANT |
| 12 | 89 | OBJECT | 4 | IS | GRANT |
| 13 | 89 | KEY | NULL | S | GRANT |
| 14 | 115 | OBJECT | 1 | IS | WAIT |

*Figure 9-3.*  *Lock requests from other sessions*

Lock partitioning may lead to prolonged blocking when a session is trying to acquire schema modification (Sch-M) or full-table locks in a busy system. SQL Server goes through all partitions in a sequential manner, waiting for the request to be granted before moving to the next partition. All other sessions that run on schedulers where requests were already granted would be blocked during this time.

The most common case when this happens is a schema alteration done online at a time when other users are accessing the system. Similarly, you can have this problem during online index rebuilds and table partitioning-related actions, such as partition function alteration and partition switches. Fortunately, low-priority locks handle lock partitioning gracefully, and they would not introduce blocking while waiting in the low-priority queue.

Finally, lock partitioning increases Lock Manager memory consumption. Non-partitioned locks are kept in each partition, which may be memory intensive in systems with a large number of schedulers. Not all row- and page-level locks are partitioned; thus, it is beneficial to keep lock escalation enabled when it does not introduce noticeable blocking in the system.

## Deadlocks Due to Lock Partitioning

When SQL Server receives a batch from a client, it assigns the batch to one or—in the case of parallel execution plans—multiple schedulers. With very rare exceptions, the batch does not change the scheduler(s) until it is completed. However, subsequent batches from the same session may be assigned to different scheduler(s). Even though SQL Server tends to reuse the same scheduler for all session requests, it is not guaranteed, especially in busy systems.

---

**Note**   You can analyze session scheduler assignments by running the `SELECT scheduler_id FROM sys.dm_exec_requests WHERE session_id = @@SPID` statement.

---

This behavior may lead to hard-to-explain deadlocks in busy systems. Let's say you have a session that starts a transaction and updates a row in a table. Let's assume that the batch is running on scheduler/logical CPU 2. This session acquires an intent exclusive (IX) table lock, which is partitioned and stored on scheduler 2 only. It also acquires a row-level exclusive (X) lock, which is not partitioned and is stored across all partitions. (I am omitting page-level intent locks again for simplicity's sake.)

Let's assume that you have a second session that is trying to alter the table and acquire a schema modification (Sch-M) lock. This lock type is non-partitioned, so the session needs to acquire it on every scheduler. It successfully acquires and holds the locks on schedulers 0 and 1, and it is blocked on scheduler 2 due to the schema modification (Sch-M) lock's incompatibility with the intent exclusive (IX) lock held there. Figure 9-4 illustrates this condition.

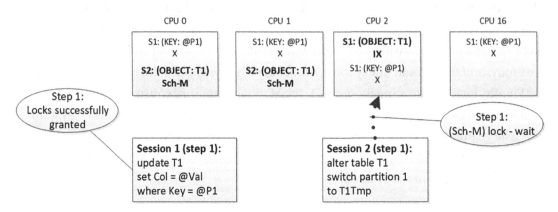

***Figure 9-4.***  *Deadlock due to lock partitioning: Step 1*

Let's now say that session 1 needs to update another row in the same table, and the batch has been assigned to another scheduler—either 0 or 1. The session will need to acquire another intent table lock in the new lock partition, but it would be blocked by the schema modification (Sch-M) lock there, which would lead to a deadlock, as shown in Figure 9-5.

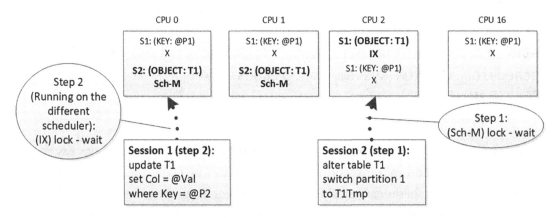

***Figure 9-5.***  *Deadlock due to lock partitioning: Step 2*

As you can guess, this deadlock occurred because the second batch from the same transaction ran on a different scheduler than the first batch. One case when this may occur is a client application that performs data modifications on a row-by-row basis in multiple separate batches. You can reduce the chance of possible deadlocks by batching all updates together; for example, with table-valued parameters. This will also help to improve the performance of the operation.

Fortunately, in many cases, SQL Server is able to *reuse* intent locks from different lock partitions and avoid such a deadlock. This behavior, however, is not documented or guaranteed. Moreover, it would not work if the second batch needed to acquire a full-table lock; a deadlock would occur in this case.

Let's look at the example and run the code from Listing 9-2. In my case, the batch is running on scheduler 13 in the session with SPID=67.

***Listing 9-2.*** Lock partitioning deadlock: Step 1

```
begin tran
    select *
    from Delivery.Orders with (repeatableread)
    where OrderId = 100;
```

As the next step, let's run the ALTER INDEX PK_Orders ON Delivery.Orders REBUILD statement in the session with SPID=68. This session successfully acquires schema modification (Sch-M) locks on partitions 0-12 and is blocked on partition 13. Figure 9-6 illustrates the status of lock requests at this point.

| | request_session_id | resource_type | resource_lock_partition | request_mode | request_status |
|---|---|---|---|---|---|
| 1 | 67 | PAGE | NULL | IS | GRANT |
| 2 | 67 | KEY | NULL | S | GRANT |
| 3 | 67 | OBJECT | 13 | IS | GRANT |
| 4 | 68 | OBJECT | 13 | Sch-M | WAIT |
| 5 | 68 | OBJECT | 12 | Sch-M | GRANT |
| 6 | 68 | OBJECT | 11 | Sch-M | GRANT |
| 7 | 68 | OBJECT | 10 | Sch-M | GRANT |
| 8 | 68 | OBJECT | 9 | Sch-M | GRANT |
| 9 | 68 | OBJECT | 8 | Sch-M | GRANT |
| 10 | 68 | OBJECT | 7 | Sch-M | GRANT |
| 11 | 68 | OBJECT | 6 | Sch-M | GRANT |
| 12 | 68 | OBJECT | 5 | Sch-M | GRANT |
| 13 | 68 | OBJECT | 4 | Sch-M | GRANT |
| 14 | 68 | OBJECT | 3 | Sch-M | GRANT |
| 15 | 68 | OBJECT | 2 | Sch-M | GRANT |
| 16 | 68 | OBJECT | 1 | Sch-M | GRANT |
| 17 | 68 | OBJECT | 0 | Sch-M | GRANT |

*Figure 9-6.* *Lock requests after the previous steps*

As the next step, let's run an UPDATE statement in the first session as shown in Listing 9-3. At this time, the batch has been executed on scheduler 10 in my system.

*Listing 9-3.* Lock partitioning deadlock: Step 2

```
update Delivery.Orders
set Pieces += 1
where OrderId = 10;
```

Even though the batch executed on a different scheduler, SQL Server was able to reuse the intent lock from partition 13, and so a deadlock did not occur. Figure 9-7 illustrates the status of the lock requests at this point. Note that SQL Server converted a table-level lock type from intent shared (IS) to intent exclusive (IX), and there is no more intent shared (IS) lock on the table despite the existence of a row-level shared (S) lock.

| | request_session_id | resource_type | resource_lock_partition | request_mode | request_status |
|---|---|---|---|---|---|
| 1 | 67 | PAGE | NULL | IS | GRANT |
| 2 | 67 | PAGE | NULL | IX | GRANT |
| 3 | 67 | KEY | NULL | S | GRANT |
| 4 | 67 | OBJECT | 13 | IX | GRANT |
| 5 | 67 | KEY | NULL | X | GRANT |
| 6 | 68 | OBJECT | 13 | Sch-M | WAIT |
| 7 | 68 | OBJECT | 12 | Sch-M | GRANT |
| 8 | 68 | OBJECT | 11 | Sch-M | GRANT |
| 9 | 68 | OBJECT | 10 | Sch-M | GRANT |
| 10 | 68 | OBJECT | 9 | Sch-M | GRANT |
| 11 | 68 | OBJECT | 8 | Sch-M | GRANT |
| 12 | 68 | OBJECT | 7 | Sch-M | GRANT |
| 13 | 68 | OBJECT | 6 | Sch-M | GRANT |
| 14 | 68 | OBJECT | 5 | Sch-M | GRANT |
| 15 | 68 | OBJECT | 4 | Sch-M | GRANT |
| 16 | 68 | OBJECT | 3 | Sch-M | GRANT |
| 17 | 68 | OBJECT | 2 | Sch-M | GRANT |
| 18 | 68 | OBJECT | 1 | Sch-M | GRANT |
| 19 | 68 | OBJECT | 0 | Sch-M | GRANT |

*Figure 9-7.*  *Lock requests after UPDATE statement*

Finally, let's trigger an operation that will need to acquire a full table-level lock with the code from Listing 9-4 running it in the first session with SPID = 67.

*Listing 9-4.*  Lock partitioning deadlock: Step 3

```
select count(*)
from Delivery.Orders with (tablock)
```

SQL Server is trying to acquire a shared intent exclusive (SIX) lock on all partitions, and it is blocked by an incompatible schema modification (Sch-M) lock held on partition 0. This leads to deadlock.

Listing 9-5 illustrates a partial resource-list section of the deadlock graph. The lockPartition attribute provides information about the lock partition on which the conflicts occurred.

***Listing 9-5.***  Deadlock graph (partial)

```
<resource-list>
  <objectlock lockPartition="13" objid=".." subresource="FULL"
      dbid=".." objectname=".." id=".." mode="IX"
      associatedObjectId="..">
    <owner-list>
      <owner id="processa4545268c8" mode="IX" />
    </owner-list>
    <waiter-list>
      <waiter id="processa475047468" mode="Sch-M" requestType="wait" />
    </waiter-list>
  </objectlock>
  <objectlock lockPartition="0" objid=".." subresource="FULL"
      dbid=".." objectname=".." id=".." mode="Sch-M"
      associatedObjectId="..">
    <owner-list>
      <owner id="processa475047468" mode="Sch-M" />
    </owner-list>
    <waiter-list>
      <waiter id="processa4545268c8" mode="SIX" requestType="wait" />
    </waiter-list>
  </objectlock>
</resource-list>
```

Lock partitioning–related deadlocks are rare, although they may happen, especially when you mix intent and full table-level locks in the same transaction. It is better to avoid such code patterns when possible.

For online index rebuilds and partition switches, you can utilize low-priority locks if they are available. Alternatively, you can implement retry logic using TRY..CATCH around DDL statements when you run them from the code. A SET DEADLOCK_PRIORITY boost could also help reduce the chance that a DDL session will be chosen as the deadlock victim. You can also implement *mutex* logic based on application locks, which we will discuss in the next chapter.

Lock partitioning is enabled by design in systems with 16 or more logical CPUs, and it cannot be disabled through documented approaches. There is the undocumented trace flag T1229 that disables it; however, using undocumented trace flags is not recommended in production. Moreover, in systems with a large number of logical CPUs, disabling lock partitioning can lead to performance issues resulting from excessive serialization during lock-structure management. It is better to keep lock partitioning enabled.

# Summary

Lock partitioning is automatically enabled on servers with 16 or more logical CPUs. When lock partitioning is enabled, SQL Server uses the separate locking queues on a per-scheduler basis. Intent shared (IS), intent exclusive (IX) and schema stability (Sch-S) locks are acquired and stored in a single partition. All other lock types need to be acquired across all partitions.

SQL Server acquires non-partitioned lock types across all partitions in a sequential manner. This may lead to the situation where lock requests were granted on some partitions and blocked on partitions that held incompatible intent (I*) or schema stability (Sch-S) locks. This condition may increase the blocking during online schema alterations and may also lead to deadlocks in some cases.

# CHAPTER 10

# Application Locks

This chapter will discuss another SQL Server locking feature called application locks, which place locks on an application resource identified by name. Application locks allow you to serialize access to T-SQL code, similar to critical sections and mutexes in client applications.

## Application Locks Overview

*Application locks* allow an application to place a lock on an *application resource* that is not related to database objects and is identified by name only. The lock follows the regular rules in terms of lock compatibility, and it can be one of the following types: shared (S), update (U), exclusive (X), intent shared (IS), and intent exclusive (IX).

An application needs to call the `sp_getapplock` stored procedure to acquire the lock using the following parameters:

> `@Resource`: specifies the name of the application lock. It is case sensitive regardless of the database and server collations.

> `@LockMode`: specifies the lock type. You need to use one of the following values to specify the type: `Shared`, `Update`, `IntentShared`, `IntentExclusive`, or `Exclusive`.

> `@LockOwner`: should be one of two values—`Transaction` or `Session`—and controls the owner (and scope) of the lock

> `@LockTimeout`: specifies the timeout in milliseconds. If a stored procedure cannot acquire the lock within this interval, it would return an error.

> `@DbPrincipal`: specifies security context (The caller needs to be a member of the `database_principal`, `dbo`, or `db_owner` roles.)

© Dmitri Korotkevitch 2018
D. Korotkevitch, *Expert SQL Server Transactions and Locking*, https://doi.org/10.1007/978-1-4842-3957-5_10

This procedure returns a value greater than or equal to zero in the case of success, and a negative value in the case of failure. As with regular locks, there is the possibility of deadlocks, although this would not roll back the transaction of the session that is chosen as the victim, but rather would return the error code that indicates the deadlock condition.

An application needs to call the `sp_releaseapplock` stored procedure to release an application lock. Alternatively, in case the `@LockOwner` of the lock is `transaction`, it would be automatically released when the transaction commits or rolls back. This behavior is similar to that of regular locks.

# Application Lock Usage

There is a concept in computer science called *mutual exclusion*. It signifies that multiple threads or processes cannot execute specific code at the same time. As an example, think about a multi-threaded application in which threads use shared objects. In those systems, you often need to serialize the code that accesses those objects to prevent the race conditions that occur when multiple threads read and update the same objects simultaneously.

Every development language has a set of synchronization primitives that can accomplish such tasks (for example, mutexes and critical sections). Application locks do the same trick when you need to serialize some part of the T-SQL code.

As an example, let's think about a system that collects some data, saves it into a database, and has a set of application servers for data processing. Each application server reads the package of data, processes it, and finally deletes the processed data from the original table. Obviously, you do not want different application servers processing the same rows, and serializing the data-loading process is one of the available options. An exclusive (X) table lock would not work, because it blocks any table access, rather than just the data loading. Implementing serialization on the application-server level is not a trivial task either. Fortunately, application locks could help to solve the problem.

Let's assume that you have the table shown in Listing 10-1. For simplicity's sake, there is a column called `Attributes` that represents all of the row data.

***Listing 10-1.*** Table structure

```
create table dbo.RawData
(
    ID int not null,
    Attributes char(100) not null
        constraint DEF_RawData_Attributes
        default 'Row Data',
    ProcessingTime datetime not null
        constraint DEF_RawData_ProcessingTime
        default '2000-01-01', -- Default constraint simplifies data loading
        in the code below

    constraint PK_RawData
    primary key clustered(ID)
)
```

There are two important columns: ID, which is the primary key, and ProcessingTime, which represents the time the row was loaded for processing. You should use UTC rather than local time to support situations in which application servers reside in different time zones, as well as to prevent issues when the clock is adjusted to Daylight Saving Time. This column also helps to prevent other sessions from rereading the data while it is still processing. It is better to avoid Boolean (bit) columns for such purposes because if the application server crashes, the row would remain in the table forever. With the time column, the system can read it again after some timeout.

Now, let's create a stored procedure that reads the data, as shown in Listing 10-2.

***Listing 10-2.*** Stored procedure that reads the data

```
create proc dbo.LoadRawData(@PacketSize int)
as
begin
    set nocount, xact_abort on

    declare
        @EarliestProcessingTime datetime
        ,@ResCode int
```

```
declare
    @Data table
      (
            ID int not null primary key,
            Attributes char(100) not null
      )

begin tran
    exec @ResCode = sp_getapplock
        @Resource = 'LoadRowDataLock'
        ,@LockMode = 'Exclusive'
        ,@LockOwner = 'Transaction'
        ,@LockTimeout = 15000; -- 15 seconds

    if @ResCode >= 0 -- success
    begin
        -- We assume that app server processes the packet within 1
        minute unless crashed
        set @EarliestProcessingTime = dateadd(minute,-1,getutcdate());

        ;with DataPacket(ID, Attributes, ProcessingTime)
        as
        (
            select top (@PacketSize) ID, Attributes, ProcessingTime
            from dbo.RawData
            where ProcessingTime <= @EarliestProcessingTime
            order by ID
        )
        update DataPacket
        set ProcessingTime = getutcdate()
        output inserted.ID, inserted.Attributes into @Data(ID, Attributes);
    end
    -- we don't need to explicitly release application lock because
    @LockOwner is Transaction
    commit

    select ID, Attributes from @Data;
end
```

The stored procedure obtains an exclusive (X) application lock at the beginning of the transaction. As a result, all other sessions calling the stored procedure are blocked until the transaction is committed and the application lock is released. It guarantees that only one session can update and read the data from within the stored procedure. At the same time, other sessions can still work with the table (for example, insert new or delete processed rows). Application locks are separate from data locks, and sessions would not be blocked unless they were trying to obtain the incompatible application lock for the same @Resource with an sp_getapplock call.

Figure 10-1 demonstrates the output from the sys.dm_tran_locks data management view at a time when two sessions are calling the dbo.LoadRawData stored procedure simultaneously. The session with SPID=58 successfully obtains the application lock, while another session with SPID=63 is blocked. The Resource_type value of APPLICATION indicates an application lock.

| | request_session_id | resource_type | resource_description | request_type | request_status | request_owner_type |
|---|---|---|---|---|---|---|
| 1 | 58 | APPLICATION | 0:[LoadRowDataLock]:(039ad780) | LOCK | GRANT | TRANSACTION |
| 2 | 63 | APPLICATION | 0:[LoadRowDataLock]:(039ad780) | LOCK | WAIT | TRANSACTION |

***Figure 10-1.*** *Sys.dm_tran_locks output*

It is worth mentioning that, if our goal is to simply guarantee that multiple sessions cannot read the same rows simultaneously, rather than serializing the entire read process, there is another, simpler, solution. You can use locking table hints, as shown in Listing 10-3.

***Listing 10-3.*** Serializing access to the data with table locking hints

```
create proc dbo.LoadRawData(@PacketSize int)
as
begin
    set nocount, xact_abort on

    declare
        @EarliestProcessingTime datetime = dateadd(minute,-1,getutcdate());

    ;with DataPacket(ID, Attributes, ProcessingTime)
    as
```

```
    (
        select top (@PacketSize) ID, Attributes, ProcessingTime
        from dbo.RawData with (updlock, readpast)
        where ProcessingTime <= @EarliestProcessingTime
        order by ID
    )
    update DataPacket
    set ProcessingTime = getutcdate()
    output inserted.ID, inserted.Attributes into @Data(ID, Attributes);
end
```

The UPDLOCK hint forces SQL Server to use update (U), rather than shared (S), locks during the SELECT operation. This prevents other sessions from reading the same rows simultaneously. At the same time, the READPAST hint forces the sessions to skip the rows with incompatible locks held rather than being blocked.

Although both implementations accomplish the same goal, they use different approaches. The latter serializes access to the same rows by using data (row-level) locks. Application locks serialize access to the code and prevent multiple sessions from running the statement simultaneously.

While both approaches can be used with disk-based tables, locking hints would not work in cases where queues are implemented using memory-optimized tables. Locking hints do not work in that scenario, but application locks would help to achieve the required serialization.

---

**Note**    We will discuss the In-Memory OLTP Concurrency Model in Chapter 13.

---

When a system has a structured data access tier, application locks may help to reduce blocking and improve the user experience when some sessions acquire table-level locks. One such example is index maintenance or partition switches in SQL Server systems that do not support low-priority locks.

Consider a scenario where you have a multi-tenant system with a set of services that query data on a per-tenant basis. The code shown in Listing 10-4 tries to acquire a shared (S) application lock before querying the table. If this operation is not successful, it returns an empty result set emulating the "no new data" condition without performing any access to the table.

***Listing 10-4.*** Preventing access to the table during index rebuild: Table and stored procedure

```
create table dbo.CollectedData
(
    TenantId int not null,
    OnDate datetime not null,
    Id bigint not null identity(1,1),
    Attributes char(100) not null
        constraint DEF_CollectedData_Attributes
        default 'Other columns'
);

create unique clustered index IDX_CollectedData_TenantId_OnDate_Id
on dbo.CollectedData(TenantId,OnDate,Id);
go

create proc dbo.GetTenantData
(
    @TenantId int
    ,@LastOnDate datetime
    ,@PacketSize int
)
as
begin
    set nocount, xact_abort on

    declare
        @ResCode int

    begin tran
        exec @ResCode = sp_getapplock
            @Resource = 'TenantDataAccess'
            ,@LockMode = 'Shared'
            ,@LockOwner = 'Transaction'
            ,@LockTimeout = 0 ; -- No wait
```

```
        if @ResCode >= 0 -- success
        begin
            if @LastOnDate is null
                set @LastOnDate = '2018-01-01';

            select top (@PacketSize) with ties
                TenantId, OnDate, Id, Attributes
            from dbo.CollectedData
            where
                TenantId = @TenantId and
                OnDate > @LastOnDate
            order by
                OnDate;
        end
        else
            -- return empty resultset
            select
                convert(int,null) as TenantId
                ,convert(datetime,null) as OnDate
                ,convert(char(100),null) as Attributes
            where
                1 = 2;
    commit
end
```

The second session, which needs to acquire a full table-level lock, may obtain an exclusive (X) application lock first, as shown in Listing 10-5. This will prevent the stored procedure from being blocked when querying the table for the duration of the index rebuild.

***Listing 10-5.*** Preventing access to the table during index rebuild: Obtaining exclusive access to the table

```
begin tran
    exec sp_getapplock
        @Resource = 'TenantDataAccess'
        ,@LockMode = 'Exclusive'
```

```
    ,@LockOwner = 'Transaction'
    ,@LockTimeout = -1 ; -- Indefinite wait

  alter index IDX_CollectedData_TenantId_OnDate_Id
  on dbo.CollectedData rebuild;
commit
```

This approach may improve the user experience by eliminating possible query timeouts in the system. Moreover, it may reduce the time it takes for an exclusive table lock to be obtained. SQL Server does not use lock partitioning with application locks, and therefore the application lock request needs to be granted just within the single locking queue rather than on each partition sequentially.

Finally, it is worth noting that there is still the possibility of blocking if a stored procedure needs to be compiled at a time when ALTER INDEX REBUILD is running. The compilation process will need to acquire a table-level lock, which will be blocked by the schema modification (Sch-M) lock held by the index rebuild.

# Summary

Application locks allow an application to place a lock on an application resource that is not related to the database objects and is identified by the name. It is a useful tool that helps you implement mutual exclusion code patterns that serialize access to T-SQL code, similar to critical sections and mutexes in client applications.

You can create and release application locks using the sp_getapplock and sp_releaseapplock stored procedures, respectively. Application locks can have either session or transaction scope, and they follow the regular lock compatibility rules.

# CHAPTER 11

# Designing Transaction Strategies

A properly implemented transaction strategy would benefit every system. This chapter will provide a set of generic guidelines on the subject and discuss how you can improve concurrency in a system.

## Transaction Strategy Design Considerations

Consistent transaction and error-handling strategies always benefit the system. They help to reduce blocking and simplify troubleshooting when blocking does occur.

As we already discussed in Chapter 2, the choice between client- and server-side transaction management greatly depends on the data access tier architecture. A stored procedure–based implementation may benefit from explicit transactions started from within the stored procedures. A client-side implementation with ORM frameworks or code generators, on the other hand, would require transactions to be managed in the client code.

There is a common misconception that autocommitted transactions may benefit the system. Even though such an approach may somewhat reduce blocking—after all, every statement runs in its own transaction, and exclusive (X) locks are held for a shorter amount of time—it is hardly the best choice. The large number of small transactions could significantly increase transaction log activity and reduce the performance of the system.

More important, autocommitted transactions may introduce data-quality issues when multiple related data modifications partially fail due to errors. Such issues are extremely hard to diagnose and address when they occur in production. In the vast majority of cases it is better to use explicit transactions in the system.

© Dmitri Korotkevitch 2018
D. Korotkevitch, *Expert SQL Server Transactions and Locking*, https://doi.org/10.1007/978-1-4842-3957-5_11

---

**Tip**  Avoid autocommitted transactions and use explicit transactions instead.

---

You can further reduce the chance of having data-quality issues by using the
SET XACT_ABORT ON option. As you will remember, this setting makes a transaction
uncommittable if there is any error. This prevents explicit transactions from committing
when some data modifications have not been completed successfully.

---

**Tip**  Use SET XACT_ABORT ON in the code.

---

Recall the nested behavior of BEGIN TRAN/COMMIT statements. You do not need to
check the @@TRANCOUNT variable and the existence of an active transaction if you call
BEGIN TRAN and COMMIT in the same module. Do not forget, however, that the ROLLBACK
statement rolls back the entire transaction regardless of the @@TRANCOUNT nested level. It
is better to check if a transaction is active before rolling it back.

Listing 11-1 shows an example of the code that checks if there is an active transaction
before starting it. This is completely unnecessary due to the nested behavior of BEGIN
TRAN/COMMIT statements, so you can remove IF statements from the implementation.

***Listing 11-1.***  Implementation with unnecesary check for active transaction

```
create proc dbo.Proc1
as
begin
    set xact_abort on
    declare
        @CurrentTranCount = @@TRANCOUNT;

    if @CurrentTranCount = 0 -- IF is not required and can be removed
        begin tran;

    /* Some logic here */

    if @CurrentTranCount = 0  -- IF is not required and can be removed
        commit;
end
```

Listing 11-2 shows the template of a stored procedure that performs server-side transaction management and error handling. This approach works regardless of whether this stored procedure is called from outside or within the active transaction, assuming, of course, that the calling code handles exceptions correctly.

It is important to note that the CATCH block is checking that @@TRANCOUNT is greater than zero. One of the common errors is using the IF @@TRANCOUNT = 1 ROLLBACK pattern, which does not work with nested BEGIN TRAN calls.

***Listing 11-2.*** Server-side transaction management

```
create proc dbo.MyProc
as
begin
    set xact_abort on
    begin try
        begin tran
            /* Some logic here  */
        commit
    end try
    begin catch
        if @@TRANCOUNT > 0 -- Transaction is active
            rollback;
        /* Optional error-handling  code */
        throw;
    end catch;
end;
```

The client-side transaction management implementation would depend on the technology and architecture of the system. However, it is always beneficial to use a TRY..CATCH block and explicitly commit or roll back the transaction there. Listing 11-3 demonstrates this approach with the classic ADO.Net.

***Listing 11-3.*** ADO.Net transaction management

```
using (SqlConnection conn = new SqlConnection(connString))
{
    conn.Open();
    using (SqlTransaction tran =
    conn.BeginTransaction(IsolationLevel.ReadCommitted))
    {
        try
        {
            SqlCommand cmd = conn.CreateCommand("exec dbo.MyProc @Param1");
            cmd.Parameters.Add("@Param1",SqlDbType.VarChar,255).
            Value = "Param Value";
            cmd.Transaction = tran;
            cmd.ExecuteNonQuery();
            tran.Commit();
        }
        catch (Exception ex)
        {
            tran.Rollback();
            throw;
        }
    }
}
```

Despite the fact that the client code needs to perform several actions in between the BeginTransaction() and ExecuteNonQuery() calls, it would not introduce any inefficiencies in the system. SQL Server considers a transaction to be started at the time of the first data access operation rather than at the time of the BEGIN TRAN call. Moreover, it would not log the beginning of the transaction (LOP_BEGIN_XACT) in the transaction log until the transaction completed the first data modification.

You should remember such behavior with SNAPSHOT transactions, which work with a "snapshot" of the data at the time when the transaction started. In practice, it means that such transactions would see the data as of the time of the first data access operation— whether a read or write one.

# Choosing Transaction Isolation Level

Choosing the right transaction isolation level is not a trivial task. You should find the right balance between blocking and `tempdb` overhead and the required level of data consistency and isolation in the system. The system must provide reliable data to the customers, and you should not compromise by choosing an isolation level that cannot guarantee it just because you want to reduce blocking.

You should choose the *minimally required* isolation level that provides the required level of data consistency. In many cases the default `READ COMMITTED` isolation level is *good enough*, especially if queries are optimized and do not perform unnecessary scans. Avoid using `REPEATABLE READ` or `SERIALIZABLE` isolation levels in OLTP systems unless you have legitimate reasons to use them. Those isolation levels hold shared (S) locks until the end of the transaction, which can lead to severe blocking issues with volatile data. They can also trigger shared (S) lock escalation during scans.

It is completely normal to use different isolation levels in a system. For example, financial management systems may need to use `REPEATABLE READ` or even `SERIALIZABLE` isolation levels when they perform operations that may affect the balances of customers' accounts. However, other use cases, such as changing customer profile information, may be completely fine with the `READ COMMITTED` level.

As a general rule, it is better to avoid the `READ UNCOMMITTED` isolation level. Even though many database professionals try to reduce blocking by switching to this isolation level, either explicitly or with (`NOLOCK`) hints, this is rarely the right choice. First, `READ UNCOMMITTED` does not address the blocking issues introduced by writers. They still acquire update (U) locks during scans. Most important, however, by using `READ UNCOMMITTED`, you are stating that data consistency is not required at all, and it is not only about reading uncommitted data. SQL Server can choose execution plans that use an *allocation map scan* on large tables, which can lead to missing rows and duplicated reads due to page splits, especially in busy systems with volatile data.

In a majority of the cases, optimistic isolation levels, especially `READ COMMITTED SNAPSHOT`, are a better choice than `READ UNCOMMITTED`, `REPEATABLE READ`, or `SERIALIZABLE`, even in OLTP systems. It provides statement-level data consistency without readers/writers blocking involved. Historically, I have been very cautious suggesting RCSI in OLTP systems due to its `tempdb` overhead; however, nowadays, it becomes a lesser issue because of modern hardware and flash-based disk arrays. You should still factor additional index fragmentation and `tempdb` overhead into your analysis though. It is also worth repeating that READ COMMITTED SNAPSHOT is enabled in Azure SQL Databases by default.

As a general rule, I recommend you do not use the SNAPSHOT isolation level in OLTP systems due to its excessive tempdb usage unless transaction-level consistency is absolutely required. It could be a good choice for data warehouse and reporting systems where data is static most of the time.

You should be very careful with transaction management if you enable optimistic isolation levels in the database. Bugs in the code that led to uncommitted transactions can prevent tempdb version store clean-up and lead to excessive growth of tempdb data files. It can happen even if you do not use optimistic isolation levels in the system, as long as READ_COMMITTED_SNAPSHOT or ALLOW_SNAPSHOT_ISOLATION database settings were enabled.

Optimistic isolation levels, however, often *mask* poorly optimized queries in the system. Even though those queries contribute to the poor system performance, they are not involved in the blocking conditions and thus are often ignored. It is not uncommon to see cases where people "solve" the readers/writers blocking by enabling READ COMMITTED SNAPSHOT and do not address the root cause of the blocking afterward. You should remember this and perform query optimization regardless of whether you have blocking in the system or not.

For data warehouse systems, transaction strategy greatly depends on how data is updated. For static read-only data, any isolation level will work because readers do not block other readers. You can even switch the database or filegroups to read-only mode to reduce the locking overhead. Otherwise, optimistic isolation levels are the better choice. They provide either transaction- or statement-level consistency for report queries, and they reduce the blocking during ETL processes. You should also consider utilizing table partitioning and using partition switches during ETL processes when this approach is feasible.

# Patterns That Reduce Blocking

Blocking occurs when multiple sessions compete for the same set of resources. Sessions try to acquire incompatible locks on them, which leads to lock collision and blocking.

As you already know, SQL Server acquires the locks when it *processes* data. It matters less how many rows need to be modified or returned to the client. What matters more is how many rows SQL Server *accesses* during statement execution. It is entirely possible that a query that selected or updated just a single row acquired thousands or even millions of locks due to excessive scans it performed.

Proper query optimization and index tuning reduce the number of rows SQL Server needs to access during query execution. This, in turn, reduces the number of locks acquired and the chance that lock conflicts will occur.

---

**Tip**  Optimize the queries. It will help to improve concurrency, performance, and user experience in the system.

---

Another method to reduce the chance of lock conflicts is to reduce the time locks are held. Exclusive (X) locks are always held until the end of the transaction. The same is true for the shared (S) locks in REPEATABLE READ and SERIALIZABLE isolation levels. The longer locks are held, the bigger the chance is that lock conflicts and blocking will occur.

You need to make transactions as short as possible and avoid any long-time operations and interactions with users through the UI while a transaction is active. You also need to be careful when dealing with external resources that use CLR or linked servers. For example, when a linked server is down, it can take a long time before a connection timeout occurs, and you would like to avoid the situation where locks are kept all that time.

---

**Tip**  Make transactions as short as possible.

---

Update the data as close to the end of the transaction as possible. This reduces the time that exclusive (X) locks are held. In some cases, it might make sense to use temporary tables as the staging place, inserting data there and updating the actual tables at the very end of the transaction.

---

**Tip**  Modify data as close to the end of the transaction as possible.

---

One particular variation of this technique is an UPDATE statement that is impossible or impractical to optimize. Consider a situation where the statement scans a large number of rows, but updates just a handful of them. You can change the code, storing the clustered index key values of the rows that need to be updated in a temporary table, running an UPDATE based on those collected key values afterward.

Listing 11-4 shows an example of a statement that could lead to a clustered index scan during execution. SQL Server will need to acquire an update (U) lock on every row of the table.

***Listing 11-4.*** Reducing blocking with temporary table: Original statement

```
update dbo.Orders
set
    Cancelled = 1
where
    (PendingCancellation = 1) or
    (Paid = 0 and OrderDate < @MinUnpaidDate) or
    (Status = 'BackOrdered' and EstimatedStockDate > @StockDate)
```

You can change the code to be similar to that shown in Listing 11-5. The SELECT statement either acquires shared (S) locks or does not acquire row-level locks at all, depending on the isolation level. The UPDATE statement is optimized, and it acquires just a handful of update (U) and exclusive (X) locks.

***Listing 11-5.*** Reducing blocking with a temporary table: Using a temporary table to stage key values for the update

```
create table #OrdersToBeCancelled
( OrderId int not null primary key );

insert into #OrdersToBeCancelled(OrderId)
    select OrderId
    from dbo.Orders
    where
        (PendingCancellation = 1) or
        (Paid = 0 and OrderDate < @MinUnpaidDate) or
        (Status = 'BackOrdered' and EstimatedStockDate > @StockDate);

update dbo.Orders
set Cancelled = 1
where OrderId in (select OrderId from #OrdersToBeCancelled);
```

You need to remember that while this approach helps to reduce blocking, creating and populating temporary tables can introduce significant I/O overhead, especially when a large amount of data involved. In some cases, you can avoid that overhead by using a CTE, as shown in Listing 11-6.

***Listing 11-6.*** Reducing blocking with a CTE

```
;with UpdateIds(OrderId)
as
(
    select OrderId
    from dbo.Orders
    where
        (PendingCancellation = 1) or
        (Paid = 0 and OrderDate < @MinUnpaidDate) or
        (Status = 'BackOrdered' and EstimatedStockDate > @StockDate);
)
update o
set o.Cancelled = 1
from UpdateIds u inner loop join dbo.Orders o on
    o.OrderId = u.OrderId
```

Similar to the previous example, the SELECT statement does not acquire update (U) locks during the scan. The inner loop join hint guarantees that exclusive (X) locks are held only on the rows that need to be modified. Remember that join hints force the order of joins in the statement. In our case, the CTE needs to be specified as the *left* (please make left in italic) input/table of the join to generate correct execution plan.

Both approaches may reduce blocking at the cost of the additional overhead they introduce. This overhead would increase with the amount of data to update, and you should not use these approaches if you expect to update a large percentage of the rows in the table. Remember that creating the right indexes is the better option in the majority of cases.

---

**Tip**    Avoid update scans on large tables.

---

You should avoid updating the row multiple times within the same transaction when UPDATE statements modify data in different nonclustered indexes. Remember that SQL Server acquires locks on a per-index basis when index rows are updated. Having multiple updates increases the chance of deadlock when other sessions access updated rows.

> **Tip**   Do not update data rows multiple times in a single transaction.

You need to understand whether lock escalation affects your system, especially in the case of OLTP workload. You can monitor object-level blocking conditions and locking waits, then correlate it with *lock_escalation* Extended and Trace Events. Remember that lock escalation helps to reduce memory consumption and improve performance in the system. You should analyze why lock escalation occurs and how it affects the system before making any decisions. In many cases, it is better to change the code and workflows rather than disabling it.

> **Tip**   Monitor lock escalation in the system.

You should avoid mixing statements that can lead to having row- and object-level locks in the same transaction in general, and mixing DML and DDL statements in particular. This pattern can lead to blocking between intent and full object-level locks as well as to deadlock conditions. This is especially important when servers have 16 or more logical CPUs, which enables lock partitioning.

> **Tip**   Do not mix DDL and DML statements in one transaction.

You need to analyze the root cause of deadlocks if you have them in your system. In most cases, query optimization and code refactoring would help to address them. You should also consider implementing retry logic around critical use cases in the system.

> **Tip**   Find the root cause of deadlocks. Implement retry logic if query optimization and code refactoring do not address them.

It is impossible to eliminate all blocking in the system. Fortunately, understanding the root cause of the blocking helps with designing a solution that mitigates the issue.

# Summary

Consistent transaction and error-handling strategies reduce blocking and simplify troubleshooting of concurrency issues. The choice between client- and server-side implementation depends on the data access tier architecture; however, as a general rule, you should use explicit rather than autocommitted transactions.

Business requirements should dictate the data consistency and isolation rules in the system. You should choose the *minimally required* isolation level that satisfies them. Do not use READ UNCOMMITTED unless it is absolutely necessary.

Optimistic isolation levels can be acceptable, even with OLTP workload, as long as the system can handle additional tempdb overhead. It is better to use READ COMMITTED SNAPSHOT unless transactional-level consistency is required.

Having proper query optimization and index tuning helps to improve concurrency in a majority of cases. Properly optimized queries acquire fewer locks, which reduces the chance of lock conflicts and blocking in the system. You should also keep transactions as short as possible and modify data close to the end of the transactions to reduce the amount of time locks are held.

Every system is unique, and it is impossible to provide generic advice that can be applied everywhere. However, a good understanding of the SQL Server concurrency model will help you to design the right transaction strategy and address any blocking and concurrency issues in the system.

# CHAPTER 12

# Troubleshooting Concurrency Issues

System troubleshooting is both an art and a science. It is also a very big and complex topic. If I had to write a book covering all aspects of system troubleshooting, it would have more pages than the one you are currently reading.

The processes of system troubleshooting and performance tuning require you to take a holistic view of the system. SQL Server never lives in a vacuum, and the root cause of a problem may not necessarily reside in the database. Inadequate hardware, improper OS and SQL Server configuration, inefficient database and application design—all these factors may lead to various issues and bad system performance.

Concurrency is just a small piece of this puzzle. Every multi-user database will suffer from some degree of blocking. Nevertheless, concurrency issues may or may not be the main source of the problem, and you can often get a better ROI by focusing on other areas in the system.

This chapter will discuss a common troubleshooting technique called *wait statistics analysis*. Even though we will focus on locking-related waits and concurrency issues, this technique is extremely useful during general troubleshooting. I would suggest you read more about this technique and other wait types that may exist in the system.

Remember, however, about taking a holistic view, and analyze the entire system—hardware and software—before focusing on in-database problems.

## SQL Server Execution Model

From a high level, the architecture of SQL Server includes six different components, as shown in Figure 12-1.

225

© Dmitri Korotkevitch 2018
D. Korotkevitch, *Expert SQL Server Transactions and Locking*, https://doi.org/10.1007/978-1-4842-3957-5_12

| Protocol Layer (Client Communication) | | Utilities (DBCC, Backup, Restore, BCP, etc) |
|---|---|---|
| Query Processor | | |
| Query Optimization (Plan Generation, Costing, Statistics, etc) | Query Execution (Parallelism, Memory Grants, etc) | |
| Storage Engine (Data Access, Locking Manager, Tran Log Management, etc) | In-Memory OLTP Engine | |
| SQLOS / PAL (Scheduling, Resource Management, Deadlock Detection, etc) | | |

**Figure 12-1.** *High-level SQL Server architecture*

The *Protocol layer* handles communications between SQL Server and client applications. The data is transmitted in an internal format called *Tabular Data Stream (TDS)* using one of the standard network communication protocols, such as TCP/IP or Named Pipes. Another communication protocol, called *Shared Memory*, can be used when both SQL Server and the client applications run locally on the same server.

The *Query Processor* layer is responsible for query optimization and execution.

The *Storage Engine* consists of components related to data access and data management in SQL Server. It works with the data on disk, handles transactions and concurrency, manages the transaction log, and performs several other functions.

The *In-Memory OLTP Engine* was introduced in SQL Server 2014. This lock- and latch-free technology helps to improve the performance of OLTP workloads. It works with memory-optimized tables that store all the data in memory. We will talk about the In-Memory OLTP Concurrency Model in the next chapter.

SQL Server includes a set of *utilities*, which are responsible for backup and restore operations, bulk loading of data, full-text index management, and several other actions.

Finally, the vital component of SQL Server is the *SQL Server Operating System (SQLOS)*. SQLOS is the layer between SQL Server and the OS (Windows or Linux), and it is responsible for scheduling and resource management, synchronization, exception handling, deadlock detection, CLR hosting, and more. For example, when any SQL Server component needs to allocate memory, it does not call the OS API function directly, but rather it requests memory from SQLOS, which in turn uses the memory allocator component to fulfill the request.

SQLOS was initially introduced in SQL Server 2005 to improve the efficiency of scheduling in SQL Server and to minimize context and kernel mode switching. The major difference between Windows and SQLOS is the scheduling model. Windows is a general-purpose operating system that uses preemptive scheduling. It controls what processes are currently running, suspending and resuming them as needed. Alternatively, with the exception of CLR code, SQLOS uses cooperative scheduling when processes yield voluntarily on a regular basis.

Linux support in SQL Server 2017 led to the further transformation of SQLOS and the introduction of the *Platform Abstraction Layer* (SQL PAL). It works as a gateway in between SQLOS and the operating system, providing the abstraction for OS API/Kernel calls. With very few exceptions in performance-critical code, SQLOS does not call the OS API directly, but rather uses PAL instead.

SQLOS creates a set of *schedulers* when it starts. The number of schedulers is equal to the number of logical CPUs in the system, with one extra scheduler for a dedicated admin connection. For example, if a server has two quad-core CPUs with hyper-threading enabled, SQL Server creates 17 schedulers. Each scheduler can be in either an `ONLINE` or `OFFLINE` state based on the processor affinity settings and core-based licensing model.

Even though the number of schedulers matches the number of CPUs in the system, there is no strict one-to-one relationship between them unless the processor affinity settings are enabled. In some cases, and under heavy load, it is possible to have more than one scheduler running on the same CPU. Alternatively, when processor affinity is set, schedulers are bound to CPUs in a strict one-to-one relationship.

Each scheduler is responsible for managing working threads called *workers*. The maximum number of workers in a system is specified by the *Max Worker Thread* configuration option. The default value of *zero* indicates that SQL Server calculates the maximum number of worker threads based on the number of schedulers in the system. In a majority of the cases, you do not need to change this default value.

Each time there is a task to execute, it is assigned to a worker in an idle state. When there are no idle workers, the scheduler creates a new one. It also destroys idle workers after 15 minutes of inactivity or in the case of memory pressure. It is also worth noting that each worker would use 512 KB of RAM in 32-bit and 2 MB of RAM in 64-bit SQL Server for the thread stack.

Workers do not move between schedulers. Moreover, a task is never moved between workers. SQLOS, however, can create child tasks and assign them to different workers; for example, in the case of parallel execution plans.

Each task can be in one of six different states:

*Pending*: Task is waiting for an available worker.

*Done*: Task is completed.

*Running*: Task is currently executing on the scheduler.

*Runnable*: Task is waiting for the scheduler to be executed.

*Suspended*: Task is waiting for an external event or resource.

*Spinloop*: Task is processing a spinlock. Spinlocks are synchronization objects that protect some internal objects. SQL Server may use them when it expects that access to the object will be granted very quickly, thus avoiding context switching for the workers.

Each scheduler has at most one task in a *running* state. In addition, it has two different queues—one for *runnable* tasks and one for *suspended* tasks. When the running task needs some resources—a data page from a disk, for example—it submits an I/O request and changes the state to *suspended*. It stays in the *suspended* queue until the request is fulfilled and the page is read. The task is moved to the *runnable* queue when it is ready to resume execution.

A grocery store is, perhaps, the closest real-life analogy to the SQL Server Execution Model. Think of cashiers as representing schedulers and customers in checkout lines as tasks in the runnable queue. A customer who is currently checking out is similar to a task in the running state.

If an item is missing a UPC code, a cashier sends a store worker to do a price check. The cashier suspends the checkout process for the current customer, asking her or him to step aside (to the suspended queue). When the worker comes back with the price information, the customer who had stepped aside moves to the end of the checkout line (end of the runnable queue).

It is worth mentioning that the SQL Server process is much more efficient as compared to real life, when others wait patiently in line during a price check. However, a customer who is forced to move to the end of the runnable queue would probably disagree with such a conclusion.

Figure 12-2 illustrates a typical task lifecycle in the SQL Server Execution Model. The total task execution time can be calculated as a summary of the time the task spent in the running state (when it ran on the scheduler), runnable state (when it waited for an available scheduler), and suspended state (when it waited for a resource or external event).

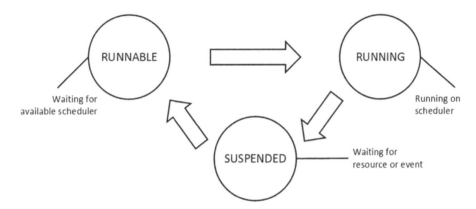

***Figure 12-2.*** *Task lifecycle*

SQL Server tracks the cumulative time tasks spend in a suspended state for different types of waits and exposes this through the sys.dm_os_wait_tasks view. This information is collected as of the time of the last SQL Server restart or since it was cleared with the DBCC SQLPERF('sys.dm_os_wait_stats', CLEAR) command.

Listing 12-1 shows how to find the *top* wait types in the system, which are the wait types for which workers spent the most time waiting. It filters out some nonessential wait types, mainly those related to internal SQL Server processes. Even though it is beneficial to analyze some of them during advanced performance tuning, you rarely focus on them during the initial stage of system troubleshooting.

**Note**   Every new version of SQL Server introduces new wait types. You can see a list of wait types at `https://docs.microsoft.com/en-us/sql/relational-databases/system-dynamic-management-views/sys-dm-os-wait-stats-transact-sql`. Make sure to select the appropriate version of SQL Server.

*Listing 12-1.* Detecting top wait types in the system

```
;with Waits
as
(
  select
    wait_type, wait_time_ms, waiting_tasks_count,signal_wait_time_ms
    ,wait_time_ms - signal_wait_time_ms as resource_wait_time_ms
    ,100. * wait_time_ms / SUM(wait_time_ms) over() as Pct
    ,row_number() over(order by wait_time_ms desc) as RowNum
  from sys.dm_os_wait_stats with (nolock)
  where
    wait_type not in /* Filtering out non-essential system waits */
    (N'BROKER_EVENTHANDLER',N'BROKER_RECEIVE_WAITFOR'
    ,N'BROKER_TASK_STOP',N'BROKER_TO_FLUSH'
    ,N'BROKER_TRANSMITTER',N'CHECKPOINT_QUEUE',N'CHKPT'
    ,N'CLR_SEMAPHORE',N'CLR_AUTO_EVENT'
    ,N'CLR_MANUAL_EVENT',N'DBMIRROR_DBM_EVENT'
    ,N'DBMIRROR_EVENTS_QUEUE',N'DBMIRROR_WORKER_QUEUE'
    ,N'DBMIRRORING_CMD',N'DIRTY_PAGE_POLL'
    ,N'DISPATCHER_QUEUE_SEMAPHORE',N'EXECSYNC'
    ,N'FSAGENT',N'FT_IFTS_SCHEDULER_IDLE_WAIT'
    ,N'FT_IFTSHC_MUTEX',N'HADR_CLUSAPI_CALL'
    ,N'HADR_FILESTREAM_IOMGR_IOCOMPLETION'
    ,N'HADR_LOGCAPTURE_WAIT'
    ,N'HADR_NOTIFICATION_DEQUEUE'
    ,N'HADR_TIMER_TASK',N'HADR_WORK_QUEUE'
    ,N'KSOURCE_WAKEUP',N'LAZYWRITER_SLEEP'
```

```
,N'LOGMGR_QUEUE',N'MEMORY_ALLOCATION_EXT'
,N'ONDEMAND_TASK_QUEUE'
,N'PARALLEL_REDO_WORKER_WAIT_WORK'
,N'PREEMPTIVE_HADR_LEASE_MECHANISM'
,N'PREEMPTIVE_SP_SERVER_DIAGNOSTICS'
,N'PREEMPTIVE_OS_LIBRARYOPS'
,N'PREEMPTIVE_OS_COMOPS'
,N'PREEMPTIVE_OS_CRYPTOPS'
,N'PREEMPTIVE_OS_PIPEOPS'
, N'PREEMPTIVE_OS_AUTHENTICATIONOPS'
,N'PREEMPTIVE_OS_GENERICOPS'
,N'PREEMPTIVE_OS_VERIFYTRUST
',N'PREEMPTIVE_OS_FILEOPS'
,N'PREEMPTIVE_OS_DEVICEOPS'
,N'PREEMPTIVE_OS_QUERYREGISTRY'
,N'PREEMPTIVE_OS_WRITEFILE'
,N'PREEMPTIVE_XE_CALLBACKEXECUTE'
,N'PREEMPTIVE_XE_DISPATCHER'
,N'PREEMPTIVE_XE_GETTARGETSTATE'
,N'PREEMPTIVE_XE_SESSIONCOMMIT'
,N'PREEMPTIVE_XE_TARGETINIT'
,N'PREEMPTIVE_XE_TARGETFINALIZE'
,N'PWAIT_ALL_COMPONENTS_INITIALIZED'
,N'PWAIT_DIRECTLOGCONSUMER_GETNEXT'
,N'QDS_PERSIST_TASK_MAIN_LOOP_SLEEP'
,N'QDS_ASYNC_QUEUE'
,N'QDS_CLEANUP_STALE_QUERIES_TASK_MAIN_LOOP_SLEEP'
,N'REQUEST_FOR_DEADLOCK_SEARCH'
,N'RESOURCE_QUEUE',N'SERVER_IDLE_CHECK'
,N'SLEEP_BPOOL_FLUSH',N'SLEEP_DBSTARTUP'
,N'SLEEP_DCOMSTARTUP'
,N'SLEEP_MASTERDBREADY',N'SLEEP_MASTERMDREADY'
,N'SLEEP_MASTERUPGRADED',N'SLEEP_MSDBSTARTUP'
, N'SLEEP_SYSTEMTASK', N'SLEEP_TASK'
,N'SLEEP_TEMPDBSTARTUP',N'SNI_HTTP_ACCEPT'
,N'SP_SERVER_DIAGNOSTICS_SLEEP'
```

```
        ,N'SQLTRACE_BUFFER_FLUSH'
        ,N'SQLTRACE_INCREMENTAL_FLUSH_SLEEP'
        ,N'SQLTRACE_WAIT_ENTRIES',N'WAIT_FOR_RESULTS'
        ,N'WAITFOR',N'WAITFOR_TASKSHUTDOWN'
        ,N'WAIT_XTP_HOST_WAIT'
        ,N'WAIT_XTP_OFFLINE_CKPT_NEW_LOG'
        ,N'WAIT_XTP_CKPT_CLOSE',N'WAIT_XTP_RECOVERY'
        ,N'XE_BUFFERMGR_ALLPROCESSED_EVENT'
        , N'XE_DISPATCHER_JOIN',N'XE_DISPATCHER_WAIT'
        ,N'XE_LIVE_TARGET_TVF',N'XE_TIMER_EVENT')
)
select
    w1.wait_type as [Wait Type]
    ,w1.waiting_tasks_count as [Wait Count]
    ,convert(decimal(12,3), w1.wait_time_ms / 1000.0)
            as [Wait Time]
    ,convert(decimal(12,1), w1.wait_time_ms / w1.waiting_tasks_count)
            as [Avg Wait Time]
    ,convert(decimal(12,3), w1.signal_wait_time_ms / 1000.0)
            as [Signal Wait Time]
    ,convert(decimal(12,1), w1.signal_wait_time_ms / w1.waiting_tasks_count)
            as [Avg Signal Wait Time]
    ,convert(decimal(12,3), w1.resource_wait_time_ms / 1000.0)
            as [Resource Wait Time]
    ,convert(decimal(12,1), w1.resource_wait_time_ms
            / w1.waiting_tasks_count) as [Avg Resource Wait Time]
    ,convert(decimal(6,3), w1.Pct) as [Percent]
    ,convert(decimal(6,3), w1.Pct + IsNull(w2.Pct,0)) as [Running Percent]
from
    Waits w1 cross apply
    (
        select sum(w2.Pct) as Pct
        from Waits w2
        where w2.RowNum < w1.RowNum
    ) w2
```

```
where
  w1.RowNum = 1 or w2.Pct <= 99
order by
  w1.RowNum
option (recompile);
```

Figure 12-3 illustrates the output of the script from one of the production servers at the beginning of the troubleshooting process.

| | Wait Type | Wait Count | Wait Time | Avg Wait Time | Signal Wait Time |
|---|---|---|---|---|---|
| 1 | LCK_M_U | 548216435 | 2430865.645 | 4.0 | 148157.438 |
| 2 | CXPACKET | 696649076 | 1991476.659 | 2.0 | 224445.736 |
| 3 | LCK_M_S | 609624311 | 327349.394 | 0.0 | 326909.609 |
| 4 | HADR_SYNC_COMMIT | 393862506 | 277294.283 | 0.0 | 128633.010 |
| 5 | PAGEIOLATCH_EX | 155976551 | 229145.101 | 1.0 | 3258.831 |
| 6 | BACKUPIO | 84529112 | 161681.111 | 1.0 | 2084.816 |
| 7 | ASYNC_IO_COMPLETION | 48377 | 157225.551 | 3250.0 | 86.153 |
| 8 | LATCH_EX | 171800900 | 141038.765 | 0.0 | 34869.237 |
| 9 | PAGEIOLATCH_SH | 97400378 | 120563.694 | 1.0 | 1936.229 |
| 10 | BACKUPBUFFER | 120290500 | 109741.003 | 0.0 | 7385.949 |
| 11 | PAGELATCH_EX | 3103005547 | 89580.939 | 0.0 | 84153.002 |
| 12 | BACKUPTHREAD | 527984 | 69381.750 | 131.0 | 180.629 |
| 13 | LCK_M_IX | 21926 | 53148.574 | 2423.0 | 25.892 |

| Avg Signal Wait Time | Resource Wait Time | Avg Resource Wait Time | Percent | Running Percent |
|---|---|---|---|---|
| 0.0 | 2282708.207 | 4.0 | 37.644 | 37.644 |
| 0.0 | 1767030.923 | 2.0 | 30.840 | 68.484 |
| 0.0 | 439.785 | 0.0 | 5.069 | 73.553 |
| 0.0 | 148661.273 | 0.0 | 4.294 | 77.847 |
| 0.0 | 225886.270 | 1.0 | 3.548 | 81.395 |
| 0.0 | 159596.295 | 1.0 | 2.504 | 83.899 |
| 1.0 | 157139.398 | 3248.0 | 2.435 | 86.334 |
| 0.0 | 106169.528 | 0.0 | 2.184 | 88.518 |
| 0.0 | 118627.465 | 1.0 | 1.867 | 90.385 |
| 0.0 | 102355.054 | 0.0 | 1.699 | 92.084 |
| 0.0 | 5427.937 | 0.0 | 1.387 | 93.472 |
| 0.0 | 69201.121 | 131.0 | 1.074 | 94.546 |
| 1.0 | 53122.682 | 2422.0 | 0.823 | 95.369 |

*Figure 12-3.* Output of the script from one of the production servers

The process of analyzing top waits in the system is called wait statistics analysis. This is one of the most frequently used troubleshooting and performance-tuning techniques in SQL Server, which allows you to quickly identify potential problems in the system. Figure 12-4 illustrates a typical wait statistics analysis troubleshooting cycle.

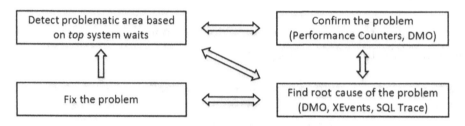

***Figure 12-4.*** *Wait statistics analysis troubleshooting cycle*

As a first step, look at the wait statistics, which detect the top waits in the system. This narrows the area of concern for further analysis. After that, confirm the problem using other tools, such as DMVs, Windows Performance Monitor, SQL Traces, and Extended Events, and detect the root cause of the problem. When the root cause is confirmed, fix it and analyze the wait statistics again, choosing a new target for analysis and improvement.

Let's look at locking-related wait types in detail.

---

**Note**   My *Pro SQL Server Internals* book provides deeper coverage of wait statistics analysis and explains how to troubleshoot various non-locking-related issues in the system.

You can also download a whitepaper on wait statistics analysis from `http://download.microsoft.com/download/4/7/a/47a548b9-249e-484c-abd7-29f31282b04d/performance_tuning_waits_queues.doc`. Even though it focuses on SQL Server 2005, the content is valid for any version of SQL Server.

---

# Lock Waits

Every lock type in the system has a corresponding wait type with the name starting with LCK_M_ followed by the lock type. For example, LCK_M_U and LCK_M_IS indicate waits for update (U) and intent exclusive (IX) locks, respectively.

Lock waits occur during blocking when lock requests are waiting in the queue. SQL Server does not generate lock waits when requests can be granted immediately and blocking does not occur.

You need to pay attention to both total wait time and number of times waits occurred. It is entirely possible to have wait types with a large total wait time generated by just a handful of long waits. You may decide to troubleshoot or ignore them based on your objectives.

You should also remember that wait statistics are accumulated from the time of the last SQL Server restart. Servers with prolonged uptime may have wait statistics that are not representative of the current load. In many cases it may be beneficial to clear wait statistics with the DBCC SQLPERF('sys.dm_os_wait_stats', CLEAR) command, collecting recent wait information before troubleshooting. You should obviously have a representative workload in the system when you do that.

Let's look at locking wait types and discuss what may lead to such waits and how we can troubleshoot them.

# LCK_M_U Wait Type

The LCK_M_U wait type is, perhaps, one of the most common locking-related wait types in OLTP systems, as it indicates a wait for update (U) locks.

As you may remember, SQL Server uses update (U) locks during update scans when it looks for the rows that need to be updated or deleted. SQL Server acquires an update (U) lock when it reads the row, releasing or converting it to an exclusive (X) lock afterward. In the majority of cases, a large number of LCK_M_U waits indicates the existence of poorly optimized writer queries (UPDATE, DELETE, MERGE) in the system.

You can correlate the data with PAGEIOLATCH* wait types. These waits occur when SQL Server is waiting for the data page to be read from disk. A high amount of such waits points to high disk I/O, which is often another sign of non-optimized queries in the system. There are other conditions besides non-optimized queries that may generate such waits, and you should not make the conclusion without performing additional analysis.

The PAGEIOLATCH* wait type indicates physical I/O in the system. It is common nowadays to have servers with enough memory to cache the active data in the buffer pool. Non-optimized queries in such environments would not generate physical reads and PAGEIOLATCH* waits. Nevertheless, they may suffer from blocking and generate LCK_M_U waits during update scans.

Poorly optimized queries need to process a large amount of data, which increases the cost of the execution plan. In many cases, SQL Server would generate parallel execution plans for them. A high CXPACKET wait indicates a large amount of parallelism, which may be another sign of poorly optimized queries in OLTP systems.

You should remember, however, that parallelism is completely normal and expected. A CXPACKET wait does not necessarily indicate a problem, and you should take the system workload into consideration during analysis. It is also worth noting that the default value of the *Cost Threshold for Parallelism* setting is extremely low and needs to be increased in the majority of cases nowadays.

There are several ways to detect poorly optimized I/O-intensive queries using standard SQL Server tools. One of the most common approaches is by capturing system activity using SQL Traces or Extended Events, filtering the data by the number of reads and/or writes. This approach, however, requires you to perform additional analysis after the data is collected. You should check how frequently queries are executed when determining targets for optimization.

---

**Important**    Extended Events sessions and SQL Traces that capture query execution statistics may lead to significant overhead in busy systems. Use them with care and do not keep them running unless you are doing performance troubleshooting.

---

Another very simple and powerful method of detecting resource-intensive queries is the sys.dm_exec_query_stats data management view. SQL Server tracks various statistics for cached execution plans, including the number of executions and I/O operations, elapsed times, and CPU times, and exposes them through that view. Furthermore, you can join it with other data management objects and obtain the SQL text and execution plans for those queries. This simplifies the analysis, and it can be helpful during the troubleshooting of various performance and plan-cache issues in the system.

Listing 12-2 shows a query that returns the 50 most I/O-intensive queries, which have plans cached at the moment of execution. It is worth noting that the sys.dm_exec_query_stats view has slightly different columns in the result set in different versions of SQL Server. The query in Listing 12-2 works in SQL Server 2008R2 and above. You can remove the last four columns from the SELECT list to make it compatible with SQL Server 2005-2008.

***Listing 12-2.*** Using `sys.dm_exec_query_stats`

```
select top 50
    substring(qt.text, (qs.statement_start_offset/2)+1,
    ((
        case qs.statement_end_offset
            when -1 then datalength(qt.text)
            else qs.statement_end_offset
        end - qs.statement_start_offset)/2)+1) as SQL
    ,qp.query_plan as [Query Plan]
    ,qs.execution_count as [Exec Cnt]
    ,(qs.total_logical_reads + qs.total_logical_writes) /
            qs.execution_count as [Avg IO]
    ,qs.total_logical_reads as [Total Reads], qs.last_logical_reads
            as [Last Reads]
    ,qs.total_logical_writes as [Total Writes], qs.last_logical_writes
            as [Last Writes]
    ,qs.total_worker_time as [Total Worker Time], qs.last_worker_time
            as [Last Worker Time]
    ,qs.total_elapsed_time / 1000 as [Total Elapsed Time]
    ,qs.last_elapsed_time / 1000 as [Last Elapsed Time]
    ,qs.creation_time as [Cached Time], qs.last_execution_time
            as [Last Exec Time]
    ,qs.total_rows as [Total Rows], qs.last_rows as [Last Rows]
    ,qs.min_rows as [Min Rows], qs.max_rows as [Max Rows]
from
    sys.dm_exec_query_stats qs with (nolock)
        cross apply sys.dm_exec_sql_text(qs.sql_handle) qt
        cross apply sys.dm_exec_query_plan(qs.plan_handle) qp
order by
    [Avg IO] desc
```

As you can see in Figure 12-5, it allows you to easily define optimization targets based on resource usage and the number of executions. For example, the second query in the result set is the best candidate for optimization because of how frequently it runs. Obviously, we need to focus on data modification queries if our target is to reduce the amount of update lock waits in the system.

| | SQL | Query Plan | Exec Cnt | Avg IO | Total Reads | Last Reads | Total Writes | Last Writes | Total Worker Time | Last Worker T... |
|---|---|---|---|---|---|---|---|---|---|---|
| 1 | select Subj, cast(ReceiverUID ... | <ShowPlanXML xmlns="http... | 1 | 8816382 | 8816296 | 8816296 | 86 | 86 | 24297389 | 24297389 |
| 2 | select UID, DOCTYPE_ID, REG... | <ShowPlanXML xmlns="http... | 26455 | 4143503 | 109616393555 | 4224687 | 0 | 0 | 154369131409 | 5074290 |
| 3 | DELETE TOP (@delete_batch... | <ShowPlanXML xmlns="http... | 1 | 4096631 | 4096468 | 4096468 | 163 | 163 | 26536518 | 26536518 |
| 4 | insert into #tmpReportIncoming... | <ShowPlanXML xmlns="http... | 62 | 3690210 | 228750206 | 3954680 | 42859 | 1012 | 3351099613 | 28477617 |
| 5 | update #tmpReportIncomingCo... | <ShowPlanXML xmlns="http... | 62 | 3139967 | 194677952 | 3140931 | 7 | 0 | 2406888686 | 27503573 |

*Figure 12-5. Sys.dm_exec_query_stats results*

Unfortunately, the sys.dm_exec_query_stats view does not return any information for the queries that do not have execution plans cached. Usually, this is not an issue, because our optimization targets are not only resource intensive, but they are also frequently executed queries. Plans for those queries usually stay in the cache due to their frequent reuse. However, SQL Server does not cache plans in the case of a statement-level recompile; therefore, sys.dm_exec_query_stats misses them. You should use Extended Events and/or SQL Traces to capture them. I usually start with queries from the sys.dm_exec_query_stats output and crosscheck the optimization targets with Extended Events later.

Query plans can be removed from the cache and, therefore, are not included in the sys.dm_exec_query_stats result in cases of a SQL Server restart, memory pressure, recompilations due to a statistics update, and a few other cases. It is beneficial to analyze the creation_time and last_execution_time columns in addition to the number of executions.

In SQL Server 2016 and above, you can use the *Query Store* to collect execution statistics for all queries in the system. It provides a rich set of reports and data management views, which you can use to quickly identify inefficient queries in the system. The data from the Query Store is persisted in the database and would survive SQL Server restart. The Query Store is an extremely powerful tool that helps dramatically during troubleshooting.

You can also use the Blocking Monitoring Framework we discussed in Chapter 4. You can analyze the data for update (U) lock waits, choosing the targets for optimization. We will talk about this framework in more detail later in the chapter.

As we already discussed, it is also possible that blocking conditions and locking waits occur due to incorrect transaction management in the system. Long transactions may hold locks for a long period of time, blocking other sessions from acquiring incompatible locks on affected rows. Remember this behavior and factor it into the analysis and troubleshooting.

# LCK_M_S Wait Type

The LCK_M_S wait type indicates waits for shared (S) locks. This lock type is acquired by SELECT queries in the READ COMMITTED, REPEATABLE READ, and SERIALIZABLE isolation levels.

In many cases, the root cause of LCK_M_S waits are similar to those for LCK_M_U waits. Poorly optimized SELECT queries may scan a large amount of data and may be blocked by exclusive (X) locks held by other sessions. You can use the same troubleshooting techniques as we just discussed to identify such queries.

In cases where queries are running in the READ COMMITTED isolation level, you can consider enabling the READ_COMMITTED_SNAPSHOT database option to eliminate readers/writers blocking. In this mode, SQL Server does not acquire shared (S) locks in the READ COMMITTED isolation level, relying on row versioning instead. Remember that this approach does not address the root cause of the issue, instead masking problems introduced by poorly optimized queries. Also remember the additional overhead it introduces.

---

**Note**   Do not use a (NOLOCK) hint or the READ UNCOMMITTED isolation level unless data consistency is not required.

---

In some cases, LCK_M_S waits may be generated by waits for table-level locks acquired by SQL Server during some operations or because of a (TABLOCK) hint in the code. One such example is an online index rebuild process, which acquires a short-term shared (S) table-level lock at the beginning of execution. The volatility of the data in busy OLTP systems may lead to a blocking condition in such a scenario, especially with lock partitioning involved.

Such cases may present themselves in wait statistics as wait types with a relatively low number of occurrences and high average wait time. Nevertheless, you should not rely only on wait statistics to drive the conclusion. It is beneficial to analyze individual blocking cases, and the Blocking Monitoring Framework may be very useful in such scenarios.

# LCK_M_X Wait Type

The LCK_M_X wait type indicates the waits for exclusive (X) locks. As strange as it sounds, in OLTP systems with volatile data, LCK_M_X waits may occur less frequently than LCK_M_U waits.

As you already know, SQL Server usually uses update (U) locks during update scans. This behavior, however, is not guaranteed. In some cases, SQL Server may decide to omit update (U) locks, using exclusive (X) locks instead. One such example is point-lookup searches, when a query updates a single row using a predicate on the indexed column. In that case, SQL Server may acquire an exclusive (X) lock immediately without using an update (U) lock. Blocking in this condition would lead to an LCK_M_X wait.

You may also have LCK_M_X waits during the conversion from an update (U) to an exclusive (X) lock. Update (U) and shared (S) locks are compatible with each other, and, therefore, a query may acquire an update (U) lock on a row with a shared (S) lock held. SQL Server, however, would be unable to convert it to an exclusive (X) lock if the row needed to be updated.

This condition happens when a SELECT query uses a REPEATABLE READ or SERIALIZABLE isolation level and shared (S) locks are held until the end of the transaction. It may also occur in the READ COMMITTED level when a SELECT query sometimes holds shared (S) locks for the duration of the statement; for example, when it reads LOB columns.

LCK_M_X waits may occur when multiple sessions work with the same data. One of the common scenarios is a *counters table* implementation, when multiple sessions are trying to increment the same counter simultaneously or even to use a (TABLOCKX) hint. You can address this collision by switching to SEQUENCE objects or identity columns.

As usual, you should analyze individual blocking cases and understand the root cause of the blocking when you see a large amount of LCK_M_X waits in the system.

## LCK_M_SCH_S and LCK_M_SCH_M Wait Types

LCK_M_SCH_S and LCK_M_SCH_M wait types indicate waits for schema stability (Sch-S) and schema modification (Sch-M) locks. These waits should not occur in the system on a large scale.

SQL Server acquires schema modification (Sch-M) locks during schema alterations. This lock requires exclusive access to the table, and requests would be blocked, generating the wait, until all other sessions disconnected from the table.

There are several common cases when such blocking may occur:

> Database schema changes that are done online, with other users connected to the system. Remember, in this case the schema modification (Sch-M) lock is held until the end of the transaction.

Offline index rebuild.

Partition switch or final phase of online index rebuild. A schema modification (Sch-M) lock is required to modify metadata in the database. You can reduce blocking by using low-priority locks if they are supported.

Schema stability (Sch-S) locks are used to avoid table alterations when tables are in use. SQL Server acquires them during query compilation and during the execution of SELECT queries in isolation levels that do not use intent locks, such as in READ UNCOMMITTED, READ COMMITTED SNAPSHOT, and SNAPSHOT.

Schema stability (Sch-S) locks are compatible with any other lock type except schema modification (Sch-M) locks. The existence of LCK_M_SCH_S waits always indicates blocking introduced by schema modifications.

If you encounter a significant amount of schema lock waits in the system, you should identify what caused this blocking. In the majority of cases, you could address them by changing deployment or database maintenance strategies in the system or by switching to low-priority locks.

# Intent LCK_M_I* Wait Types

Intent lock wait types indicate waits for intent locks in the system. Each intent lock type has a corresponding wait type. For example, LCK_M_IS indicates intent shared (IS) lock waits, and LCK_M_IX indicates intent exclusive (IX) lock waits.

SQL Server acquires intent locks on the object (table) and page levels. On the table level, blocking may occur in two conditions. First, the session cannot acquire an intent lock due to an incompatible schema modification (Sch-M) lock held on the object. Usually, in this case you would also see some schema lock waits, and you would need to troubleshoot the reason why they occurred in the system.

Another case is the existence of an incompatible full lock on the table. For example, neither of the intent locks can be acquired while the table has a full exclusive (X) lock held.

In some cases, this may occur due to table-level locking hints in the code, such as (TABLOCK) or (TABLOCKX). However, this condition may also be triggered by successful lock escalation during large batch modifications. You can confirm this by monitoring lock_escalation Extended Events and address this by disabling lock escalation on some of the critical tables. I will also demonstrate later in the chapter how to identify tables involved in object-level blocking using the Blocking Monitoring Framework.

It is also possible to have intent-lock blocking when a session requests an intent lock on a page with an incompatible full lock held. Consider a situation where SQL Server needs to run a SELECT statement that scans the entire table. In this scenario, SQL Server may choose to use page-level instead of row-level locking, acquiring full shared (S) locks on the pages. This would introduce blocking if another session tried to modify a row by acquiring an intent exclusive (IX) lock on the page.

As usual, you need to identify and address the root cause of the blocking when you encounter such issues.

# Locking Waits: Summary

Table 12-1 summarizes possible root causes and troubleshooting steps for common lock-related wait types.

*Table 12-1.* *Most Common Lock-Related Wait Types*

| Wait Type | Possible Root Cause | Troubleshooting Steps |
| --- | --- | --- |
| LCK_M_U | Update scans due to poorly optimized queries | Detect and optimize poorly optimized queries using Query Store, sys.dm_exec_query_stats, xEvent sessions, Blocking Monitoring Framework |
| LCK_M_X | Multiple sessions work with the same data | Change the code |
| | Update scans due to poorly optimized queries | Detect and optimize poorly optimized queries using Query Store, sys.dm_exec_query_stats, xEvent sessions, Blocking Monitoring Framework |
| LCK_M_S | Select scans due to poorly optimized queries | Detect and optimize poorly optimized queries using Query Store, sys.dm_exec_query_stats, xEvent sessions, Blocking Monitoring FrameworkConsider switching to optimistic isolation levels |
| LCK_M_U, LCK_M_S, LCK_M_X | Incorrect transaction management with long-running transactions holding incompatible locks | Redesign transaction strategy. Optimize the queries |

*(continued)*

***Table 12-1.*** (*continued*)

| Wait Type | Possible Root Cause | Troubleshooting Steps |
|---|---|---|
| LCK_M_SCH_S, LCK_M_SCH_M | Blocking due to database schema alteration or index or partition maintenance | Evaluate deployment and maintenance strategies. Switch to low-priority locks if possible |
| LCK_M_I* | Blocking due to database schema alteration or index or partition maintenance | Evaluate deployment and maintenance strategies |
| | Lock Escalation | Analyze and disable lock escalations on affected tables |

As I already mentioned, every lock type in the system has a corresponding wait type. You may encounter other lock-related wait types that we have not covered in this chapter. Nevertheless, knowledge of the SQL Server Concurrency Model will help you in troubleshooting. Analyze blocking conditions that may generate such lock types and identify the root cause of the blocking.

# Data Management Views

SQL Server provides a large set of data management views that expose information about system health and the SQL Server state. I would like to mention several views that we have not yet covered.

## sys.db_exec_requests View

The sys.dm_exec_requests view provides a list of currently executed requests. This view is extremely useful during troubleshooting and provides you with great visibility of the sessions that are currently running on the server. The most notable columns in the view are as follows:

> The session_id column provides ID of the session. The user sessions in the system will always have a session_id greater than 50, although it is possible that some of the system sessions may also have a session_id greater than 50. You can get information about

the session and client application by joining results with the
sys.dm_exec_sessions and sys.dm_exec_connections views.

The start_time, total_elapsed_time, cpu_time, reads, logical_
reads, and writes columns provide execution statistics for the
request.

The sql_handle, statement_start_offset, and statement_end_
offset columns allow you to get information about the query.
In SQL Server 2016 and above, you can use it together with the
function sys.dm_exec_input_buffer to obtain information
about currently running SQL statements. You can also use the
sys.dm_exec_sql_text function for such a purpose, as you have
already seen in this book.

The plan_handle column allows you to obtain the execution plan
of the statement using the sys.dm_exec_query_plan and sys.
dm_exec_text_query_plan functions.

The status column provides you with the status of the worker. For
blocked sessions in SUSPENDED status, you can use the wait_type,
wait_time, wait_resource, and blocking_session_id columns
to get information about session wait and blocker. Moreover,
the last_wait_type column will show the last wait type for the
session.

There are many scenarios where the sys.dm_exec_requests view may help with
troubleshooting. One of them is when analyzing the state of a long-running statement.
You can look at the status and wait-related columns to see if a request is running or being
blocked, identifying a blocking session by the blocking_session_id column.

---

**Note**   You can get more information about the sys.dm_exec_requests view
at https://docs.microsoft.com/en-us/sql/relational-databases/
system-dynamic-management-views/sys-dm-exec-requests-
transact-sql.

---

# sys.db_os_waiting_tasks View

You can get more information about blocked sessions by using the `sys.dm_os_waiting_tasks` view. This view returns data on the tasks/workers level, which is beneficial when you analyze blocking for queries with parallel execution plans. The output includes one row per blocked worker and provides information about wait type and duration, blocked resource, and ID of the blocking session.

---

**Note**    You can get more information about the `sys.dm_os_waiting_tasks` view at `https://docs.microsoft.com/en-us/sql/relational-databases/system-dynamic-management-views/sys-dm-os-waiting-tasks-transact-sql`.

---

# sys.db_exec_session_wait_stats view and wait_info xEvent

In some cases, you may want to track waits on the session level; for example, when you troubleshoot the performance of long-running queries. Detailed wait information will allow you to understand what may cause the delays and adjust your tuning strategy accordingly.

SQL Server 2016 and above provide you this information with the `sys.dm_exec_session_wait_stats` view. This view, in a nutshell, returns similar data as `sys.dm_os_wait_stats` does, collected on the session level. It clears the information when the session is opened or when the polled connection is reset.

The `sys.dm_exec_session_wait_stats` view is useful when you suspect that a query suffers from a large number of short-term blocking waits. Such waits may not trigger a *blocked process report*; however, they may lead to a large cumulative blocking time.

In SQL Server prior to 2016, you can track session-level waits with the `wait_info` Extended Event using the `opcode=1` predicate, which indicates the end of the wait. As you can guess, this session may generate an enormous amount of information, which can impact server performance. Do not keep it running unless you are troubleshooting, and do not use the `event_file` target due to the I/O system latency it would introduce.

You may set the predicate on the duration field, capturing only long-term waits—for example, waits longer than 50ms. You can also reduce the amount of collected information by using a session_id filter. Unfortunately, session_id is an action for a wait_type event, which adds some overhead during data collection. SQL Server executes actions after it evaluates the predicates on Extended Event fields, and it is beneficial to remove unnecessary wait types from the processing.

Listing 12-3 provides a list of map values that correspond to each wait type, which you can use as the filter for the wait types.

***Listing 12-3.*** Wait_type map values

```
select name, map_key, map_value
from sys.dm_xe_map_values
where name = 'wait_types'
order by map_key
```

Finally, another External Event, wait_type_external, captures information about preemptive waits (PREEMPTIVE* wait types). Those waits are associated with external OS calls; for example, when SQL Server needs to zero-initialize a log file or authenticate a user in Active Directory. In some cases, you need to troubleshoot them; however, those cases are not related to blocking and concurrency issues.

---

**Note**   You can get more information about the sys.dm_exec_session_wait_ stats view at https://docs.microsoft.com/en-us/sql/relational-databases/system-dynamic-management-views/sys-dm-exec-session-wait-stats-transact-sql. You can read about Extended Events at https://docs.microsoft.com/en-us/sql/relational-databases/extended-events/extended-events.

---

# sys.db_db_index_operational_stats and sys.dm_db_index_usage_stats Views

SQL Server tracks index usage statistics with the sys.dm_db_index_usage_stats and sys.dm_db_index_operational_stats views. They provide information about index access patterns, such as number of seeks, scans, and lookups; number of data modifications in the index; latching and locking statistics; and many other useful metrics.

The `sys.dm_db_index_usage_stats` view focuses mainly on index access patterns, counting the number of queries that utilize the index. The `sys.dm_db_index_operational_stats` view, on the other hand, tracks operations on a per-row basis. For example, if you ran a query that updated ten index rows in a single batch, the `sys.dm_db_index_usage_stats` view would count it as one data modification and increment the `user_updates` column by one, while the `sys.dm_db_index_operational_stats` view would increment the `leaf_update_count` column by ten based on the number of rows affected by the operation.

Both views are extremely useful during index analysis and allow you to detect unused and inefficient indexes. Moreover, the `sys.dm_db_index_operational_stats` view gives you very useful insight into index operational metrics and helps to identify the indexes that suffer from a large amount of blocking, latching, and physical disk activity.

From a locking standpoint, the `sys.dm_db_index_operational_stats` view includes three different set of columns:

- `row_lock_count`, `row_lock_wait_count`, and `row_lock_wait_ms` indicate the number of row-level locks requested in the index along with lock wait statistics.

- `page_lock_count`, `page_lock_wait_count`, and `page_lock_wait_ms` show locking information on the page level.

- `index_lock_promotion_ count` and `index_lock_promotion_attempt_count` return lock escalation statistics.

You can correlate this information with other venues during troubleshooting. For example, when you analyze the impact of lock escalations in the system, you can look at `index_lock_promotion_count` column values and identify the indexes that triggered lock escalation most often.

Listing 12-4 shows a query that returns ten indexes with the highest row- and page-level lock wait times, helping you to identify the indexes that suffer the most from blocking.

***Listing 12-4.*** Indexes with the highest lock wait times

```
select top 10
    t.object_id
    ,i.index_id
    ,sch.name + '.' + t.name as [table]
```

```
    ,i.name as [index]
    ,ius.user_seeks
    ,ius.user_scans
    ,ius.user_lookups
    ,ius.user_seeks + ius.user_scans + ius.user_lookups as reads
    ,ius.user_updates
    ,ius.last_user_seek
    ,ius.last_user_scan
    ,ius.last_user_lookup
    ,ius.last_user_update
    ,ios.*
from
    sys.tables t with (nolock) join sys.indexes i with (nolock) on
        t.object_id = i.object_id
    join sys.schemas sch with (nolock)  on
        t.schema_id = sch.schema_id
    left join sys.dm_db_index_usage_stats ius with (nolock) on
        i.object_id = ius.object_id and
        i.index_id = ius.index_id
    outer apply
    (
        select
            sum(range_scan_count) as range_scan_count
            ,sum(singleton_lookup_count) as singleton_lookup_count
            ,sum(row_lock_wait_count) as row_lock_wait_count
            ,sum(row_lock_wait_in_ms) as row_lock_wait_in_ms
            ,sum(page_lock_wait_count) as page_lock_wait_count
            ,sum(page_lock_wait_in_ms) as page_lock_wait_in_ms
            ,sum(page_latch_wait_count) as page_latch_wait_count
            ,sum(page_latch_wait_in_ms) as page_latch_wait_in_ms
            ,sum(page_io_latch_wait_count) as page_io_latch_wait_count
            ,sum(page_io_latch_wait_in_ms) as page_io_latch_wait_in_ms
        from sys.dm_db_index_operational_stats(db_id(),i.object_id,
        i.index_id,null)
    ) ios
```

order by

```
    ios.row_lock_wait_in_ms + ios.page_lock_wait_in_ms desc
```

Figure 12-6 shows the partial output of the query from one of the production servers. Note that the first index in the output has a very low number of reads and high update overhead and may potentially be removed from the system.

| | table | index | user_seeks | user_scans | user_lookups | reads | user_updates | row_lock_wait_in_ms | page_lock_wait_in_ms |
|---|---|---|---|---|---|---|---|---|---|
| 1 | | | 0 | 15 | 0 | 15 | 150903156 | 151979666 | 1640 |
| 2 | | | 79848367 | 99668779 | 26512194 | 206029340 | 120133196 | 101905474 | 577 |
| 3 | | | 61668323 | 54044320 | 19 | 115712662 | 99450931 | 55669084 | 206 |
| 4 | | | 2537432 | 4 | 0 | 2537436 | 335183755 | 20396562 | 16344 |
| 5 | | | 88422269 | 0 | 0 | 88422269 | 2466503 | 20039239 | 16 |
| 6 | | | 4672688 | 79 | 0 | 4672767 | 161933538 | 0 | 18439998 |
| 7 | | | 133516988 | 0 | 0 | 133516988 | 674140935 | 5378803 | 3513 |
| 8 | | | 2272649286 | 2087478 | 974519 | 2275711283 | 399097304 | 2243821 | 2912199 |
| 9 | | | 53437035 | 11540688 | 0 | 64977723 | 36468984 | 4414070 | 4717 |
| 10 | | | 0 | 1425633 | 0 | 1425633 | 323368305 | 3702137 | 84056 |

***Figure 12-6.*** *Indexes with the highest lock wait times*

You can detect the queries that utilize a specific index by using the code from Listing 12-5. The results are not bulletproof, however; this code analyzes the cached execution plans and may miss queries that do not have plans cached for some reason. You can adjust it to use Query Store DMVs, if it is enabled in the system.

As a word of caution, this code is CPU intensive. Be careful when you run it on CPU-bound production servers with a large number of plans in the cache.

***Listing 12-5.*** Identifying queries that use a specific index

```
declare
  @IndexName sysname = quotename('IDX_CI'); -- Add Index Name here

;with xmlnamespaces(default 'http://schemas.microsoft.com/
sqlserver/2004/07/showplan')
,CachedData
as
(
  select distinct
    obj.value('@Database','sysname') as [Database]
    ,obj.value('@Schema','sysname') + '.' +
        obj.value('@Table','sysname') as [Table]
    ,obj.value('@Index','sysname') as [Index]
```

```
    ,obj.value('@IndexKind','varchar(64)') as [Type]
    ,stmt.value('@StatementText', 'nvarchar(max)') as [Statement]
    ,convert(nvarchar(max),qp.query_plan) as query_plan
    ,cp.plan_handle
  from
    sys.dm_exec_cached_plans cp with (nolock)
      cross apply sys.dm_exec_query_plan(plan_handle) qp
      cross apply query_plan.nodes
        ('/ShowPlanXML/BatchSequence/Batch/Statements/StmtSimple')
        batch(stmt)
      cross apply stmt.nodes
        ('.//IndexScan/Object[@Index=sql:variable("@IndexName")]') idx(obj)
)
select
  cd.[Database]
  ,cd.[Table]
  ,cd.[Index]
  ,cd.[Type]
  ,cd.[Statement]
  ,convert(xml,cd.query_plan) as query_plan
  ,qs.execution_count
  ,(qs.total_logical_reads + qs.total_logical_writes) /
      qs.execution_count as [Avg IO]
  ,qs.total_logical_reads
  ,qs.total_logical_writes
  ,qs.total_worker_time
  ,qs.total_worker_time / qs.execution_count /
      1000 as [Avg Worker Time (ms)]
  ,qs.total_rows
  ,qs.creation_time
  ,qs.last_execution_time
from
  CachedData cd
    outer apply
```

```
  (
    select
      sum(qs.execution_count) as execution_count
      ,sum(qs.total_logical_reads) as total_logical_reads
      ,sum(qs.total_logical_writes) as total_logical_writes
      ,sum(qs.total_worker_time) as total_worker_time
      ,sum(qs.total_rows) as total_rows
      ,min(qs.creation_time) as creation_time
      ,max(qs.last_execution_time) as last_execution_time
    from sys.dm_exec_query_stats qs with (nolock)
    where qs.plan_handle = cd.plan_handle
  ) qs
option (recompile, maxdop 1)
```

Both the sys.dm_db_index_usage_stats and the sys.dm_db_index_operational_ stats views provide the information, which is very useful during performance troubleshooting. The data, however, may be incomplete. The views do not include usage statistics from those queries that run on readable secondaries in Availability Groups. Nor does SQL Server persist the data in the database to survive SQL Server restart. Finally, in SQL Server 2012 RTM-SP3 CU2, SQL Server 2014 RTM and SP1, the views clear at the time of index rebuild operations.

Use the data with care and correlate results with other venues during analysis.

---

**Note**    You can get more information about the sys.dm_db_index_ usage_stats view at https://docs.microsoft.com/en-us/sql/ relational-databases/system-dynamic-management-views/sys-dm-db-index-usage-stats-transact-sql. Information about the sys.dm_db_ index_operational_stats view is available at https://docs.microsoft. com/en-us/sql/relational-databases/system-dynamic-management-views/sys-dm-db-index-operational-stats-transact-sql.

---

# Blocking Chains

One of the common challenges experienced during the troubleshooting of concurrency issues is that of *blocking chains*, which represent a case of multi-level blocking. As you remember, a lock request can be granted only when it is compatible with all other requests on the resource, regardless of whether they are in a granted or pending state.

Figure 12-7 illustrates this situation. Session 1 holds an intent exclusive (IX) lock on the table, which is incompatible with the schema modification (Sch-M) lock requested by session 2. The schema modification (Sch-M) lock is incompatible with all lock types and thus blocks all other sessions trying to access the table, even when their lock requests are compatible with the intent exclusive (IX) lock held by session 1.

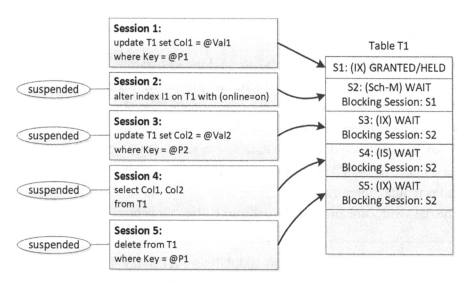

***Figure 12-7.*** *Blocking chain*

When this condition occurs, session 2 may become the *blocking session* for a large number of other sessions in the system. It will be exposed as the *blocker* in data management views and in the blocked process report. Session 1, on the other hand, would become the blocking session only for session 2, which may be misleading during troubleshooting.

Let's illustrate this with a slightly more complicated example in code. Listing 12-6 updates one row from the Delivery.Customers table in the session with SPID=53.

***Listing 12-6.*** Blocking chain: Step 1 (SPID=53)

```
begin tran
    update Delivery.Customers
    set Phone = '111-111-1234'
    where CustomerId = 1;
```

As the next step, let's run the code from Listing 12-7 in the session with SPID=56. The first statement acquires an intent exclusive (IX) lock on the Delivery.Orders table. The second statement scans the Delivery.Customers table and is blocked due to an incompatible exclusive (X) lock from the first session with SPID=53.

***Listing 12-7.*** Blocking chain: Step 2 (SPID=56)

```
begin tran
    update Delivery.Orders
    set Pieces += 1
    where OrderId = 1;

    select count(*)
    from Delivery.Customers with (readcommitted);
```

Next, we will run the code from Listing 12-8 in the session with SPID=57. This code is trying to acquire a shared (S) lock on the Delivery.Orders table and will be blocked by the incompatible intent exclusive (IX) lock held by the session with SPID=56.

***Listing 12-8.*** Blocking chain: Step 3 (SPID=57)

```
select count(*)
from Delivery.Orders with (tablock);
```

Finally, let's run the code from Listing 12-9 in several sessions with SPID=60 and above (you may use a different OrderId in each session). Those sessions will need to acquire intent exclusive (IX) locks on the Delivery.Orders table and will be blocked due to the incompatible shared (S) lock request held by the session with SPID=57.

***Listing 12-9.*** Blocking chain: Step 4 (SPID>=60)

```
update Delivery.Orders
set Pieces += 1
where OrderId = 5000;
```

Figure 12-8 demonstrates the partial output of the `sys.dm_os_waiting_tasks` and `sys.dm_exec_requests` DMVs. It may appear that the session with `SPID=57` is the source of the blocking. This is incorrect, however, and you need to unwind the blocking chain up to the session with `SPID=53` during troubleshooting.

| | session_id | blocking_session_id | wait_type | resource_description |
|---|---|---|---|---|
| 1 | 56 | 53 | LCK_M_S | rldlock fileid=3 pageid=24 dbid=5 id=lo... |
| 2 | 57 | 56 | LCK_M_S | objectlock lockPartition=0 objid=5655... |
| 3 | 60 | 57 | LCK_M_IX | objectlock lockPartition=0 objid=5655... |
| 4 | 61 | 57 | LCK_M_IX | objectlock lockPartition=0 objid=5655... |
| 5 | 62 | 57 | LCK_M_IX | objectlock lockPartition=0 objid=5655... |
| 6 | 63 | 57 | LCK_M_IX | objectlock lockPartition=0 objid=5655... |

| | session_id | status | blocking_session_id | wait_type | wait_resource |
|---|---|---|---|---|---|
| 1 | 56 | suspended | 53 | LCK_M_S | RID: 5:3:24:0 |
| 2 | 57 | suspended | 56 | LCK_M_S | OBJECT: 5:565577053:0 |
| 3 | 60 | suspended | 57 | LCK_M_IX | OBJECT: 5:565577053:0 |
| 4 | 61 | suspended | 57 | LCK_M_IX | OBJECT: 5:565577053:0 |
| 5 | 62 | suspended | 57 | LCK_M_IX | OBJECT: 5:565577053:0 |
| 6 | 63 | suspended | 57 | LCK_M_IX | OBJECT: 5:565577053:0 |

***Figure 12-8.*** *Output of sys.dm_os_waiting_tasks and sys.dm_exec_requests views*

It is also worth noting that the root blocker with `SPID=53` is not present in the output. The `sys.dm_os_waiting_tasks` and `sys.dm_exec_requests` views show currently suspended and executed requests, respectively. In our case, the session with `SPID=53` is in the *sleeping* state, and therefore neither of the views includes it.

Figure 12-9 shows the partial output of the blocked process reports for sessions with an `SPID` of 60, 57, or 56. You can detect the blocking chain condition by the `suspended` status of the blocking process with a locking-related `waitresource`.

```
<!-- Blocked Process Report for SPID=60 -->
<blocked-process-report>
    <blocked-process>
        <process id="processdfe65a7c28" waitresource="OBJECT: 5:565577053:0" spid="60" lockMode="IX" />
    </blocked-process>
    <blocking-process>
        <process status="suspended" waitresource="OBJECT: 5:565577053:0 " spid="57" />
    </blocking-process>
</blocked-process-report>

<!-- Blocked Process Report for SPID=57 -->
<blocked-process-report>
    <blocked-process>
        <process id="processdfe9b164e8" waitresource="OBJECT: 5:565577053:0" spid="57" lockMode="S" />
    </blocked-process>
    <blocking-process>
        <process status="suspended" waitresource="RID: 5:3:24:0" spid="56" />
    </blocking-process>
</blocked-process-report>

<!-- Blocked Process Report for SPID=56 -->
<blocked-process-report>
    <blocked-process>
        <process id="processdfe65a7848" waitresource="RID: 5:3:24:0" spid="56" lockMode="S" />
    </blocked-process>
    <blocking-process>
        <process status="sleeping" spid="53"   >
            <inputbuf>
                begin tran
                    update Delivery.Customers
                    set Phone = '111-111-1234'
                    where CustomerId = 1;
            </inputbuf>
        </process>
    </blocking-process>
</blocked-process-report>
```

***Figure 12-9.*** *Blocked process reports*

Even though blocking chains may add additional complexity, they do not change your troubleshooting approach. You need to unwind the blocking chain to identify the root cause of the blocking and address the issue.

# AlwaysOn Availability Groups and Blocking

AlwaysOn Availability Groups have perhaps become the most common High Availability technology used with SQL Server. This technology provides database group–level protection and stores a separate copy of the databases on each server/node. This eliminates the single point of failure on the SQL Server level; however, there is still a dependency on Windows or Linux Failover Clustering internally.

The implementation and maintenance of AlwaysOn Availability Groups are worth a separate book. There are, however, a couple of things that may affect blocking and concurrency in the system.

# Synchronous Commit Latency

AlwaysOn Availability Groups consist of one *primary* and one or more *secondary* nodes/ servers. All data modifications are done on the primary node, which sends a stream of transactional log records to the secondaries. Those log records are saved (*hardened*) in transaction logs on the secondary nodes and asynchronously reapplied to the data files there by a set of *REDO threads*. Assuming there is no latency, each server in the Availability Group would store exact byte-to-byte copies of the databases.

The secondary nodes may be configured using *asynchronous* or *synchronous commit*. With asynchronous commit, a transaction is considered to be committed when the COMMIT log record is hardened on the primary node. SQL Server then sends the COMMIT record to a secondary node; however, it does not wait for confirmation that the record has been hardened in the log there. This process is shown in Figure 12-10.

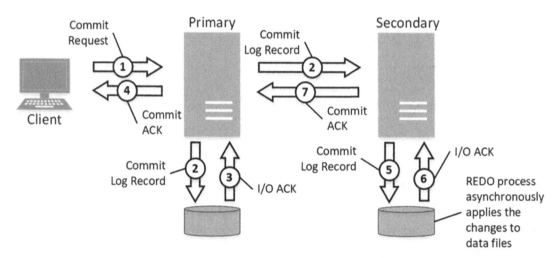

***Figure 12-10.*** *Asynchonous commit*

As you can guess, this behavior will reduce the overhead introduced by Availability Groups at the cost of possible data loss in the event of a primary node crash/data corruption before some of the log records have been sent to the secondaries.

This behavior changes when you use synchronous commit, as shown in Figure 12-11. In this mode, SQL Server does not consider a transaction to be committed until it receives the confirmation that the COMMIT log record is hardened in the log on the secondary node. While this approach allows you to avoid data loss, it would lead to additional commit latency while the primary node is waiting for acknowledgement from the secondary server(s).

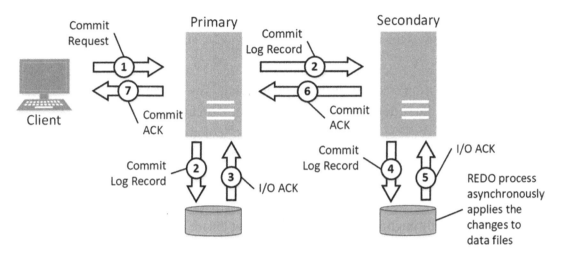

***Figure 12-11.*** *Synchonous commit*

The high synchronous commit latency may introduce subtle and hard to understand concurrency issues in the system. SQL Server keeps the transaction active and does not release the locks until commit acknowledgements are received. This would increase the chance of competing lock requests and blocking in the system.

There is another potential problem. Some operations—for example, index maintenance—may generate an enormous number of transaction log records and saturate the send queue. This may lead to extremely high commit latency and introduce severe blocking in the system.

---

**Tip**   You can throttle the log-generation rate of index maintenance operations by reducing the MAXDOP option for the statement. Remember that this will increase the time the operation will take.

---

You can monitor synchronous commit latency with the HADR_SYNC_COMMIT wait. The average wait time from the sys.dm_os_wait_stats view would provide you with latency information. Remember that latency may seriously deviate during atypical, log-intensive workloads; consider clearing wait statistics with the DBCC SQLPERF('sys.dm_os_wait_ stats', CLEAR) command when you troubleshoot the latency at a particular time.

High commit latency troubleshooting requires you to locate the bottleneck and identify what consumes the most time during the process. There are three main factors that contribute to it:

1. The time a log record waits in the send queue. You can analyze this with the code in Listing 12-10 using the data from the [Send Queue Size(KB)] and [Send Rate KB/Sec] columns. It is worth noting that the queue management process is CPU intensive, which may lead to additional latency in systems with high CPU load.

2. Network throughput. You can troubleshoot it with network-related performance counters. There are also several Availability Group–related performance counters that indicate the amount of data sent between the nodes.

3. I/O latency on secondary nodes. Synchronous commit requires a COMMIT log record to be hardened in the transaction log before acknowledgement is sent back to the primary node. You can monitor the write latency of transaction log files using the sys. dm_io_virtual_file_stats view. I am including the script that allows you to do this in the companion materials for this book.

*Listing 12-10.* Analyze Availability Group queues

```
select
    ag.name as [Availability Group]
    ,ar.replica_server_name as [Server]
    ,db_name(drs.database_id) as [Database]
    ,case when ars.is_local = 1 then 'Local' else 'Remote' end
    ,case as [DB Location]
    ,ars.role_desc as [Replica Role]
    ,drs.synchronization_state_desc as [Sync State]
    ,ars.synchronization_health_desc as [Health State]
    ,drs.log_send_queue_size as [Send Queue Size (KB)]
    ,drs.log_send_rate as [Send Rate KB/Sec]
    ,drs.redo_queue_size as [Redo Queue Size (KB)]
    ,drs.redo_rate as [Redo Rate KB/Sec]
```

```
from
    sys.availability_groups ag with (nolock)
        join sys.availability_replicas ar  with (nolock) on
            ag.group_id = ar.group_id
        join sys.dm_hadr_availability_replica_states ars  with (nolock) on
            ar.replica_id = ars.replica_id
        join sys.dm_hadr_database_replica_states drs  with (nolock) on
            ag.group_id = drs.group_id and drs.replica_id = ars.replica_id
order by
    ag.name, drs.database_id, ar.replica_server_name
```

While network and I/O performance may sometimes be addressed by hardware upgrades, it is much harder to deal with the latency introduced by a large number of log records in very busy OLTP systems. You can reduce the impact of queue management by utilizing CPUs with higher clock speed; however, there are some limits on what you can achieve with hardware.

There are several things you can do when you experience this situation:

- Make sure that SQL Server schedulers are evenly balanced across NUMA nodes. For example, if SQL Server is using 10 cores on a 2-NUMA-node server with 8 cores per node, set the affinity mask to use 5 cores per node. Unevenly balanced schedules may introduce various performance issues in the system and affect Availability Group throughput.

- Reduce the number of log records generated in the system. Some options are to redesign the transaction strategy to avoid autocommitted transactions; remove unused and redundant indexes; and fine-tune the index FILLFACTOR property to reduce the page splits in the system.

- Rearchitect data tier in the system. It is very common that different data in the system may have different RPO (*recovery point objective*) requirements and tolerances to the data loss. You may consider moving some data to another Availability Group that does not require synchronous commit and/or utilize NoSQL technologies for some entities.

Finally, if you are using SQL Server prior to 2016, you should consider upgrading to the latest version of the product. SQL Server 2016 has several internal optimizations that dramatically increase Availability Group throughput over that of SQL Server 2012 and 2014. It may be the simplest solution in many cases.

---

**Note**  You may experience the same commit latency problems with synchronous database mirroring. You should monitor the DBMIRROR_SEND wait type in this case.

---

# Readable Secondaries and Row Versioning

The Enterprise Edition of SQL Server allows you to configure read-only access to the secondary nodes in AlwaysOn Availability Groups, thus scaling the read-only workload in the system. This, however, may lead to unexpected side effects on the primary node in the group.

When you run queries against secondary nodes, SQL Server always uses the SNAPSHOT isolation level, ignoring the SET TRANSACTION ISOLATION LEVEL statement and locking hints. It allows it to eliminate possible readers/writers blocking, and it happens even if you did not enable the ALLOW_SNAPSHOT_ISOLATION database option.

It also means that SQL Server will use row versioning on the primary node. You may not be able to use optimistic isolation levels *programmatically* when they are not enabled; nevertheless, SQL Server would use row versioning internally. The databases on the primary and secondary nodes are exactly the same, and it is impossible to use row versioning only on the secondary nodes.

As you will remember from Chapter 6, this behavior will introduce additional tempdb load to support the version store. It may also increase index fragmentation due to the 14-byte pointers appended to the data rows during data modifications. However, it also leads to another phenomenon. Long-running SNAPSHOT transactions on *secondary* nodes may defer ghost and version-store cleanup on the *primary* node. SQL Server cannot remove deleted rows and reuse the space, because of the possibility that a SNAPSHOT transaction on the secondary node will need to access the old versions of the rows.

Let's look at an example and create two tables in the database, as shown in Listing 12-11. The table dbo.T1 will have 65,536 rows and will use 65,536 pages—one row per data page.

***Listing 12-11.*** Readable secondaries: Tables creation

```
create table dbo.T1
(
    ID int not null,
    Placeholder char(8000) null,

    constraint PK_T1
    primary key clustered(ID)
);

create table dbo.T2
(
    Col int
);

;with N1(C) as (select 0 union all select 0) -- 2 rows
,N2(C) as (select 0 from N1 as T1 cross join N1 as T2) -- 4 rows
,N3(C) as (select 0 from N2 as T1 cross join N2 as T2) -- 16 rows
,N4(C) as (select 0 from N3 as T1 cross join N3 as T2) -- 256 rows
,N5(C) as (select 0 from N4 as T1 cross join N4 as T2 ) -- 65,536 rows
,IDs(ID) as (select row_number() over (order by (select null)) from N5)
insert into dbo.T1(ID)
    select ID from IDs;
```

As the next step, let's start a transaction on the *secondary* node and run the query against the dbo.T2 table, as shown in Listing 12-12. Even though we are using explicit transactions, the same behavior will occur with long-running statements in autocommitted transactions.

***Listing 12-12.*** Readable secondaries: Starting transaction on secondary node

```
begin tran
    select * from dbo.T2;
```

Next, let's delete all data from the dbo.T1 table and then run a query that will do a *Clustered Index Scan* on the primary node. The code is shown in Listing 12-13.

***Listing 12-13.*** Readable secondaries: Deleting data and performing CI Scan

```
delete from dbo.T1;
go

-- Waiting 1 minute
waitfor delay '00:01:00.000';

set statistics io on
select count(*) from dbo.T1;
set statistics io off
```

**--Output: Table 'T1'. Scan count 1, logical reads 65781**

As you can see, despite the fact that the table is empty, the data pages have not been deallocated. This leads to significant I/O overhead on the primary node.

Finally, let's look at the index statistics using the code from Listing 12-14.

***Listing 12-14.*** Readable secondaries: Analyzing index statistics

```
select index_id, index_level, page_count, record_count, version_ghost_
record_count
from sys.dm_db_index_physical_stats(db_id(),object_id(N'dbo.
T1'),1,NULL,'DETAILED');
```

Figure 12-12 shows the output of the query. As you can see, the leaf index level shows 65,536 rows in the version_ghost_record_count column. This column contains the number of ghosted rows that cannot be removed due to the active transactions in the system that rely on row versioning. In our case, this transaction runs on a different (secondary) node.

| | index_id | index_level | page_count | record_count | version_ghost_record_count |
|---|---|---|---|---|---|
| 1 | 1 | 0 | 65536 | 0 | 65536 |
| 2 | 1 | 1 | 243 | 65536 | 0 |
| 3 | 1 | 2 | 1 | 243 | 0 |

***Figure 12-12.*** *Index statistics*

There is nothing special about this behavior. The ghost and version store cleanup tasks would behave the same way if SNAPSHOT transactions were running on the primary node. It is very common, however, to see systems in which people offload non-optimized reporting queries to secondary nodes without understanding the potential impact it may have on the primary node.

Remember this behavior when you plan to use readable secondaries, and apply the same considerations as when you enable optimistic isolation levels in the system. On the flip side, there is absolutely no reason to avoid using optimistic isolation levels when you have readable secondaries enabled. SQL Server already uses row versioning internally, even if you do not enable it in the database.

# Working with the Blocking Monitoring Framework

Wait statistics analysis provides a holistic picture of system health and may help to identify bottlenecks in all areas of the system, including locking and blocking. You may be able to evaluate how badly a system suffers from concurrency issues; however, in the end, you will need to detect and address individual blocking and deadlock cases to solve the problems.

As we have already discussed in Chapters 4 and 5 of this book, troubleshooting is relatively straightforward. You need to understand the root cause of the issue by reverse engineering the blocking or deadlock condition. You need to identify the resources, lock types, and processes involved and analyze why the processes acquired, held, and competed for locks on the same resources. In the majority of cases, it requires you to analyze the queries and their execution plans.

Both blocked process reports and deadlock graphs contain required information. They, however, have dependencies on the SQL Server state at the time of the event. In many cases, you need to query the plan cache and other data management views to obtain the text and plan of the queries. The longer you wait, the less likely it will be that the information will be available.

There are plenty of monitoring tools present on the market, and many of them will capture and provide you the data. As another option, you can install the Blocking Monitoring Framework, which I have already mentioned in this book. This framework use Event Notifications, and it parses the blocking process report and deadlock graph, persisting the data in a set of tables. The parsing happens at the time the event occurred, while the information is still available through data management views.

At the time of writing this book, the framework consists of three main tables:

- The dbo.BlockedProcessesInfo table stores information about blocking occurrences based on blocked process reports. It includes duration of the blocking, resources and lock types involved, and blocking and blocked sessions details, along with queries and their execution plans.

- The dbo.Deadlocks table stores information about deadlock events in the system.

- The dbo.DeadlockProcesses table provides information about the processes involved in the deadlock, including text and execution plans of the statements that triggered it.

You can use the captured data to troubleshoot individual blocking occurrences. Moreover, you can aggregate it to identify the queries most commonly involved in blocking or deadlock cases.

Listing 12-15 shows code that returns ten queries that have been blocked the most in the last three days. It groups the data by plan_hash, which combines queries with *similar* execution plans. Consider ad-hoc queries that have different parameter values but end up with similar execution plans, as in the example.

The code returns the first query and execution plan that matches the plan_hash value, along with blocking statistics. Alternatively, in SQL Server 2016 and above, you can join the data with Query Store data management views to correlate information from multiple sources.

---

**Note**   You can use the dbo.DeadlockProcesses table instead of the dbo.BlockedProcessesInfo table to obtain information about queries most frequently involved in deadlocks.

---

***Listing 12-15.*** Getting top 10 queries that were blocked the most

```
;with Data
as
(
    select top 10
        i.BlockedPlanHash
        ,count(*) as [Blocking Counts]
        ,sum(WaitTime) as [Total Wait Time (ms)]
    from
        dbo.BlockedProcessesInfo i
    group by
        i.BlockedPlanHash
    order by
        sum(WaitTime) desc
)
select
    d.*, q.BlockedSql
from
    Data d
        cross apply
        (
            select top 1 BlockedSql
            from dbo.BlockedProcessesInfo i2
            where i2.BlockedPlanHash = d.BlockedPlanHash
            order by EventDate desc
        ) q;
```

Listing 12-16 shows code that returns a list of tables most frequently involved in blocking resulting from waiting for object-level intent (I*) locks. This blocking may occur due to lock escalation, and you may benefit from disabling it on affected tables.

Do not forget that schema modification (Sch-M) locks will also block all other object-level lock requests—factor it into your analysis.

***Listing 12-16.*** Identifying the tables that may suffer from lock escalation–related blocking

```
;with Objects(DBID,ObjID,WaitTime)
as
(
    select
        ltrim(rtrim(substring(b.Resource,8,o.DBSeparator - 8)))
        ,substring(b.Resource, o.DBSeparator + 1, o.ObjectLen)
        ,b.WaitTime
    from
        dbo.BlockedProcessesInfo b
            cross apply
            (
                select
                    charindex(':',Resource,8) as DBSeparator
                    ,charindex(':',Resource, charindex(':',Resource,8) + 1) -
                            charindex(':',Resource,8) - 1 as ObjectLen
            ) o
    where
        left(b.Resource,6) = 'OBJECT' and
        left(b.BlockedLockMode,1) = 'I'
)
select
    db_name(DBID) as [database]
    ,object_name(ObjID, DBID) as [table]
    ,count(*) as [# of events]
    ,sum(WaitTime) / 1000 as [Wait Time(Sec)]
from Objects
group by
    db_name(DBID), object_name(ObjID, DBID);
```

The Blocking Monitoring Framework is an extremely useful tool for the analysis and troubleshooting of concurrency issues. I would recommend installing it on your servers.

**Note**   The current (August 2018) version of the framework is included in the companion materials for this book. You can download the latest version from my blog: `http://aboutsqlserver.com/bmframework/`.

# Summary

Databases do not live in a vacuum. They are part of a large ecosystem that includes various hardware and software components. Slowness and unresponsiveness of client applications are not necessarily database- or SQL Server–related issues. The root cause of the problem can be found anywhere in the system, from hardware misconfiguration to incorrect application code.

It is important to check the entire system infrastructure as an initial step in the troubleshooting process. This includes the performance characteristics of the hardware, network topology and throughput, operating system and SQL Server configuration, and the processes and databases running on the server.

SQL Server consists of several major components, including the protocol layer, query processor, storage engine, utilities, and SQL Server Operating System (SQLOS). SQLOS is the layer between the OS and all other SQL Server components, and it is responsible for scheduling, resource management, and several other low-level tasks.

SQLOS creates a number of schedulers equal to the number of logical processors in the system. Every scheduler is responsible for managing a set of workers that perform a job. Every task is assigned to one or more workers for the duration of the execution.

Tasks stay in one of three major states during execution: RUNNING (currently executing on scheduler), RUNNABLE (waiting for scheduler to execute), and SUSPENDED (waiting for the resource). SQL Server tracks the cumulative waiting time for the different types of waits and exposes this information to the users. Wait statistics analysis is a common performance troubleshooting technique that analyzes top system wait types and eliminates the root causes of waits.

Every lock type has a corresponding wait type, which helps you to identify what type of blocking happens the most in the system. Nevertheless, you need to analyze individual blocking and deadlock cases, understand the root causes of the events, and address them during troubleshooting.

# CHAPTER 13

# In-Memory OLTP Concurrency Model

The In-Memory OLTP technology, introduced in SQL Server 2014, can significantly improve the performance and throughput of OLTP systems. The key technology component—memory-optimized tables—stores the data in-memory, utilizing lock- and latch-free multi-versioning concurrency control.

This chapter will provide an overview of the In-Memory OLTP Concurrency Model and explain how the Engine handles transactions internally.

## In-Memory OLTP Overview

Way back when SQL Server and other major databases were originally designed, hardware was very expensive. Servers at that time had just one or very few CPUs and a small amount of installed memory. Database servers had to work with data that resided on disk, loading it into memory on demand.

The situation has changed dramatically since then. During the last 30 years, memory prices have dropped by a factor of ten every five years, and hardware has become more affordable. While it is also true that databases have become larger, it is often possible for *active* operational data to fit into memory.

Obviously, it is beneficial to have data cached in the buffer pool. It reduces the load on the I/O subsystem and improves system performance. However, when systems work under a heavy concurrent load, it is often not enough to obtain required throughput. SQL Server manages and protects page structures in memory, which introduces large overhead and does not scale well. Even with row-level locking, multiple sessions cannot modify data on the same data page simultaneously; they must wait for each other.

269

D. Korotkevitch, *Expert SQL Server Transactions and Locking*, https://doi.org/10.1007/978-1-4842-3957-5_13

Perhaps the last sentence needs to be clarified. Obviously, multiple sessions can modify data rows on the same data page, holding exclusive (X) locks on different rows simultaneously. However, they cannot update *physical* data-page and row objects simultaneously because it could corrupt the in-memory page structure. SQL Server addresses this problem by protecting pages with *latches*. Latches work in a similar manner to locks, protecting internal SQL Server data structures on the physical level by serializing write access to them so only one thread can update data on the data page in memory at any given point in time.

In the end, this limits the improvements that can be achieved with the current database engine's architecture. Although you can scale hardware by adding more CPUs and cores, that serialization quickly becomes a bottleneck and a limiting factor in improving system scalability.

---

**Note**   You can monitor PAGELATCH* waits for the resources in users' databases to understand the impact of latch contention in the system.

---

The In-Memory OLTP Engine, introduced in SQL Server 2014, addresses that issue. The core component of the Engine—memory-optimized tables—stores and manages all data completely in-memory, persisting it on disk only for durability purposes. The data rows are, in a nutshell, individual in-memory objects. They are not stored on the data pages; the rows are linked together through chains of memory pointers—one chain per index. It is also worth noting that memory-optimized tables do not share memory with disk-based tables and live outside of the buffer pool.

Let's illustrate this with an example and create a memory-optimized table, as shown in Listing 13-1.

---

**Note**   This technology requires you to create another filegroup in the database to store In-Memory OLTP data. The database-creation script is included in the companion material for this book.

---

***Listing 13-1.*** Creating the memory-optimized table

```
create table dbo.People
(
    Name varchar(64) not null
        constraint PK_People
        primary key nonclustered
        hash with (bucket_count = 1024),
    City varchar(64) not null,

    index IDX_City nonclustered hash(City)
    with (bucket_count = 1024),
)
with (memory_optimized = on, durability = schema_and_data);
```

This table has two hash indexes defined on the Name and City columns. Hash indexes are the new type of index supported by In-Memory OLTP. We are not going to discuss them in depth in this book, but as a general overview, they consist of a hash table (an array of hash buckets, each of which contains a memory pointer to the data row). SQL Server applies a hash function to the index-key columns, and the result of the function determines to which bucket a row belongs. All rows that have the same hash value and belong to the same bucket are linked together in a row chain; every row has a pointer to the next row in the chain.

---

**Note**    It is extremely important to properly size a hash table in the hash index. You should define bucket_count to be about 1.5–2 times bigger than the number of unique key values in the index.

In-Memory OLTP also supports nonclustered indexes, which have a relatively similar structure to B-Tree indexes in disk-based tables. They are a good choice when index selectivity cannot be estimated.

---

Figure 13-1 illustrates this. Solid arrows represent pointers in the index on the Name column. Dotted arrows represent pointers in the index on the City column. For simplicity's sake, let's assume that the hash function generates a hash value based on the first letter of the string. Two numbers, displayed in each row, indicate row lifetime, which I will explain shortly.

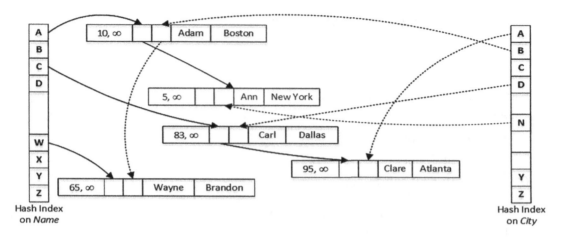

***Figure 13-1.*** *Memory-optimized table with two hash indexes*

# Multi-Version Concurrency Control

As I just mentioned, every row in a memory-optimized table has two values, called BeginTs and EndTs, which define the lifetime of the row. A SQL Server instance maintains the *Global Transaction Timestamp* value, which is auto-incremented when the transaction commits and is unique for every committed transaction. BeginTs stores the Global Transaction Timestamp of transactions that insert a row, and EndTs stores the timestamp of transactions that delete a row. A special value called Infinity is used as the EndTs for rows that have not been deleted.

The rows in memory-optimized tables are never updated. The update operation creates a new version of the row, with a new Global Transaction Timestamp set as BeginTs, and marks the old version of the row as deleted by populating the EndTs timestamp with the same value.

At the time when a new transaction starts, In-Memory OLTP assigns the *logical start time* for the transaction, which represents the Global Transaction Timestamp value at the time when the transaction starts. It dictates what version of the rows is visible to the transaction. A transaction can see a row only when its logical start time (Global Transaction Timestamp value at time when the transaction starts) is between the BeginTs and EndTs timestamps of the row.

To illustrate that, let's assume that we ran the statement shown in Listing 13-2 and committed the transaction when the Global Transaction Timestamp value was 100.

***Listing 13-2.*** Updating data in the dbo.People table

```
update dbo.People
set City = 'Cincinnati'
where Name = 'Ann'
```

Figure 13-2 illustrates the data in the table after this update transaction has been committed. As you can see, we now have two rows with Name='Ann' and different lifetimes. The new row has been appended to the row chain referenced by the hash bucket for the value of A in the index on the Name column. The hash index on the City column did not have any rows referenced by the C bucket; therefore, the new row becomes the first in the row chain referenced from that bucket.

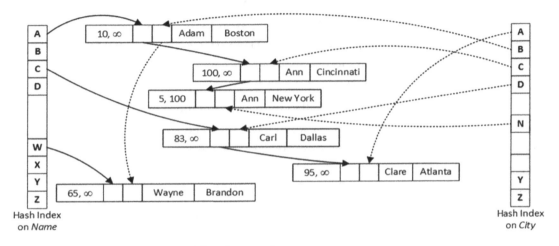

***Figure 13-2.*** *Data in the table after update*

Let's assume that you need to run a query that selects all rows with Name='Ann' in the transaction with the logical start time (Global Transaction Timestamp at time when transaction started) of 110. SQL Server calculates the hash value for Ann, which is A, and finds the corresponding bucket in the hash index on the Name column. It follows the pointer from that bucket, which references a row with Name='Adam'. This row has a BeginTs of 10 and an EndTs of Infinity; therefore, it is visible to the transaction. However, the Name value does not match the predicate, and the row is ignored.

In the next step, SQL Server follows the pointer from the Adam index pointer array, which references the first Ann row. This row has a BeginTs of 100 and an EndTs of Infinity; therefore, it is visible to the transaction and needs to be selected.

As a final step, SQL Server follows the next pointer in the index. Even though the last row also has Name='Ann', it has an EndTs of 100 and is invisible to the transaction.

SQL Server keeps track of the active transactions in the system and detects stale rows with an EndTs timestamp older than the logical start time of the *oldest active transaction* in the system. Stale rows are invisible for active transactions in the system, and eventually they are removed from the index row chains and deallocated by the *garbage collection* process.

As you should have already noticed, this concurrency behavior and data consistency corresponds to the SNAPSHOT transaction isolation level when every transaction *sees* the data as of the time the transaction started. SNAPSHOT is the default transaction isolation level in the In-Memory OLTP Engine, which also supports the REPEATABLE READ and SERIALIZABLE isolation levels. However, REPEATABLE READ and SERIALIZABLE transactions in the In-Memory OLTP behave differently than they do with disk-based tables. In-Memory OLTP raises an exception and rolls back a transaction if REPEATABLE READ or SERIALIZABLE data-consistency rules were violated rather than blocking a transaction, as with disk-based tables.

In-Memory OLTP documentation also indicates that autocommitted (single statement) transactions can run in the READ COMMITTED isolation level. However, this is a bit misleading. SQL Server promotes and executes such transactions in the SNAPSHOT isolation level and does not require you to explicitly specify the isolation level in your code. Similar to SNAPSHOT transactions, the autocommitted READ COMMITTED transaction would not see the changes committed after the transaction started, which is a different behavior compared to READ COMMITTED transactions performed against disk-based tables.

Let's look at transaction isolation levels and the In-Memory OLTP Concurrency Model in more detail.

# Transaction Isolation Levels in In-Memory OLTP

In-Memory OLTP supports three transaction isolation levels: SNAPSHOT, REPEATABLE READ, and SERIALIZABLE. However, In-Memory OLTP uses a completely different approach to enforcing data-consistency rules as compared to disk-based tables. Rather than block or be blocked by other sessions, In-Memory OLTP validates data consistency at the transaction COMMIT time and throws an exception and rolls back the transaction if rules were violated:

- In the SNAPSHOT isolation level, any changes made by other sessions are invisible to the transaction. A SNAPSHOT transaction always works with a snapshot of the data as of the time when the transaction started. The only validation at the time of commit is checking for primary-key violations, which is called *snapshot validation*.

- In the REPEATABLE READ isolation level, In-Memory OLTP validates that the rows that were read by the transaction have not been modified or deleted by other transactions. A REPEATABLE READ transaction would not be able to commit if this was the case. That action is called *repeatable read validation* and is executed in addition to snapshot validation.

- In the SERIALIZABLE isolation level, SQL Server performs repeatable read validation and also checks for phantom rows that were possibly inserted by other sessions. This process is called *serializable validation* and is executed in addition to snapshot validation.

Let's look at a few examples that demonstrate this behavior. As a first step, shown in Listing 13-3, let's create a memory-optimized table and insert a few rows. We will run that script, resetting the data to its original state before each test.

***Listing 13-3.*** Data consistency and transaction isolation levels: Table creation

```
drop table if exists dbo.HKData;

create table dbo.HKData
(
    ID int not null
        constraint PK_HKData
        primary key nonclustered hash with (bucket_count=64),
    Col int not null
)
with (memory_optimized=on, durability=schema_only);

insert into dbo.HKData(ID, Col) values(1,1),(2,2),(3,3),(4,4),(5,5);
```

Table 13-1 shows how concurrency works in the REPEATABLE READ transaction isolation level. It is important to note that SQL Server starts a transaction at the moment of the first data access rather than at the time of the BEGIN TRAN statement. Therefore, the session 1 transaction starts at the time when the first SELECT operator executes.

***Table 13-1.*** *Concurrency in the* REPEATABLE READ *Transaction Isolation Level*

| Session 1 | Session 2 | Results |
|---|---|---|
| begin tran<br>  select ID, Col<br>  from dbo.HKData<br>    with (repeatableread) | | |
| | update dbo.HKData<br>set Col = -2<br>where ID = 2 | |
| select ID, Col<br>from dbo.HKData<br>  with (repeatableread) | | Return old version of a row<br>(Col = 2) |
| commit | | Msg 41305, Level 16, State 0,<br>Line 0<br>The current transaction failed<br>to commit due to a repeatable<br>read validation failure. |
| begin tran<br>  select ID, Col<br>  from dbo.HKData<br>    with (repeatableread) | | |
| | insert into dbo.HKData<br>values(10,10) | |
| select ID, Col<br>from dbo.HKData<br>  with (repeatableread) | | Does not return new row<br>(10,10) |
| commit | | Success |

As you can see, with memory-optimized tables, other sessions were able to modify data that was read by the active REPEATABLE READ transaction. This led to a transaction abort at the time of COMMIT when the repeatable read validation failed. This is a completely different behavior than that of disk-based tables, where other sessions are blocked, unable to modify data until the REPEATABLE READ transaction successfully commits.

It is also worth noting that in the case of memory-optimized tables, the REPEATABLE READ isolation level protects you from the *phantom read* phenomenon, which is not the case with disk-based tables. The BeginTs value of the newly inserted rows would exceed the logical start time of the active transaction (more on it later), making them invisible for the transaction.

As a next step, let's repeat these tests in the SERIALIZABLE isolation level. You can see the code and the results of the execution in Table 13-2. Remember to rerun the initialization script from Listing 13-3 before the test.

***Table 13-2.*** *Concurrency in the* SERIALIZABLE *Transaction Isolation Level*

| Session 1 | Session 2 | Results |
|---|---|---|
| begin tran<br>  select ID, Col<br>  from dbo.HKData<br>    with (serializable) | | |
| | update dbo.HKData<br>set Col = -2<br>where ID = 2 | |
|   select ID, Col<br>  from dbo.HKData<br>    with (serializable) | | Return old version of a row<br>(Col = 2) |
| commit | | Msg 41305, Level 16, State 0,<br>Line 0<br>The current transaction failed<br>to commit due to a repeatable<br>read validation failure. |

*(continued)*

***Table 13-2.*** *(continued)*

| Session 1 | Session 2 | Results |
|-----------|-----------|---------|
| begin tran<br>  select ID, Col<br>  from dbo.HKData<br>   with (serializable) | | |
| | insert into dbo.HKData<br>values(10,10) | |
|   select ID, Col<br>  from dbo.HKData<br>   with (serializable) | | Does not return new row<br>(10,10) |
| commit | | Msg 41325, Level 16, State 0,<br>Line 0<br>The current transaction failed<br>to commit due to a serializable<br>validation failure. |

As you can see, the SERIALIZABLE isolation level prevents the session from committing a transaction when another session inserts a new row and violates the serializable validation. Like the REPEATABLE READ isolation level, this behavior is different from that of disk-based tables, where the SERIALIZABLE transaction successfully blocks other sessions until the transaction is complete.

Finally, let's repeat the tests in the SNAPSHOT isolation level. The code and results are shown in Table 13-3.

***Table 13-3.*** *Concurrency in the* SNAPSHOT *Transaction Isolation Level*

| Session 1 | Session 2 | Results |
| --- | --- | --- |
| begin tran<br>  select ID, Col<br>  from dbo.HKData<br>    with (snapshot) | | |
| | update dbo.HKData<br>set Col = -2<br>where ID = 2 | |
| select ID, Col<br>from dbo.HKData<br>  with (snapshot) | | Return old version of a row<br>(Col = 2) |
| commit | | Success |
| begin tran<br>  select ID, Col<br>  from dbo.HKData<br>    with (snapshot) | | |
| | insert into dbo.HKData<br>values(10,10) | |
| select ID, Col<br>from dbo.HKData<br>  with (snapshot) | | Does not return new row (10,10) |
| commit | | Success |

The SNAPSHOT isolation level behaves in a similar manner to disk-based tables, and it protects from the non-repeatable reads and phantom reads phenomena. As you can guess, it does not need to perform repeatable read and serializable validations at the commit stage, and therefore it reduces the load on SQL Server. However, there is still snapshot validation, which checks for primary-key violations and is done in any transaction isolation level.

Table 13-4 shows the code that leads to the primary-key violation condition. In contrast to disk-based tables, the exception is raised at the commit stage rather than at the time of the second INSERT operation.

*Table 13-4.* *Primary Key Violation*

| Session 1 | Session 2 | Results |
|---|---|---|
| begin tran<br>  insert into dbo.<br>  HKData<br>    with (snapshot)<br>      (ID, Col)<br>  values(100,100) | | |
| | begin tran<br>    insert into dbo.HKData<br>    with (snapshot)<br>        (ID, Col)<br>    values(100,100) | |
| commit | | Successfully commit the first session |
| | commit | Msg 41325, Level 16, State 1, Line 0<br>The current transaction failed to commit due to a serializable validation failure. |

It is worth mentioning that the error number and message are the same as with the serializable validation failure even though SQL Server validated a different rule.

Write/write conflicts work the same way regardless of the transaction isolation level in In-Memory OLTP. SQL Server does not allow a transaction to modify a row that has been modified by other uncommitted transactions. Table 13-5 illustrates this behavior. It uses the SNAPSHOT isolation level; however, the behavior does not change with different isolation levels.

***Table 13-5.*** *Write/Write Conflicts in In-Memory OLTP*

| Session 1 | Session 2 | Results |
|---|---|---|
| begin tran<br>  select ID, Col<br>  from dbo.HKData<br>    with (snapshot) | | |
| | begin tran<br>  update dbo.HKData<br>    with (snapshot)<br>    set Col = -3<br>    where ID = 2<br>commit | |
| update dbo.HKData<br>  with (snapshot)<br> set Col = -2<br> where ID = 2 | | Msg 41302, Level 16, State 110, Line 1<br>The current transaction attempted to update a record that has been updated since this transaction started. The transaction was aborted.<br>Msg 3998, Level 16, State 1, Line 1<br>Uncommittable transaction is detected at the end of the batch. The transaction is rolled back.<br>The statement has been terminated. |
| begin tran<br>  select ID, Col<br>  from dbo.HKData<br>    with (snapshot) | | |
| | begin tran<br>  update dbo.HKData<br>    with (snapshot)<br>  set Col = -3<br>  where ID = 2 | |

*(continued)*

**Table 13-5.** *(continued)*

| Session 1 | Session 2 | Results |
|---|---|---|
| update dbo.HKData<br>  with (snapshot)<br>set Col = -2<br>where ID = 2 | | Msg 41302, Level 16, State 110, Line 1<br>The current transaction attempted to update a record that has been updated since this transaction started. The transaction was aborted.<br>Msg 3998, Level 16, State 1, Line 1<br>Uncommittable transaction is detected at the end of the batch. The transaction is rolled back.<br>The statement has been terminated. |
| | commit | Successful commit of Session 2 transaction |

# Cross-Container Transactions

The In-Memory OLTP Engine is fully integrated in SQL Server, and it works side-by-side with the classic Storage Engine. The databases may include both disk-based and memory-optimized tables, and you can query them transparently regardless of their technologies.

Transactions that involve both disk-based and memory-optimized tables are called *cross-container transactions*. You can use different transaction isolation levels for disk-based and memory-optimized tables. However, not all combinations are supported. Table 13-6 illustrates possible combinations for transaction isolation levels in cross-container transactions.

**Table 13-6.** *Isolation Levels Allowed for Cross-Container Transactions*

| Isolation Levels for Disk-based Tables | Isolation Levels for Memory-optimized Tables |
|---|---|
| READ UNCOMMITTED, READ COMMITTED, READ COMMITTED SNAPSHOT | SNAPSHOT, REPEATABLE READ, SERIALIZABLE |
| REPEATABLE READ, SERIALIZABLE | SNAPSHOT only |
| SNAPSHOT | Not supported |

As you already know, internal implementations of REPEATABLE READ and SERIALIZABLE isolation levels are very different for disk-based and memory-optimized tables. Data-consistency rules with disk-based tables rely on locking, while In-Memory OLTP uses pre-commit validation. It leads to a situation in cross-container transactions where SQL Server only supports SNAPSHOT isolation levels for memory-optimized tables, while disk-based tables require REPEATABLE READ or SERIALIZABLE isolation levels.

Moreover, SQL Server does not allow access to memory-optimized tables when disk-based tables require SNAPSHOT isolation. Cross-container transactions, in a nutshell, consist of two internal transactions: one for disk-based and another one for memory-optimized tables. It is impossible to start both transactions at exactly the same time and guarantee the state of the data at the moment the transaction starts.

As a general guideline, it is recommended to use the READ COMMITTED/SNAPSHOT combination in cross-container transactions during a regular workload. This combination provides minimal blocking and the least pre-commit overhead and should be acceptable in a large number of use cases. Other combinations are more appropriate during data migrations when it is important to avoid the non-repeatable and phantom reads phenomena.

As you may have already noticed, SQL Server requires you to specify the transaction isolation level with a table hint when you are accessing memory-optimized tables. This does not apply to individual statements that execute outside of the explicitly started (with BEGIN TRAN) transaction. As with disk-based tables, such statements are executed in the individual *autocommitted transactions,* which are active for the duration of the statement execution.

An isolation level hint is not required for statements running in autocommitted transactions. When the hint is omitted, the statement runs in the SNAPSHOT isolation level.

---

**Note**   Implicit transactions are not supported in In-Memory OLTP.

---

SQL Server allows you to keep a NOLOCK hint while accessing memory-optimized tables from autocommitted transactions. That hint is ignored. A READUNCOMMITTED hint, however, is not supported and triggers an error.

There is a useful database option called MEMORY_OPTIMIZED_ELEVATE_TO_SNAPSHOT, which is disabled by default. When this option is enabled, SQL Server allows you to omit the isolation level hint in non-autocommitted transactions. SQL Server uses the SNAPSHOT isolation level, as with autocommitted transactions, if the isolation level hint is not specified and the MEMORY_OPTIMIZED_ELEVATE_TO_SNAPSHOT option is enabled. Consider enabling this option when you port an existing system to In-Memory OLTP and have T-SQL code that accesses tables that become memory-optimized.

# Transaction Lifetime

Although I have already discussed a few key elements used by In-Memory OLTP to manage data access and the concurrency model, let's review them here:

- *Global Transaction Timestamp* is an auto-incremented value that uniquely identifies every transaction in the system. SQL Server increments and obtains this value at the transaction commit stage.

- Every row has BeginTs and EndTs timestamps, which correspond to the Global Transaction Timestamp of the transaction that created or deleted this version of the row.

At the time when a new transaction starts, In-Memory OLTP generates a TransactionId value, which uniquely identifies the transaction. Moreover, In-Memory OLTP assigns the *logical start time* for the transaction, which represents the Global Transaction Timestamp value at the time when the transaction starts. It dictates what version of the rows is visible to the transaction. The logical start time should be in between the BeginTs and EndTs in order for the row to be visible.

When the transaction issues a COMMIT statement, In-Memory OLTP increments the Global Transaction Timestamp value and assigns it to the transaction's *logical end time*. The logical end time will become the BeginTs for the rows inserted and the EndTs for the rows deleted by the transaction after it is committed.

Figure 13-3 shows the lifetime of a transaction that works with memory-optimized tables.

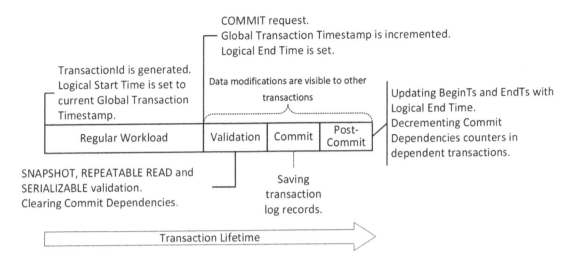

*Figure 13-3.* *Transaction lifetime*

When a transaction needs to delete a row, it updates the EndTs timestamp with the TransactionId value. Remember that the transaction's logical end time is unknown at this phase, and therefore In-Memory OLTP uses the TransactionId as the temporary value. The insert operation creates a new row with the BeginTs of the TransactionId and the EndTs of Infinity. Finally, the update operation consists of delete and insert operations internally. It is also worth noting that during data modifications, transactions raise an error if there are any uncommitted versions of the rows they are modifying. It prevents write/write conflicts when multiple sessions modify the same data.

When another transaction—call it Tx1—encounters uncommitted rows with a TransactionId within the BeginTs and EndTs timestamps (TransactionId has a flag that indicates such a condition), it checks the status of the transaction with that TransactionId. If that transaction is committing and the logical end time is already set, those uncommitted rows may become visible for the Tx1 transaction, which leads to a situation called *commit dependency*. Tx1 is not blocked; however, it does not return data to the client nor commit until the original transaction on which it has a commit dependency commits itself. I will talk about commit dependencies shortly.

Let's look at a transaction lifetime in detail. Figure 13-4 shows the data rows after we created and populated the dbo.HKData table in Listing 13-3, where we inserted five different rows into the table: (1,1), (2,2), (3,3), (4,4), (5,5). Let's assume that the rows were created by a transaction with the Global Transaction Timestamp of 5. (The hash index structure is omitted for simplicity's sake.)

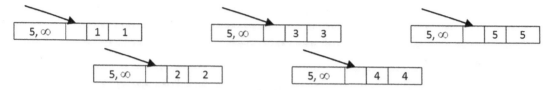

**Figure 13-4.** *Data in the dbo.HKData table after insert*

Let's assume that the transaction performs the operations shown in Listing 13-4. The explicit transaction has already started, and the BEGIN TRAN statement is not included in the listing. All three statements are executing in the context of a single active transaction.

**Listing 13-4.** Data modification operations

```
insert into dbo.HKData with (snapshot) (ID, Col) values(10,10);
update dbo.HKData with (snapshot) set Col = -2 where ID = 2;
delete from dbo.HKData with (snapshot) where ID = 4;
```

Figure 13-5 illustrates the state of the data after data modifications. An INSERT statement created a new row, a DELETE statement updated the EndTs value in the row with ID=4, and an UPDATE statement changed the EndTs value of the row with ID=2 and created a new version of the row with the same ID. I am using a negative value of TransactionId (-8) to indicate that the transaction is active and that a logical end time has not yet been assigned.

It is important to note that the transaction maintains a *write set*, or pointers to rows that have been inserted and deleted by a transaction, which is used to generate transaction log records.

In addition to the write set, in the REPEATABLE READ and SERIALIZABLE isolation levels, transactions maintain a *read set* of the rows read by a transaction and use it for repeatable read validation. Finally, in the SERIALIZABLE isolation level, transactions maintain a *scan set*, which contains information about predicates used by the queries in the transaction. The scan set is used for serializable validation.

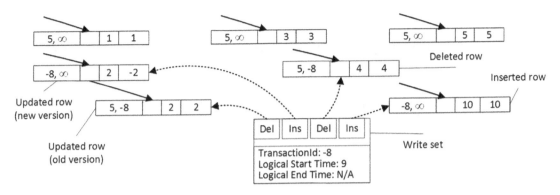

**Figure 13-5.** *Data in the dbo.HKData table after modifications*

When a COMMIT request is issued, the transaction starts the validation phase. First, it autoincrements the current Global Transaction Timestamp value, which becomes the logical end time of the transaction. Figure 13-6 illustrates this state, assuming that the new Global Transaction Timestamp value is 11. Note that the BeginTs and EndTs timestamps in the rows still have TransactionId (-8) at this stage.

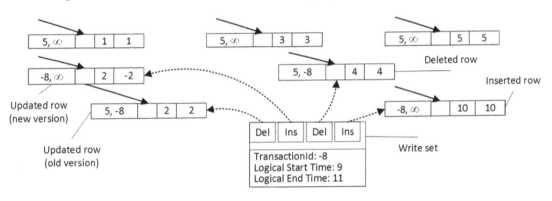

**Figure 13-6.** *Start of validation phase*

As the next step, the transaction starts a validation phase. SQL Server performs several validations based on the isolation level of the transaction, as shown in Table 13-7.

***Table 13-7.*** *Yes/No Done in the Different Transaction Isolation Levels*

| | **Snapshot Validation** | **Repeatable Read Validation** | **Serializable Validation** |
|---|---|---|---|
| | Checking for primary-key violations | Checking for non-repeatable reads | Checking for phantom reads |
| SNAPSHOT | YES | NO | NO |
| REPEATABLE READ | YES | YES | NO |
| SERIALIZABLE | YES | YES | YES |

**Important**    Repeatable read and serializable validations add overhead to the system. Do not use REPEATABLE READ and SERIALIZABLE isolation levels unless you have a legitimate use case for such data consistency.

After the required rules have been validated, the transaction waits for the commit dependencies to clear and the transaction on which it depends to commit. If those transactions fail to commit for any reason—for example, validation rules violation—the dependent transaction is also rolled back, and an Error 41301 is generated.

At this moment, the rows modified by transactions become visible to other transactions in the system even though the transaction has yet to be committed, which can lead to commit dependencies. Again, we will talk about them shortly.

Figure 13-7 illustrates a commit dependency scenario. Transaction Tx2 can access uncommitted rows from transaction Tx1 during the Tx1 validation and commit phases, and therefore Tx2 has a commit dependency on Tx1. After the Tx2 validation phase is complete, Tx2 has to wait for Tx1 to commit and the commit dependency to clear before entering the commit phase.

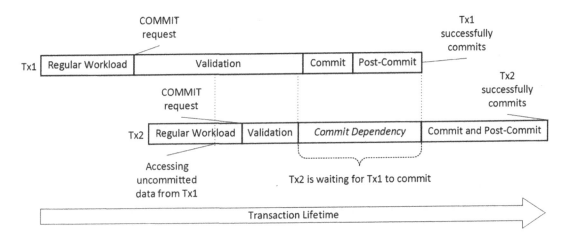

***Figure 13-7.***  *Commit dependency: Successful commit*

If Tx1, for example, failed to commit due to a serializable validation violation, Tx2 would be rolled back with Error 41301, as shown in Figure 13-8.

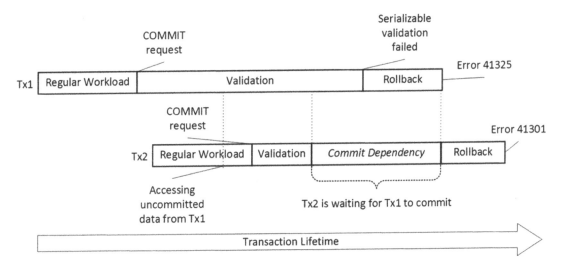

***Figure 13-8.***  *Commit dependency: Validation error*

A commit dependency is technically a case of blocking in In-Memory OLTP. However, the validation and commit phases of the transactions are relatively short, and such blocking should not be excessive.

SQL Server allows a maximum of eight commit dependencies on a single transaction. When this number is reached, other transactions that try to take a dependency would fail with Error 41839.

> **Note**   You can track commit dependencies using the `dependency_`
> `acquiredtx_event` and `waiting_for_dependenciestx_event` Extended
> Events.

When all commit dependencies are cleared, the transaction moves to the commit phase, generates one or more log records, saves them to the transaction log, then moves to the post-commit phase.

It is worth noting that In-Memory OLTP transaction logging is significantly more efficient than that for disk-based tables. The In-Memory OLTP Engine combines multiple data modifications in one or a few transaction log records and writes them to the transaction log only if the transaction has been successfully committed. Nothing is logged for rolled-back transactions.

In the post-commit phase, the transaction replaces BeginTs and EndTs timestamps with the logical end time value and decrements commit dependencies counters in the dependent transactions. Figure 13-9 illustrates the final state of the transaction.

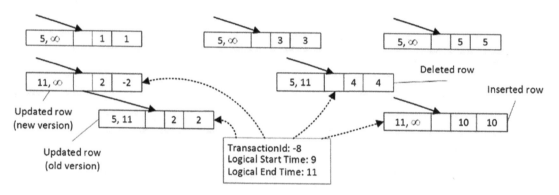

***Figure 13-9.*** *Completed transaction*

Finally, if a transaction is rolled back either due to an explicit ROLLBACK command or because of a validation violation, In-Memory OLTP resets the EndTs timestamp of the deleted rows back to Infinity. The new versions of the rows inserted by the transaction become ghosted. They will be deallocated by the regular garbage-collection process running in the system.

# Referential Integrity Enforcement

It is impossible to enforce referential integrity in *pure* SNAPSHOT isolation level because transactions are completely isolated from each other. Consider a situation where a transaction deletes a row that is referenced by a newly inserted row in another transaction that started after the original one. This newly inserted row would be invisible to the SNAPSHOT transaction that executes the DELETE statement during referential integrity check.

In-Memory OLTP addresses this problem by maintaining read and/or scan sets in the SNAPSHOT isolation level for the tables and queries that were affected by referential integrity validation.

In contrast to REPEATABLE READ and SERIALIZABLE transactions, those read and scan sets are maintained only for affected tables rather than for entire transactions. They, however, would include all rows that were read and all predicates that were applied during the referential integrity check.

This behavior can lead to issues when the referencing table does not have an index on the foreign key column(s). Similar to disk-based tables, SQL Server will have to scan the entire referencing (detail) table when you delete a row in the referenced (master) table. In addition to performance impact, the transaction will maintain the read set, which includes all rows it read during the scan, regardless of whether those rows referenced the deleted row. If any other transactions update or delete any rows from the read set, the original transaction would fail with a *repeatable read rule violation* error.

Let's look at the example and create two tables with the code in Listing 13-5.

*Listing 13-5.* Referential integrity validation: Tables creation

```
create table dbo.Branches
(
    BranchId int not null
        constraint PK_Branches
        primary key nonclustered hash with (bucket_count = 4)
)
with (memory_optimized = on, durability = schema_only);

create table dbo.Transactions
(
    TransactionId int not null
        constraint PK_Transactions
```

```
        primary key nonclustered hash with (bucket_count = 4),
    BranchId int not null
        constraint FK_Transactions_Branches
        foreign key references dbo.Branches(BranchId),
    Amount money not null
)
with (memory_optimized = on, durability = schema_only);

insert into dbo.Branches(BranchId) values(1),(10);
insert into dbo.Transactions(TransactionId,BranchId,Amount)
values(1,1,10),(2,1,20);
```

The dbo.Transactions table has a foreign key constraint referencing the dbo. Branches table. There are no rows, however, referencing the row with BranchId = 10. As the next step, let's run the code shown in Listing 13-6, deleting this row from the dbo. Branches table and leaving the transaction active.

**Listing 13-6.** Referential integrity validation: First session code

```
begin tran
    delete from dbo.Branches with (snapshot) where BranchId = 10;
```

The DELETE statement would validate the foreign key constraint and would complete successfully. The dbo.Transactions table, however, does not have an index on the BranchId column, and the validation will need to scan the entire table, as you can see in Figure 13-10.

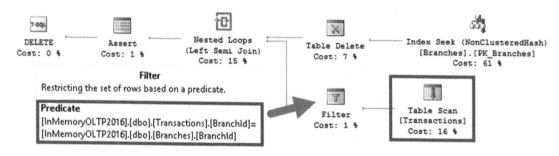

**Figure 13-10.** *Referential integrity validation: Execution plan of DELETE statement*

At this time, all rows from the dbo.Transactions table would be included in the transaction read set. If another session updated one of the rows from the read set with the code shown in Listing 13-7, it would succeed, and the first session would fail to commit, offering a *repeatable read rule violation* error.

***Listing 13-7.*** Referential integrity validation: Second session code

```
update dbo.Transactions with (snapshot)
set Amount = 30
where TransactionId = 2;
```

---

**Important**   Similar to disk-based tables, you should always create an index on the foreign key columns in the referencing table to avoid this problem.

---

# Additional Resources

In-Memory OLTP is a fascinating technology that may significantly improve the performance and scalability of OLTP systems. This chapter focused on only one aspect of the technology—the In-Memory OLTP Concurrency Model—and did not even scratch the surface of other technology areas.

I have published another book with Apress, *Expert SQL Server In-Memory OLTP*, which provides a deep overview of the technology. You might consider reading it if you are planning to utilize In-Memory OLTP in your systems. The first edition focuses on SQL Server 2014 implementation. The second edition covers SQL Server 2016 and 2017's technology enhancements.

# Summary

In-Memory OLTP supports three transaction isolation levels, SNAPSHOT, REPEATABLE READ, and SERIALIZABLE. In contrast to disk-based tables, where non-repeatable and phantom reads are addressed by acquiring and holding locks, In-Memory OLTP validates data-consistency rules at the transaction commit stage. An exception will be raised and the transaction will be rolled back if rules were violated.

Repeatable read validation and serializable validation add overhead to transaction processing. It is recommended to use the SNAPSHOT isolation level during a regular workload unless REPEATABLE READ or SERIALIZABLE data consistency is required.

SQL Server performs repeatable read and serializable validations to enforce referential integrity in the system. Always create an index on the foreign key columns in the referencing tables to improve performance and avoid validation errors.

You can use different transaction isolation levels for disk-based and memory-optimized tables in cross-container transactions; however, not all combinations are supported. The recommended practice is to use the READ COMMITTED isolation level for disk-based and the SNAPSHOT isolation level for memory-optimized tables.

# CHAPTER 14

# Locking in Columnstore Indexes

Columnstore indexes are a type of index that stores data on a per-column rather than per-row basis. This storage format benefits query processing in data warehousing, reporting, and analytics environments where, although queries typically read a very large number of rows, they work with just a subset of the columns from a table.

This chapter will provide an overview of column-based storage and discuss the locking behavior of columnstore indexes and their usage in OLTP systems.

## Column-Based Storage Overview

Even though every database system is unique, there are two generic workloads—OLTP and Data Warehouse. OLTP, which stands for *Online Transactional Processing*, describes systems that support the operational activity of a business. Such systems usually handle a large number of simultaneous requests in short transactions and deal with volatile data.

Data Warehouse systems, on the other hand, support the reporting and analytical activities of a business. The data in these systems is relatively static and is often updated based on some schedule. The queries are complex, and they usually perform aggregations and process large amounts of data.

For example, consider a company that sells items to customers. A typical OLTP query from the company's *point-of-sale* (POS) system might have the following semantic: *Provide a list of orders that were placed by this particular customer this month.* Alternatively, a typical query in a Data Warehouse system might read as follows: *Provide the total amount of sales year to date, grouping the results by item category and customer region.*

© Dmitri Korotkevitch 2018
D. Korotkevitch, *Expert SQL Server Transactions and Locking*, https://doi.org/10.1007/978-1-4842-3957-5_14

The separation between OLTP and Data Warehouse systems is relatively thin though. Almost every OLTP system has some reporting queries. It is also not uncommon to see OLTP queries in Data Warehouse systems. Finally, there is another category of tasks called *Operational Analytics*, which run analytical queries against *hot* OLTP data. Think about a point-of-sale system in which you want to monitor up-to-date sales and dynamically adjust items' sale price based on their popularity.

Performance tuning a system with a mixed workload is not a trivial task. OLTP and Data Warehouse queries would take advantage of different database schema designs and indexing strategies, and they may also benefit from different storage technologies.

In the classic row-based storage format, the data from all columns is stored together in a single *data row* object. This approach works great in cases with volatile data—the data from all columns is grouped together, and INSERT, UPDATE, and DELETE operations may be done as a single action. B-Tree indexes are good for OLTP workload, when queries typically deal with one or just a handful of rows from large tables.

Row-based storage, however, is not optimal for Data Warehouse queries that scan a large amount of data. Such queries usually work with just a subset of the columns from a table, and it is impossible to avoid reading entire data row objects while skipping unnecessary columns.

Data compression may help to reduce the size of the data and I/O overhead. However, with row-based storage, PAGE compression works on a data-page scope. The data from different columns is not similar enough for compression to be effective, and PAGE compression rarely compresses the data more than 2 or 2.5 times.

SQL Server 2012 introduced a new type of index-the *columnstore index*-which keeps data in a *column-based storage* format. These indexes store data on a per-column rather than on a per-row basis. Data in each column is stored together, separate from other columns, as shown in Figure 14-1.

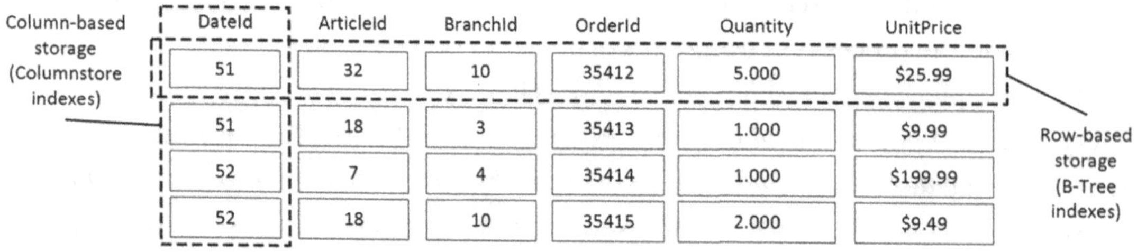

*Figure 14-1.* Row-based and column-based storage

Data in columnstore indexes is heavily compressed using algorithms that provide significant space savings, even when compared to PAGE compression. Moreover, SQL Server can skip columns that are not requested by a query, and it does not load the data from those columns into memory, significantly reducing the I/O footprint of the query.

Moreover, the new data storage format of columnstore indexes allows SQL Server to implement a new *batch mode* execution model. In this model, SQL Server processes data in groups of rows, or *batches*, rather than one row at a time. The size of the batches varies to fit into the CPU cache, which reduces the number of times that the CPU needs to request *external* data from memory, or other components. All these enhancements significantly reduce the CPU load and execution time of Data Warehouse queries.

Columnstore indexes are a relatively new feature in SQL Server and have been evolving rapidly. Initial implementation in SQL Server 2012 supported just read-only *nonclustered columnstore indexes* that stored a copy of the data from a table in a column-based storage format. Those indexes essentially made tables read-only, and the only way to import data was via *partition switch*. We are not going to discuss those indexes; from a locking standpoint, their behavior was straightforward.

As of SQL Server 2014, you can create tables with clustered columnstore indexes and store entire tables in a column-based storage format. These indexes are updatable; however, you cannot define any nonclustered indexes on those tables.

This limitation has been removed in SQL Server 2016, where you can utilize different storage technologies for the indexes defined on a table. You can support a mixed workload by creating nonclustered B-Tree indexes on the tables with clustered columnstore indexes or, alternatively, you can create updateable nonclustered columnstore indexes on B-Tree tables. It is worth noting that you can create columnstore indexes in memory-optimized tables, thus improving the performance of Operational Analytics queries in In-Memory OLTP.

# Columnstore Index Internals Overview

Each data column in column-based storage is stored separately in a set of structures called *row groups*. Each row group stores data for up to approximately one million—or, to be precise, $2^{20}=1,048,576$—rows. SQL Server tries to populate row groups completely during index creation, leaving the last row group partially populated. For example, if a table has five million rows, SQL Server creates four row groups of 1,048,576 rows each and one row group with 805,696 rows.

In practice, you can have more than one partially populated row group when multiple threads create columnstore indexes using a parallel execution plan. Each thread will work with its own subset of data, creating separate row groups. Moreover, in the case of partitioned tables, each table partition will have its own set of row groups.

After row groups are built, SQL Server encodes and compresses the column data in each row group. The rows within a row group can be rearranged if that helps to achieve a better compression rate.

Column data within a row group is called a *segment*. SQL Server loads an entire segment to memory when it needs to access columnstore data. SQL Server also keeps information about data in the segments' metadata—for example, minimum and maximum values stored in the segment—and can skip the segments that do not have the required data.

The data that belong to the same data row are identified by the *offset* within the segments. For example, the first row in the table consists of the first values from all segments from the first row group on the first table partition. The second row consists of the second values from all segments from the same row group, and so forth. The combination of `partition_id`, `row_group_id`, and `offset` uniquely identifies the row and is called a `row-id` in columnstore indexes.

The data in columnstore indexes is heavily compressed and can introduce significant space savings compared to page compression. It is common to see column-based storage providing a more than 10X compression rate over the row-based data. Moreover, SQL Server 2014 introduced another compression option called *archival compression* that reduces storage space even further. It uses the Xpress 8 compression library, which is an internal Microsoft implementation of the LZ77 algorithm. This compression works directly with row-group data without having any knowledge of the underlying SQL Server data structures.

Updateable columnstore indexes have two additional elements to support data modifications. The first is the *delete bitmap*, which stores the `row-id` of the rows that were deleted from a table. The second structure is the *delta store*, which stores the newly inserted rows. In disk-based columnstore indexes, both the delta store and the delete bitmap are implemented as regular heap tables.

**Note**   The internal structure of columnstore indexes defined on memory-optimized tables is conceptually the same; however, the delta store and delete bitmap are implemented differently. Such indexes support In-Memory OLTP multi-version concurrency control and do not introduce any locking in memory-optimized tables. You can read more about them in my *Expert SQL Server In-Memory OLTP* book; we are not going to focus on them in this book.

Figure 14-2 illustrates the structure of an updateable columnstore index in a table that has two partitions. Each partition can have a single delete bitmap and multiple delta stores. This structure makes each partition self-contained and independent from other partitions, which allows you to perform a partition switch on tables that have columnstore indexes defined.

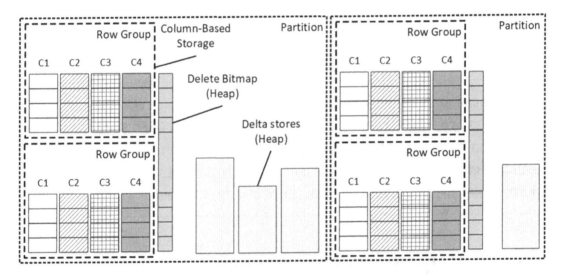

***Figure 14-2.*** *Updateable columnstore index structure*

It is worth noting that delete bitmaps and delta stores are created *on-demand*. For example, a delete bitmap would not be created unless some of the rows in the row groups were deleted.

Every time you delete a row that is stored in a compressed row group (not in a delta store), SQL Server adds information about the deleted row to the delete bitmap. Nothing happens to the original row. It is still stored in a row group. However, SQL Server checks the delete bitmap during query execution, excluding deleted rows from the processing.

As already mentioned, when you insert data into a columnstore index, it goes into a delta store, which is a heap table. Updating a row that is stored in a row group does not change the row data either. Such an update triggers the deletion of a row, which is, in fact, insertion into a delete bitmap marking old version as *deleted*, and insertion of a new version of the row into a delta store. However, any data modifications of the rows in a delta store are done in-place as in regular heap tables by updating and deleting actual rows there.

Each delta store can be in either an *open* or a *closed* state. Open delta stores accept new rows and allow modifications and deletions of data. SQL Server closes a delta store when it reaches 1,048,576 rows, which is the maximum number of rows that can be stored in a row group. Another SQL Server process, called *tuple mover*, runs every five minutes and converts closed delta stores to row groups that store data in a column-based storage format.

Both large delta stores and delete bitmaps may affect query performance. SQL Server must access delete bitmaps to check if compressed rows were deleted, and it reads the rows from delta stores during query execution. Consider rebuilding indexes on affected partitions if ETL processes lead to large delta stores and delete bitmaps.

---

**Tip**   You can examine the state of row groups and delta stores with the `sys.column_store_row_groups` view. Rows in an OPEN or CLOSED state correspond to delta stores. Rows in a COMPRESSED state correspond to row groups with data in a column-based storage format. Finally, the `deleted_rows` column provides statistics about deleted rows stored in a delete bitmap.

---

# Locking Behavior in Columnstore Indexes

Storage space savings and the updateable nature of clustered columnstore indexes make them appealing as a replacement for large transactional tables in OLTP environments. Their locking behavior, however, is very different than that of B-Tree indexes, and it may not scale well in environments with a large number of concurrent transactions.

Let's look at a few examples. As a first step, shown in Listing 14-1, we will create a table with a clustered columnstore index and insert about four million rows there. After the columnstore index is created, we will try to insert another row into the table, rolling back the transaction afterward. This will create an empty delta store in the index. Finally, we will analyze the state of the row groups using the sys.column_store_row_groups view.

***Listing 14-1.*** Creating a test table

```
create table dbo.Test
(
    ID int not null,
    Col int not null
);

;with N1(C) as (select 0 union all select 0) -- 2 rows
,N2(C) as (select 0 from N1 as T1 cross join N1 as T2) -- 4 rows
,N3(C) as (select 0 from N2 as T1 cross join N2 as T2) -- 16 rows
,N4(C) as (select 0 from N3 as T1 cross join N3 as T2) -- 256 rows
,N5(C) as (select 0 from N4 as T1 cross join N4 as T2 ) -- 65,536 rows
,N6(C) AS (select 0 from N5 as T1 cross join N3 as T2 cross join N2 as T3)
-- 4,194,304 rows
,IDs(ID) as (select row_number() over (order by (select null)) from N6)
insert into dbo.Test(ID, Col)
    select ID, ID from IDs;

create clustered columnstore index CCI_Test
on dbo.Test
with (maxdop = 1);

begin tran
    insert into dbo.Test(ID, Col) values(-1,-1);
rollback
go

select *
from sys.column_store_row_groups
where object_id = object_id(N'dbo.Test');
```

Figure 14-3 illustrates the output from the view. Four row groups in a COMPRESSED state store the data in a column-based format. An empty row group with row_group_id = 4 in the OPEN state is in the delta store.

| | object_id | index_id | partition_number | row_group_id | delta_store_hobt_id | state | state_description | total_rows | deleted_rows | size_in_bytes |
|---|---|---|---|---|---|---|---|---|---|---|
| 1 | 981578535 | 1 | 1 | 4 | 5260204372965785600 | 1 | OPEN | 0 | NULL | 16384 |
| 2 | 981578535 | 1 | 1 | 3 | NULL | 3 | COMPRESSED | 1048576 | 0 | 5593584 |
| 3 | 981578535 | 1 | 1 | 2 | NULL | 3 | COMPRESSED | 1048576 | 0 | 5593584 |
| 4 | 981578535 | 1 | 1 | 1 | NULL | 3 | COMPRESSED | 1048576 | 0 | 5593584 |
| 5 | 981578535 | 1 | 1 | 0 | NULL | 3 | COMPRESSED | 1048576 | 0 | 5593584 |

***Figure 14-3.*** *Row groups after table was created*

Now, let's run a few tests and analyze the locking behavior of the index.

# Inserting Data into Clustered Columnstore Index

Columnstore indexes support two types of data load. The first, and most efficient, method requires you to utilize a BULK INSERT API for loading data in large batches. In this mode, SQL Server creates a new row group for each batch, compressing data into a column-based format on the fly. Since every batch becomes an individual row group, multiple inserts would not block each other and could run in parallel.

The minimum size of the batch that triggers this behavior is about 102,000 rows; however, you will get the best results if you use batches that match the maximum row group size, which is 1,048,576 rows.

With smaller batches and single-row inserts, SQL Server uses *trickle inserts*, placing data into delta stores. Each table partition will have separate delta stores, and in some cases you may have several open delta stores per partition. SQL Server closes the delta store and compresses its data into a column-based format when it reaches 1,048,576 rows or when you run an index rebuild operation.

Let's insert a single row into a table and then analyze what locks get acquired during the process. The code is shown in Listing 14-2.

***Listing 14-2.*** Inserting data into the table

```
begin tran
    insert into dbo.Test(ID, Col)
    values(-1,-1);

    select
        resource_type, resource_description
        ,request_mode, request_status
        ,resource_associated_entity_id
```

```
    from sys.dm_tran_locks
    where
        request_session_id = @@SPID;
rollback
```

As you can see in Figure 14-4, the locking behavior is similar to locking in heap tables. SQL Server acquired an exclusive (X) lock on the newly inserted row, along with intent exclusive (IX) locks on the page and HOBT (allocation unit). It also acquired an intent exclusive (IX) lock on the row group, which is conceptually similar to the object-level lock on the table.

| | resource_type | resource_description | request_mode | request_status | resource_associated_entity_id |
|---|---|---|---|---|---|
| 1 | PAGE | 5:83264 | IX | GRANT | 5260204372965785600 |
| 2 | ROWGROUP | ROWGROUP: 2:47000001e3b30000:4 | IX | GRANT | 5116089184808009728 |
| 3 | HOBT | | IX | GRANT | 5260204372965785600 |
| 4 | KEY | (8194443284a0) | X | GRANT | 5260204372965785600 |

**Figure 14-4.** *Locks acquired by INSERT operation*

As you can guess, this behavior indicates that you may scale the insert workload in a way similar to how you do so with heap tables. Multiple sessions can insert data in parallel without blocking each other.

# Updating and Deleting Data from Clustered Columnstore Indexes

The situation changes when you update or delete data in the table. Unfortunately, this workload does not scale as well as inserts do.

Let's update one row in the table using the code from Listing 14-3. As you may remember, when a row is stored in a delta store, this operation is done *in-place*. Updating an already compressed row, on the other hand, will lead to two operations—marking a row as *deleted* by inserting the row-id into the delete bitmap and inserting a new version of the row into a delta store.

***Listing 14-3.*** Updating data in the table

```
begin tran
    update dbo.Test
    set Col += 1
    where ID=1;

    select
        resource_type, resource_description
        ,request_mode, request_status
        ,resource_associated_entity_id
    from sys.dm_tran_locks
    where
        request_session_id = @@SPID
rollback
```

Figure 14-5 shows the locks that are held after the operation. You can see exclusive (X) and intent exclusive (IX) locks acquired on the delta store and delete bitmap objects (both are heap tables). However, the row groups and HOBT of the delta store are protected with update intent exclusive (UIX) rather than intent exclusive (IX) locks.

| | resource_type | resource_description | request_mode | request_status | resource_associated_entity_id |
|---|---|---|---|---|---|
| 1 | PAGE | 1:100480 | IX | GRANT | 5188146778886897664 |
| 2 | PAGE | 5:83264 | IX | GRANT | 5260204372965785600 |
| 3 | KEY | (5e7c853b854b) | X | GRANT | 5188146778886897664 |
| 4 | ROWGROUP | ROWGROUP: 2:47000001e3b30000:0 | UIX | GRANT | 5116089184808009728 |
| 5 | ROWGROUP | ROWGROUP: 2:47000001e3b30000:4 | UIX | GRANT | 5116089184808009728 |
| 6 | HOBT | | IX | GRANT | 5188146778886897664 |
| 7 | HOBT | | UIX | GRANT | 5260204372965785600 |
| 8 | KEY | (61a06abd401c) | X | GRANT | 5260204372965785600 |

***Figure 14-5.*** *Locks acquired by UPDATE operation*

The same pattern would occur if you deleted a compressed row from a table. Listing 14-4 shows the code that performs that.

***Listing 14-4.*** Deleting data from the table

```
begin tran
    delete from dbo.Test where ID=1;

    select
        resource_type, resource_description
        ,request_mode, request_status
        ,resource_associated_entity_id
    from sys.dm_tran_locks
    where
        request_session_id = @@SPID
rollback
```

Figure 14-6 shows the locks held after the DELETE statement. This operation does not touch the delta store, and only the delete bitmap is affected. Nevertheless, there is still an update intent exclusive (UIX) lock on the row group from which we deleted the row.

|   | resource_type | resource_description | request_mode | request_status | resource_associated_entity_id |
|---|---|---|---|---|---|
| 1 | PAGE | 1:100480 | IX | GRANT | 5188146778886897664 |
| 2 | KEY | (5e7c853b854b) | X | GRANT | 5188146778886897664 |
| 3 | ROWGROUP | ROWGROUP: 2:47000001e3b30000:0 | UIX | GRANT | 5116089184808009728 |
| 4 | HOBT | | IX | GRANT | 5188146778886897664 |

***Figure 14-6.*** *Locks acquired by DELETE operation*

The reason why SQL Server uses update intent exclusive (UIX) locks is simple. The data in columnstore indexes is not sorted, and SQL Server has to scan it during query execution. Partition and segment elimination may allow SQL Server to skip some row groups; however, when a row group is scanned, SQL Server acquires an update intent exclusive (UIX) lock on it and runs an update scan, reading all rows from there.

Figure 14-7 proves that by showing the execution plan of the UPDATE statement from Listing 14-3. You can see the *Columnstore Index Scan* operator there.

***Figure 14-7.*** *Execution plan of UPDATE statement*

Unfortunately, update intent exclusive (UIX) locks are incompatible with each other. Moreover, they are held until the end of the transaction. This means that concurrent update and delete workloads could introduce a large amount of blocking and would not scale well in OLTP systems.

SQL Server 2016 and above allow you to create nonclustered B-Tree indexes on clustered columnstore index tables. Those indexes can eliminate update scans of column-based data by using *Nonclustered Index Seek* and *Key Lookup* operations.

---

**Note**    The key lookup operations on clustered columnstore and B-Tree indexes are conceptually similar. SQL Server locates a row in a clustered columnstore index based on `partition_id`, `row_group_id`, and `offset` from the `row-id`.

---

Let's create the index using the `CREATE NONCLUSTERED INDEX Idx_Test_ID ON dbo.Test(ID)` statement and run the code from Listing 14-3 again. Figure 14-8 illustrates an execution plan of the UPDATE statement with *Nonclustered Index Seek* and *Key Lookup* operations.

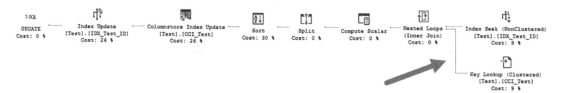

***Figure 14-8.*** *Execution plan of UPDATE statement with nonclustered index*

Figure 14-9 shows the locks that were held after this UPDATE statement. As you can see, SQL Server did not acquire update intent exclusive (UIX) locks on the row groups, using intent exclusive (IX) locks instead. This lock type is compatible with intent locks from other sessions.

| | resource_type | resource_description | request_mode | request_status | resource_associated_entity_id |
|---|---|---|---|---|---|
| 1 | PAGE | 1:100480 | IX | GRANT | 5188146778886897664 |
| 2 | KEY | (8669c8752e62) | X | GRANT | 5476377155202449408 |
| 3 | KEY | (5e7c853b854b) | X | GRANT | 5188146778886897664 |
| 4 | KEY | (5f29acedd944) | X | GRANT | 5476377155202449408 |
| 5 | ROWGROUP | ROWGROUP: 2:47000001e3b30000:0 | IX | GRANT | 5116089184808009728 |
| 6 | ROWGROUP | ROWGROUP: 2:47000001e3b30000:5 | IX | GRANT | 5116089184808009728 |
| 7 | HOBT | | IX | GRANT | 5188146778886897664 |
| 8 | PAGE | 5:92128 | IX | GRANT | 5332261967044673536 |
| 9 | HOBT | | IX | GRANT | 5332261967044673536 |
| 10 | KEY | (98ec012aa510) | X | GRANT | 5332261967044673536 |
| 11 | PAGE | 5:95200 | IX | GRANT | 5476377155202449408 |

*Figure 14-9.* *Locks held by UPDATE statement with nonclustered index*

Even though you can *technically* scale update and delete workloads with nonclustered B-Tree indexes, this approach is dangerous. The choice of using a nonclustered index would depend on index selectivity and the query. SQL Server may decide to scan a columnstore index if it expects that a large number of Key Lookups is required, which will lead to blocking in the system.

# Nonclustered Columnstore Indexes

SQL Server 2016 and above allow you to create nonclustered columnstore indexes on B-Tree tables. These indexes persist a copy of the data in column-based format, thus helping to optimize Operational Analytics and reporting workloads in OLTP systems. In contrast to SQL Server 2012 implementation, these indexes are updatable and do not make a table read-only.

Listing 14-5 shows the code that drops a clustered columnstore index on the dbo. Test table, creating clustered B-Tree and nonclustered columnstore indexes after that. As before, we are running an INSERT statement and rolling back the transaction to create an empty delta store in the index.

*Listing 14-5.* Creating nonclustered columnstore index on table

```
drop index IDX_Test_ID on dbo.Test;

drop index CCI_Test on dbo.Test;

create unique clustered index CI_Test_ID
on dbo.Test(ID);
```

```
create nonclustered columnstore index NCCI_Test
on dbo.Test(ID,Col)
with (maxdop=1);

begin tran
    insert into dbo.Test(ID, Col) values(-1,-1);
rollback
```

Figure 14-10 shows the output of the sys.column_store_row_groups view for the NCCI_TestData index. The data in the table remain the same, and the index consists of four compressed row groups and an empty delta store.

| | object_id | index_id | partition_number | row_group_id | delta_store_hobt_id | state | state_description | total_rows | deleted_rows | size_in_bytes |
|---|---|---|---|---|---|---|---|---|---|---|
| 1 | 981578535 | 3 | 1 | 4 | 6269010690070216704 | 1 | OPEN | 0 | NULL | 16384 |
| 2 | 981578535 | 3 | 1 | 3 | NULL | 3 | COMPRESSED | 1048576 | 0 | 5593584 |
| 3 | 981578535 | 3 | 1 | 2 | NULL | 3 | COMPRESSED | 1048576 | 0 | 5593584 |
| 4 | 981578535 | 3 | 1 | 1 | NULL | 3 | COMPRESSED | 1048576 | 0 | 5593584 |
| 5 | 981578535 | 3 | 1 | 0 | NULL | 3 | COMPRESSED | 1048576 | 0 | 5593584 |

***Figure 14-10.*** *Row groups in nonclustered columnstore index*

Figure 14-11 shows the locks held when you run the code from Listing 14-3 with the UPDATE statement again. SQL Server tracks the row locations in the nonclustered columnstore index through another internal structure called a *delete buffer*, which maps the values of clustered index keys and columnstore row-ids. This allows SQL Server to avoid update scans on column-based storage and to use intent exclusive (IX) rather than update intent exclusive (UIX) locks.

| | resource_type | resource_description | request_mode | request_status | resource_associated_entity_id |
|---|---|---|---|---|---|
| 1 | HOBT | | IX | GRANT | 6124895501912440832 |
| 2 | HOBT | | IX | GRANT | 6269010690070216704 |
| 3 | KEY | (8194443284a0) | X | GRANT | 6269010690070216704 |
| 4 | PAGE | 3:9792 | IX | GRANT | 5620492343360225280 |
| 5 | KEY | (1a2ef5c35ba2) | X | GRANT | 6124895501912440832 |
| 6 | KEY | (8194443284a0) | X | GRANT | 5620492343360225280 |
| 7 | ROWGROUP | ROWGROUP: 2:5300000200ff0000:4 | IX | GRANT | 5980780313754664960 |
| 8 | PAGE | 5:128920 | IX | GRANT | 6269010690070216704 |
| 9 | PAGE | 1:129184 | IX | GRANT | 6124895501912440832 |

***Figure 14-11.*** *Locks held after UPDATE statement*

Nonclustered columnstore indexes have been designed to work in OLTP workloads, and they would scale well without introducing additional concurrency issues in the system.

# Tuple Mover and ALTER INDEX REORGANIZE Locking

Finally, let's look at the locking behavior of the tuple mover process and the ALTER INDEX REORGANIZE operation. Both of them compress closed delta stores into compressed row groups and essentially do the same thing; however, their implementation is slightly different. Tuple mover is a single-threaded process that works in the background, preserving system resources. Alternatively, index reorganizing runs in parallel using multiple threads.

SQL Server acquires and holds a shared (S) lock on the delta store during the compression process. These locks do not prevent you from selecting the data from a table, nor do they block inserts. New data will be inserted into different and open delta stores; however, deletions and data modifications on locked delta stores would be blocked for the duration of the operation.

Figure 14-12 illustrates lock_acquired and lock_released Extended Events taken on delta stores during the ALTER INDEX REORGANIZE command. You can see the shared (S) locks taken during the operation.

| | name | timestamp | resource_type | mode | associated_object_id |
|---|---|---|---|---|---|
| 1 | lock_acquired | 2018-04-28 12:42:10.6423834 +00:00 | HOBT | S | 72057594046578688 |
| 2 | lock_released | 2018-04-28 12:42:12.2846239 +00:00 | HOBT | S | 72057594046578688 |
| 3 | lock_acquired | 2018-04-28 12:42:12.2879180 +00:00 | HOBT | S | 72057594046644224 |
| 4 | lock_released | 2018-04-28 12:42:13.9417023 +00:00 | HOBT | S | 72057594046644224 |
| 5 | lock_acquired | 2018-04-28 12:42:13.9445742 +00:00 | HOBT | S | 72057594046709760 |
| 6 | lock_released | 2018-04-28 12:42:15.5228468 +00:00 | HOBT | S | 72057594046709760 |
| 7 | lock_acquired | 2018-04-28 12:42:15.5257147 +00:00 | HOBT | S | 72057594046775296 |
| 8 | lock_released | 2018-04-28 12:42:17.1301706 +00:00 | HOBT | S | 72057594046775296 |

***Figure 14-12.*** *Locking during ALTER INDEX REORGANIZE command*

The associated_object_id column indicates delta store hobt_id, which we can confirm by analysing the sys.column_store_row_groups view. Figure 14-13 shows the state of the row groups after ALTER INDEX REORGANIZE has been completed. The row groups in the TOMBSTONE state indicate delta stores that have just been compressed and are waiting to be deallocated. As you can see, the delta_store_hobt_id values of those filegroups match resources on which shared (S) locks were taken.

| | object_id | row_group_id | delta_store_hobt_id | state | state_description | total_rows | deleted_rows | size_in_bytes |
|---|---|---|---|---|---|---|---|---|
| 1 | 693577509 | 10 | NULL | 3 | COMPRESSED | 1048576 | 0 | 5593584 |
| 2 | 693577509 | 9 | NULL | 3 | COMPRESSED | 1048576 | 0 | 5593584 |
| 3 | 693577509 | 8 | NULL | 3 | COMPRESSED | 1048576 | 0 | 5593584 |
| 4 | 693577509 | 7 | NULL | 3 | COMPRESSED | 1048576 | 0 | 5593584 |
| 5 | 693577509 | 6 | NULL | 3 | COMPRESSED | 1048576 | 0 | 5593584 |
| 6 | 693577509 | 5 | 72057594046840832 | 1 | OPEN | 994120 | NULL | 21250048 |
| 7 | 693577509 | 4 | 72057594046775296 | 4 | TOMBSTONE | 1048576 | NULL | 22405120 |
| 8 | 693577509 | 3 | 72057594046709760 | 4 | TOMBSTONE | 1048576 | NULL | 22405120 |
| 9 | 693577509 | 2 | 72057594046644224 | 4 | TOMBSTONE | 1048576 | NULL | 22405120 |
| 10 | 693577509 | 1 | 72057594046578688 | 4 | TOMBSTONE | 1048576 | NULL | 22405120 |

*Figure 14-13.*  *Row groups after ALTER INDEX REORGANIZE command*

As you can guess, this behavior would not scale well with update and delete workloads in OLTP systems.

# Wrapping Up

While it is appealing to use clustered columnstore indexes to store data in OLTP environments, this is rarely the best choice. Updateability in these indexes has been designed to simplify ETL processes and perform infrequent data modifications. While clustered columnstore indexes may handle append-only workloads, they would not scale well in generic OLTP workloads with a large number of concurrent transactions that modify data in the table.

You can still benefit from clustered columnstore indexes in OLTP systems. Many of the systems need to retain data for a prolonged period of time, and the volatility of the data and workload would change as the data becomes older. You can partition the data across several tables, combining columnstore, B-Tree, and In-Memory OLTP tables together with partitioned views. This will allow you to get the most from each technology, thus improving system performance and reducing the size of the data in the database.

**Note**    I have discussed this architecture in detail, including the methods for data movements between tables, in my *Pro SQL Server Internals* book.

# Summary

Columnstore indexes store data in a column-based format, persisting it on a per-column rather than per-row basis. This approach may significantly improve the performance of Data Warehouse, Operational Analytics, and reporting workloads in the system.

The data in columnstore indexes are heavily compressed. Clustered columnstore indexes may provide significant storage-space reduction as compared to B-Tree tables. They, however, do not scale well from a locking standpoint under OLTP workloads with multiple concurrent sessions modifying the data in parallel. You should not use them as a replacement for OLTP tables in such environments.

Finally, I would like to thank you again for reading this book! It was a pleasure to write for Thank you!

# Index

## A

ABORT_AFTER_WAIT option for
 low-priority locks, 187
ACID, 25
Allocation maps, 8
Allocation map scan, 14, 217
Allocation unit, 3
ALTER DATABASE SET ALLOW_
 SNAPSHOT_ISOLATION
 statement, 140
ALTER DATABASE SET READ_
 COMMITTED_SNAPSHOT
 statement, 139
ALTER INDEX REBUILD statement, 211
ALTER INDEX REORGANIZE
 statement in columnstore
 indexes, 309
ALTER TABLE REBUILD statement, 10
ALTER TABLE SET LOCK_ESCALATION
 statement, 169
AlwaysOn Availability Groups, 255
Application lock, 203
Archival compression in columnstore
 indexes, 298
Asynchronous commit in AlwaysOn
 Availability Groups, 256
Atomicity, transaction
 property, 25–26
Autocommitted
 transactions, 29–30, 213, 283

## B

Batch mode execution, 297
BEGIN TRAN statement, 29
BeginTs timestamp, 272, 284
Blocked process report, 82, 245, 263
blocked_process_report Extended Event,
 *see* Extended events
Blocked process threshold configuration
 option, 82
Blocking, 235
Blocking chains, 80, 252–255
Blocking monitoring
 framework, 263–266
B-Tree, *see* B-Tree index
B-Tree index, 11–16, 271
bucket_count in hash index, 271

## C

Catalog views, *see* Data management and
 catalog views
Clustered columnstore index, 297
Clustered index, 2, 11–16
Column-based storage, 296
Columnstore indexes, 1, 296, 297
Commit dependency, 285, 288
COMMIT statement, 29
Composite indexes, 17, 18
Compound indexes, *see* Composite
 indexes

313

© Dmitri Korotkevitch 2018
D. Korotkevitch, *Expert SQL Server Transactions and Locking*, https://doi.org/10.1007/978-1-4842-3957-5

Printed in the United States
By Bookmasters